JULIA ROBERTS

ABOUT THE AUTHOR

Frank Sanello has written biographies on Steven Spielberg, Jimmy Stewart, Tom Cruise, Sharon Stone, Eddie Murphy, Will Smith, Harold and Grace Robbins and the current bestseller, *Don't Call Me Marky Mark: The Unauthorised Biography of Mark Wahlberg.*

As a journalist for the past twenty-five years, Sanello has written for the *Washington Post*, the *Chicago Tribune*, the *New York Times* syndicate, *People*, *Cosmo* and *Penthouse* magazines. He was also the film critic for the *Los Angeles Daily News* and a business reporter for United Press International.

A native of Joliet, Illinois, Sanello graduated from the University of Chicago with honours and earned a Master's Degree from UCLA's film school. A purple belt in Tae Kwon Do, Sanello volunteers as a martial arts instructor at AIDS Project Los Angeles.

His upcoming biography, *Will Smith: Safe for Stardom*, examines the joys and frustrations of being the number-one box-office star in Hollywood – and a black man in a largely white industry.

A writer with wide-ranging interests, Sanello is currently working on a popular history, tentatively titled, *They Simply Addicted a Nation: China's Opium Wars with Britain*, which will apply modern theories of substance abuse to nineteenth-century politics.

The author lives in West Hollywood, California, with one dog, three cats and a kitten.

Julia Roberts

Frank Sanello

MAINSTREAM
PUBLISHING

EDINBURGH AND LONDON

First published in Great Britain in 2000 by
MAINSTREAM PUBLISHING COMPANY (EDINBURGH) LTD
7 Albany Street
Edinburgh EH1 3UG

This edition 2002

ISBN 1 84018 270 9

A catalogue record for this book is available from the
British Library

Typeset in Stone Serif

The Random House Group Limited supports The Forest Stewardship
Council (FSC®), the leading international forest certification organisation.
Our books carrying the FSC label are printed on FSC® certified paper.
FSC is the only forest certification scheme endorsed by the leading
environmental organisations, including Greenpeace. Our
paper procurement policy can be found at
www.randomhouse.co.uk/environment

MIX
Paper | Supporting
responsible forestry
FSC® C018179

Printed and bound in Great Britain by Clays Ltd, St Ives PLC

CONTENTS

Q: Whom would you rather wake up with?
A: Kate Winslet – 3%, Cameron Diaz – 11%, Uma
Thurman – 15%, Julia Roberts – 56%

   – Results of a 1997 readers' poll in Esquire *magazine*

'Those legs in *Pretty Woman*; they were certainly her
legs, weren't they?'

   *– Former French President François Mitterrand, to a dinner
guest eight days before he died and six years after* Pretty
Woman *was released*

'Julia Roberts – superstar, accomplished actress . . .
and national fetish object.'

   – Boxoffice *magazine*

Chapter One

AN UPLIFTING EVENT

From *Time* magazine in the States to the *Sunday Times* of London, the UK première of *Notting Hill* in May 1999 made international headlines. The film deserved the publicity it attracted. The romantic comedy about an American movie star who falls in love with a shy London bookshop owner reunited the principals who had made 1994's *Four Weddings and a Funeral* a $250 million hit and the most successful British film up to that time: star Hugh Grant, screenwriter Richard Curtis and producer Duncan Kenworthy. The film's director and Jane Austen populiser Roger Michell (*Persuasion*) added class to the crass appeal of *Four Weddings*.

Grant's presence at the London début guaranteed publicity if for no other reason than that his private life once famously overlapped with his public behaviour after a run-in with a Hollywood streetwalker in 1995. Accompanying him to the première was another eye-grabber, his long-time love, supermodel/actress Elizabeth Hurley, the woman who shagged both Austin Powers and the lucrative Estee Lauder account. As usual, the fabulously photogenic Hurley did not disappoint gawkers and paparazzi, showing up in a Gianni Versace gown that provided maximum exposure – slit to the thigh and made of see-through Lycra that fitted her like a coat of paint.

Both the infamous Grant and his gorgeous girlfriend, however, were upstaged by his *Notting Hill* leading lady, Julia Roberts. As the highest-paid actress in the world, and with a lovelife almost as controversial as her co-star's, Roberts had the ability to steal his and Hurley's thunder by the sheer power of her notoriety and commercial success. But it wasn't the actress's box-office appeal, her transcendent beauty or even her international fame that trumped the other stars and siphoned away the attention of the cameramen and fans outside the theatre.

Julia Roberts is such a hypnotic cynosure that all she had to do to upstage Grant and Hurley that night was skip a crucial bit of personal grooming. As she walked down the red carpet wearing a nondescript, sleeveless dress (described by one fashion reporter as 'frumpy'), Roberts graciously raised her arm to acknowledge screaming fans and revealed . . . she had failed to shave her armpits for the big event!

Hurley's dress may have left little to the imagination of leering youth, but Julia merely had to lift a limb and the act was recorded in newspapers and magazines around the world. Headline writers couldn't resist the opportunity to create banners like 'Do You Dare to Bare Your Hair?' and 'Arms and the Woman'.

The *Sunday Times* of London devoted an amazing number of column inches to 'the event', and we're not talking about the première itself. The *Times'* columnist India Knight reported that Hurley and Roberts do not get along and refused to talk to one another at the première. But Julia, so to speak, got in the last word. Or, as Knight wryly put it, Roberts 'comes up with the most divinely comical idea ever: Liz Hurley, Miss Ubiquity Herself, upstaged by an armpit'.

The *Observer's* pundit compared Roberts' hirsute appearance to performance art and the work of surrealist Meret Oppenheim, who once created a fur cup and saucer which the columnist claimed suggested oral sex. And, by implication, so did Julia's redolent pits. All this intellectualising for skipping a date with the razor!

Not surprisingly, reportage on the affair of the unshaven underarm went downmarket as well. *The Sun* set up a free phone hotline for readers to call in their votes, yea or nay, on the suitability of Roberts' controversial coiffure. *The Mirror* printed the opinions of beauty mavens and celebrities. *The Sun's* columnist Caprice clucked, 'Yuk, yuk, yuk. I shuddered when I saw Julia Roberts' hairy armpits.' Another writer called this tiny patch of skin 'the black forest' and bestowed on its owner the sobriquet 'pretty hairy woman'. Yet another complained, 'A woman's armpit is incredibly sexy to a man. Why ruin it by growing your own carpet under there?' A radio talk-show cited a survey that showed 63 per cent of men preferred their significant other hairless in that crucial erogenous zone. The *Evening Standard* noted that Roberts seemed curiously out of step with her compatriots since 'Yanks are fanatical about personal hygiene', implying that failing to go under the blade somehow reflected uncleanliness when it more likely suggests, at worst, slovenliness. *The Sun* was more forgiving. According to the tabloid, in the Liz v. Julia derby, the latter won, well, arms down. 'Hairy armpits aside,' Jane Moore wrote, 'Ms Roberts is a thoroughbred beauty compared to the look-at-me! look-at-me! coltishness of Hurley.'

News of Roberts' furry *faux pas* even crossed the Atlantic, where the usually sober-minded *Time* magazine got downright giddy and suggested Julia try a more traditional means of attention-hogging: 'The fashion press fixated on her armpits, which were visibly unshaven. Note to Julia: next time, try cleavage.'

Roberts' reaction to this tempest in an armpit was typical of her dealings with the public and the press. First she creates the furore, whether it's jilting her bridegroom near the altar or wandering around Hollywood dressed like a bag lady, then denounces all the attention her quirky behaviour attracts. 'You'd think it was like chinchilla the way they responded,' she complained back in America on Howard Stern's radio talk-show. 'It's something that I don't even think about.' That may explain the whole affair. Maybe amid the hubbub of preparing for the première, Julia simply forgot to depilate.

Smug headlines and weak puns aside, the incident at the *Notting Hill* première is significant, perhaps in spite of itself. It shows just how big a star Roberts is. No portion of her body is too unimportant – or unsexy – to go unremarked and unreported on. No bit of grooming or lack thereof fails to garner serious critique and commentary. Another American obsession, Madonna, elicited less international outrage when she appeared similarly unshaven – not to mention totally nude in the pages of *Playboy* and *Penthouse*.

After more than a decade of overexposure and a movie career with as many flops as hits, why does Julia Fiona Roberts continue to mesmerise both cynical journalists and the adoring, unwashed (but shaven) masses? What is there about this gangly near-six-footer who came from nowhere – or as close to nowhere as Smyrna, Georgia, gets – gobbled up box-office records and logged record numbers of magazine covers that keeps us forever famished for more Juliana? Why are her personal psychodramas often much more absorbing than her screen dramas?

To answer that question, we have to start at the beginning, in the Deep South of America, at the home of a financially strapped family of failed actors and *avant-garde* wannabes . . .

Chapter Two

DOWN AND OUT IN GEORGIA

———∢ᴜᴜ\ᴨᴜᴜ∘———

'I suspect she unconsciously associates acting with happy family
life and intimacy' – *a New York psychotherapist (not Julia's)*

Julia Fiona Roberts was born on Saturday, 28 October 1967, at Crawford
Long Hospital in downtown Atlanta. Betty, her thirty-three-year-old
mother, had been married to Walter, thirty-four, her father, for twelve
years. Julia was their third child. Her brother Eric had been born eleven
years earlier, and her sister Lisa two years before Julia. All three siblings
would become actors.

Acting and the theatre were in the children's blood. Both parents were
bohemian, arty types who ran several acting schools and writing work-
shops during Julia's early years.

Julia inherited her looks from her dashing father. 'Walter Roberts was
one of the most charming people I've ever met,' said Frank Wittow, an
Atlanta-based theatre director and colleague. 'He was extremely good-
looking, sort of like Armand Assante, and had very dark, piercing eyes. He
was very dynamic, very verbally adept.'

Unlike her daughter Julia, who would grow to a statuesque five foot
nine, Betty was short and blonde. Unusually for a woman of her generation (she was born in Minneapolis in 1934), Betty had enlisted in the Air
Force when she was nineteen. Her unusual career path was dictated by
her family's strained finances. She would have preferred to study drama,

but her parents couldn't afford to send her to college. She hoped to use the GI Bill after her stint in the military to pay for college acting classes. It was while stationed at the Keesler Air Force Base in Biloxi, Mississippi, that she met Airman First Class Walter Roberts, a medic who had served in Korea. With his wavy black hair, the sculpted features of a matinee idol and deep-set eyes, Roberts cut a dashing figure. Within a year of their meeting, the two GIs were married on 1 July 1955 by the Reverend Victor Augsburger at the First Presbyterian Church in Biloxi. The wedding reception took place in a friend's home on the base.

The first of a series of sour notes that would ultimately doom the relationship sounded at this time. When Betty's enlistment ended, her friends Rance and Jean Howard, parents of future Hollywood director Ron Howard, begged her to join them in Los Angeles, where they all hoped to launch acting careers. Betty wanted to go. Indeed, she had only joined the Air Force to further her acting aspirations, but Walter still had a year of military service left, and the couple, stuck in Biloxi, sadly said goodbye to the Howards, off to fulfil their dreams in Hollywood. (Rance Howard became a respected TV director, while his son became a child star on TV's *The Andy Griffith Show*, a teen star on *Happy Days* and the director of critically acclaimed box-office hits like *Apollo 13* and *Cocoon*.) As she saw her friend's career prosper in Hollywood, Betty must have wondered, as her own theatrical aspirations withered, 'What if . . .'

When Walter was finally discharged in 1956, the couple and their newborn son Eric moved to New Orleans, where Walter enrolled at Tulane University, majoring in psychology and English literature. As she would throughout much of their difficult marriage, Betty became the breadwinner of the family, supporting her college boy by working for an insurance company. She got some artistic satisfaction by taking night classes at Tulane in English literature.

As his daughter herself would later display, Walter had a temper that erupted unexpectedly and volcanically. Three months shy of receiving his bachelor's degree, he dropped out of Tulane in a huff. 'He had a great deal of animosity toward the professors and was convinced there was nothing more they could teach him,' Betty recalled years later.

Walter had always felt like a fish out of water, according to his wife.

The child of a construction worker and a housewife, Walter had a high IQ and wide-ranging intellectual interests. Sadly, most of his life would be spent 'not fitting in'. He also had a defeatist streak. Despite his desire to become a theatre director and actor, he refused to move to New York or Los Angeles, where his aspirations would have stood a better chance of being fulfilled. 'He came from nothing and was going to be something, make something of himself,' Betty said. '[But] he didn't want to leave Georgia, so he stayed and beat his brains out. He was a very talented, brilliant man who was in the wrong town to be doing what he was doing. That was his downfall.'

Instead of heading for the bright lights of Broadway or the offices of Hollywood casting agents, Walter decided to launch his career in sleepy Decatur, a suburb of Georgia, where the family moved after he dropped out of Tulane. There, in 1965, he began his foray into the world of the theatre impresario by opening an acting school. Called The Actors Workshop, it had modest beginnings. The workshop operated out of the living-room of the family's apartment on Scott Boulevard in Decatur.

That same year, the couple had their second child, Lisa, who, unlike Eric, favoured her mother's fair colouring. As an adult, Lisa would also share Betty's diminutive stature.

Both Betty and Walter had to take day jobs to keep the workshop afloat. Betty worked as a secretary in the public relations department of Emory University. Walter must have felt his artistic wings clipped and his ego bruised by taking a decidedly lowly job as a milkman with the Atlanta Dairies Co-op. It was only one of a series of jobs his temperament and temper would see him leave abruptly.

Frank Wittow, who had hired Walter as a publicist for the Academy Theater that Wittow directed, summed up the troubled young man at the time: 'He was very bright and he was king where his family was involved, but he was somewhat manipulative and I felt he had some emotional problems.'

Walter quit the Academy Theater after working there less than a year, but his surface charm landed him a new job almost immediately at the Harrington Scenic and Lighting Studio. Charles Walker, who was then an employee of the studio and now runs it in suburban Atlanta, recalled the

Roberts charisma: 'He just walked down there and introduced himself to Mr Harrington, and the next thing I knew he was working here, building scenery.'

Walter's manipulative side soon emerged, however. He used the studio's mailing list of members to solicit clients for a new acting and writing school which he launched within a year of joining the Harrington establishment. Mrs Harrington was annoyed. Charles Walker recalled, 'I remember her being quite upset about it, saying, "That renegade so-and-so tried to take our kids!"'

Walter rented a spacious, two-storey Victorian gingerbread house at 849 Juniper Street in midtown Atlanta and converted it to serve two purposes: the first floor was for his Actors and Writers Workshop, while the family occupied the second floor.

No. 849 was a pleasant place to raise a family and the fact that the Robertses lived there gave the school a warmth that a more institutional setting would have lacked. Just inside the front door was a library. Next to it a large dining-room and sun-room, plus a kitchen and a large pantry, which housed the workshop's costumes.

In the late '60s, when Walter opened his workshop, central Atlanta was home to hippies, performance artists and other arty types, a sort of Haight-Ashbury south of the Mason-Dixon Line. It was the perfect neighbourhood in which to operate an acting school.

It was into this vibrant artistic environment that Julia was born in 1967. At the time, her brother Eric was already appearing in theatre productions at the workshop. By fifteen, the youth with a precociously deep voice would be playing the title role in *Othello*, coached by his father, who had played the lethal Venetian years before.

Walter, as usual, had grand plans for his school, hoping to turn it into a southern fried version of the Lee Strasberg Institute in New York which had launched the careers of legends such as Marlon Brando and James Dean. Instead, Atlanta's bourgeoisie brought their children to the school, and Walter unwillingly found himself playing impresario to kids rather than future James Deans.

His school did attract one famous patron, Coretta Scott King, the wife of the murdered civil rights leader, Dr Martin Luther King. Mrs King became one of the school's keenest supporters and enrolled all three of her children there: Yolanda, Martin Luther III and Dexter. Betty would later proudly recall the relationship: 'She was very supportive, both emotionally and financially.'

Mrs King's financial help was sorely needed. Her daughter Yolanda, who studied speech, movement and drama there and appeared in more than forty productions, remembered the predicament of the chronically cash-strapped school: 'My mother was immediately attracted to the workshop because it was an integrated group, [but] it was a constant struggle to get funds to keep going. My mother was very much committed to them. But it was always a case of just barely getting by, paying the rent, getting the costumes.'

While providing a colourblind showcase for the performing talents of Atlanta youth, Walter was not above using the workshop to flex his own dramatic muscles in what some felt were vanity productions. Among these was his star turn in the school's first offering, *Othello*, where Walter played the Moor of Venice opposite his wife's Desdemona.

The school's constant financial distress was alleviated in part by Walter's knack for squeezing money out of charitable organisations and government agencies. With a $2,500 grant from the Guggenheim Foundation, he produced a series of children's plays, including *The Nightingale*, based on the Chinese fairytale, and various Uncle Remus folktales. In the latter, Eric played Brer Rabbit and Yolanda King Ma Alligator.

A federal grant provided by the Economic Opportunity Act allowed Walter to create a travelling theatre aboard a flatbed truck that put on plays in Atlanta's black neighbourhoods. This turned out to be the first time Julia caught a whiff of greasepaint and heard the roar of the crowd.

Betty remembered the 'showmobile' performances fondly. Years later, she described the scene: 'When we toured that summer, I would put Julia in a pushchair while I set up the sound system. In the ghetto areas the kids would come up and ask, "Can we take her for a walk?" And I'd say "Sure." Then one time someone said, "Are you sure she's coming back?" But the black children were fascinated by her because a lot of them had never seen any white kids. She was about two years old, and she had all this soft blonde hair.' Julia's early mixing with people of another race would make her a staunch defender of civil rights as an adult and stir up controversy when she condemned racism wherever she saw it.

While the workshop and showmobile provided the Robertses with artistic satisfaction and the gratitude of Atlanta's parents, the two enterprises never provided a comfortable income. Somehow, the family managed to subsist on just fifty dollars a week during Julia's early years.

Despite the poor returns on their investment, both Walter and Betty worked around the clock: 'We dealt strictly with volunteers, which could be very difficult because Walter felt they should work as hard as he did. We made our own costumes, which meant I used to spend a lot of time in thrift stores. When Julia was just a baby, I'd put her downstairs in a playpen while I worked twenty-four hours a day making costumes for the next production.'

While Betty struggled to keep the school afloat, Walter, it seemed, worked even harder to alienate the school's bread and butter, the parents. His students adored him, but the difficult theatre director managed to antagonise the people who paid their tuition. A colleague at the time later said, 'Basically, Walter's problem was that he got into theatre late so he had no patience with the people he had to work with.' Stuart Culpepper, a well-known local actor, was more blunt about Walter's people problems: 'Walter had more dreams than talent. He was one of those men I didn't want to pursue a friendship with because I never quite trusted him. He was quite pompous, something of a conman, I think. Anyway, he just didn't fit in with anything. It was a workshop for kids. I don't think there was any substance there at all. My impression was that it was a very shoe-string operation, run by family members and close friends.'

Atlanta theatre director Ed Danos offered an even harsher assessment. 'Whenever I talked to Walter, I had an idea in the back of my head that he didn't really know much. Walter was somebody on the fringes of society, and, frankly, I didn't have a good impression of him. There was something about him that was not quite on the level. He was a little sleazy, a little oily. He seemed like somebody living hand to mouth. And I remember his clothes never seemed pressed, and he always seemed to be wearing the same baggy, nondescript dark suit,' Danos told Aileen Joyce in her exhaustively researched 1993 biography, *Julia: The Untold Story of America's Pretty Woman.*

Even those observers who felt Walter's heart and hopes were in the right place also believed his talent failed to match his energy and ambition. The *Atlanta Constitution*'s theatre critic, Terry Kay, praised Walter as an *avant-garde* pioneer, but one who blazed a rather lacklustre trail. 'The workshop was a real serious attempt to create the first repertory company in Atlanta. Walter had a tremendously intense feeling towards theatre, and a zest for what he was doing . . . but, truthfully, although his ideas and ambitions were good, his productions didn't live up to them. He never had enough time [or] enough talent,' Kay said.

Walter did have one fan, who remains so to this day – his son Eric. 'My father was a gentle giant,' Eric has said. 'He was the most educated man I've ever known. And because I didn't talk so well when I was a kid, I got into reading. We didn't even have a TV. I had to go over to a friend's house to watch *Leave It to Beaver.*'

Eric, unfortunately, had inherited his mother's stutter, which plagues him to this day. He found that he could overcome his speech impediment by memorising lines in plays. His father introduced him to the world of literature, and Eric borrowed Walter's copy of *The Glass Menagerie* when he was only eight years old. 'My father was my book pal. He was my best friend, my teacher, my dad, and I loved him,' Eric has said.

Obsessed as they both were with keeping the workshop alive, Walter and Betty presented a picture of a united, happy family. They balanced and complemented one another. Betty's charm always somehow managed to clear the wreckage Walter's irritating behaviour created. It also didn't hurt that she was as gorgeous as her daughter would one day become.

'Betty looked like a movie star. She had luxurious hair and a glamorous attitude. She was just a really neat person, and Walter was very handsome, very intense. They seemed to be the perfect couple,' their friend Philip De Poy has said.

The pretty public picture hid an ugly private life. The constant financial pressure of keeping the school afloat and raising three children led to arguments that grew more violent as the marriage deteriorated. Adding to the pressure were the mortgage payments on a bungalow in Atlanta Walter somehow managed to buy in February 1971 for $17,000.

The new home failed to save the relationship, and in June 1971 Betty filed for divorce after sixteen years of marriage. In contrast to all the bickering that preceded it, the terms of the divorce were arrived at amicably. Betty got the house, the kids and their 1968 Volkswagen. She agreed to pay the mortgage, while Walter would pay $195 a month in child support. Visitation rights were sketchily spelled out with the implication that Dad could basically see the children any time he wanted. The divorce became final on 28 January 1972.

It was not a good year for Walter Roberts. It saw the failure of his marriage and the end of his theatre ambitions. After one last hurrah for the workshop, in which he horrified Atlanta's civil rights establishment by casting a black woman, Dr Martin Luther King's daughter Yolanda, no less, as a prostitute opposite a white actor in the farce *The Owl and the Pussycat*, the school closed its doors forever.

A few months later, Walter found himself living every actor's nightmare, taking a day job that became a full-time occupation. Years later, Julia recalled her father's fall from grace: 'My dad ended up selling vacuum cleaners [at Rich's department store in downtown Atlanta].' Betty began working again as a secretary, just as she had done during Walter's college days.

Julia claimed she learned a useful lesson from her parents' imploding dreams. 'They never got rich and they never got famous, but they showed me that you do things for a purpose, and if it treats you well, then all the better. But if it goes away, you won't die. You must move on. They instilled this in me: motivation is the engine in life.'

That philosophy would serve their daughter well years later when critics and pundits claimed that her rising star had prematurely burnt out.

Chapter Three

NEW BEGINNINGS, TRAGIC ENDINGS

Betty Roberts didn't remain alone long. A month after her divorce from Walter became final, she began dating a journalist named Michael Motes. They met while Betty was appearing in a community theatre production of *Arsenic and Old Lace*. Motes covered the theatre scene for the *Atlanta Constitution* at the time, and he asked Betty out after seeing her on stage.

Overweight and pasty-faced, Motes wore hornrimmed glasses. To say he lacked Walter's good looks would be too kind. Acquaintances described him as solitary, 'weird-acting, weird-looking' and lacking the ambition which consumed Walter. Since childhood, Motes had also suffered from alopecia, a kind of baldness that afflicts the entire body. A classmate from those days described him as 'strange, a sissy type. He was totally bald even in high school. With a round, clean-shaven face and this dark brown hair-piece, he was definitely weird.' In contrast to Walter's bombast, the low-key Motes, despite his unprepossessing appearance, may have appealed to Betty after all the *Sturm und Drang* with her ex-husband.

The new couple spent a great deal of time together and often left Betty's children with their father. Walter was delighted to take custody since he adored the kids and – actor that he was – loved to entertain them. They sang showtunes together and went to the movies. Walter even joined in as the kids drew pictures with crayons.

Julia has nothing but happy memories of these days, despite her parents' break-up. 'I had a great relationship with my dad. Nothing intellectual, just really caring and fun, singing the Oompa-Loompas song or drawing and painting,' she recalled years later.

By now, Walter had moved into Ansley Forest, an upmarket apartment complex not far from Betty's house. Like his ex-wife, the handsome 'bachelor' soon found companionship. A neighbour, Eileen Sellars, bumped into Walter outside the complex one day when he had Julia and Lisa in tow. Julia was entranced by the pretty Sellars, and precociously played matchmaker. 'This is my daddy,' she said to Eileen. 'His name is Walter. But you can call him Daddy!'

The attractive couple began dating regularly, but this happy period in Walter's life was short-lived. Betty was unable to make the mortgage payments on the house in Atlanta and moved the family into Michael Motes' home in rural Smyrna, a fifteen-minute drive and twenty miles north-west of the big city. Smyrna's greatest claim to fame, before Julia became its most famous citizen, is that General William Sherman, on his pyromaniacal way to the Atlantic Ocean, burned the city to the ground in 1864 during the Civil War.

*

In May 1972, Eric Roberts and Michael Motes got into an argument that soon became physical. Betty sided with her boyfriend and kicked her son out of the house. Eric called his father, who wasn't home, and ended up getting a ride to his father's place from Eileen's mother, Virginia Sellars. The youngster and the older woman had struck up a friendship after Walter and Eileen started seeing each other.

Virginia didn't pick up Eric in Smyrna, however. The plucky youth had hitchhiked all the way to downtown Atlanta before Virginia caught up with him. It was raining, and Eric was a pitiful sight. 'I felt so sorry for him,' Virginia recalled. 'He couldn't get in touch with his father, and he didn't have any money. He was just soaking wet, and he was so upset he was stuttering something awful.'

Eric and Michael had never got along since the start, and after Betty threw him out, he never spoke to Motes again. He also never lived with his mother again. Eric moved in with his father, while the girls stayed with Betty. It was the end of their happy days together.

On 13 September 1972, Betty married Michael Motes. It would be a union even more troubled than Betty's first marriage.

Walter soon sued for permanent custody of all three children. In court documents, he claimed Motes had physically abused Eric and that his ex-wife had kicked him out of the house and abandoned him. He also alleged that Motes 'has and continues to mistreat our minor children and that during the winter months our daughters had colds, appeared extremely tired and listless, and had fevers'. Walter added that his ex-wife had 'neglected the minor children by staying out late at night without providing any adult care and supervision' while she was out on the town with her husband.

Betty quickly countersued, claiming Walter had failed to pay child support and had taken furniture and other objects from her home. She also said Walter had told 'malicious lies to the minor children concerning her behaviour in order to prejudice them and induce them to leave her custody'.

Apparently, the judge believed both parents, because on 30 October 1972 Betty got temporary custody of their daughters while Eric was allowed to continue living with his father, out of reach of Michael Motes. The judge ordered both parents into therapy. Two months later, the court made the division of the family permanent. Although he retained custody of Eric, Walter came out the loser in the settlement since he was granted very limited visitation rights with his daughters – only two weeks a year.

The financial problems Betty had suffered with her first husband continued with her second. In January 1973, her house on Eighth Street was foreclosed on when she failed to make the $136-a-month mortgage payment. The couple and the girls were living in Michael Motes' house in Smyrna when the Atlanta residence was put up for auction. Motes had financial troubles of his own. Two months after he married Betty, he was sued for $260 back rent on an apartment he had occupied before moving into his present home. Two months later, a company sued Betty for failing to pay a bill.

The stress took its toll on the newlyweds. Julia and Lisa would later recall their mother and stepfather staying up late into the night fighting over finances.

The Motes' lifestyle was necessarily modest. The family spent the first five years living in low-income housing. Michael Motes had an even sketchier employment history than Walter. He flitted from one low-paid job to another and was often unemployed for long periods of time. Betty, once again, became the family's anchor and steady breadwinner. She soon found work as a secretary for the *Georgia Bulletin*, a newspaper published by the Catholic Archdiocese of Atlanta.

The family stayed put in Smyrna, a nondescript commuter town of 35,000 which *National Geographic* once labelled a 'redneck city'.

As Betty and Michael descended the socio-economic ladder in a dusty suburb, Walter's life seemed to be on the upswing. In contrast to his previous work history, he prospered as a vacuum cleaner salesman and was promoted to sales representative for the entire chain of Macy's department stores in Atlanta.

His relationship with Eileen Sellars also prospered. Just as Betty had chosen a second husband 180 degrees away from her first, Walter's girlfriend presented a dramatic contrast to his first wife. Eileen was a well-educated legal secretary with a Masters degree from Florida State University. Physically and temperamentally, Eileen couldn't have been more different from Betty. Betty was a chirpy extrovert and blonde; the dark-haired Eileen a studious introvert. 'Eileen was a very shy person, a very conservative person in both her manner and her dress. Walter brought her out. She was like a flower that bloomed,' according to Eileen's aunt, Vivien McKinley.

Eileen was not without her influence on Walter, however, whose temperamental mood swings she helped ameliorate. They were a perfect pairing of opposites. Friends and relatives said they were crazy about each other.

Their infatuation quickly turned into love, and they were married on 4 April 1974. The only fly in the ointment was Walter's limited access to the girls. Now that he was a married man again, he hoped his new status would help him gain custody of his daughters. On 20 June 1974 he petitioned the court to increase the time he was allowed to spend with Julia and Lisa.

Shortly after Walter's petition, the Motes had a nightmare run-in with the police. In the middle of the night, Smyrna's narcotics squad entered the family home, armed with a search warrant. The officers were acting on a tip-off that drugs would be found hidden in a bible at the residence. The tip-off turned out to be accurate, and the police confiscated the drugs. Inexplicably, no arrests were made.

A member of the narcotics team that invaded the house, Troy Ballinger, remembered the ugly scene. 'The husband started crying. He got really upset and began wringing his hands, saying he had young children in the house and how he would never have drugs around them. And then the wife said the stuff had probably been planted by her ex-husband,' he is quoted as saying in Aileen Joyce's 1993 biography of Julia.

'Anyway, things just didn't fit,' Ballinger said. 'So we never charged them, and the whole thing was dropped.' The narcotics detective also mentioned that the exterior of the house looked run down, but the interior was tidy and the furniture in good condition.

Although there was speculation that Walter might have planted the drugs to help him gain custody of his daughters, the allegations were never proven. And if he had, his efforts were in vain because a month after his petition for extended visitation rights, he was slapped with a restraining order which not only kept him away from the Motes residence, but the entire block surrounding it. The only benefit he gained from his petition was the right to call his daughters on the phone for half an hour each week. But Walter often failed to enjoy even that small grace. Betty frequently hung up on him or refused to tell the girls he was on the phone.

One of Walter's friends recalled, 'It was terrible, just plain meanness on Betty's part. She kept the little girls away from Walter's parents, too, for the most part. But I know that whenever Walter's mother was allowed to see them, which wasn't very often, Walter would either call and talk to them, or sneak up there to see them. I don't know how they managed to keep the secret from Betty, but somehow they did.'

His second wife's aunt, Vivien McKinley, described the toll this subterfuge took on Walter. 'It tore him up. It tormented him that he didn't get to see the little girls. And that upset Eileen. I remember her saying, "It's just not fair. He's a good father. He needs them and they need him."'

Eric also found himself denied access to his sisters, which especially hurt since the children had all been so close. Walter and Eric became obsessed with reuniting the family. One friend recalled: 'Eric used to talk about how he was going to go to Hollywood and become a big star, and they'd all live together happily ever after. But, of course, even though Eric did become a movie star, it never happened, did it?'

Eric also confided his dream of reuniting the family to his stepmother, with whom he enjoyed a loving relationship. 'When I'm famous I'm going to buy a big home in Hollywood and we can all live out there,' he told Eileen.

Sadly, the childhood separation would evolve into a nasty adulthood estrangement from his sister, with accusations and counter-accusations aired in the press after both siblings became famous.

Although Walter wasn't given much opportunity to be with his daughters, he spent a lot of time trying to make their lives happy. He and Eric built a huge doll's-house as a surprise Christmas gift for Julia and Lisa. They spent nearly six months constructing the little palace for the girls. Father and son also made big plans for the two weeks during the summer which they were allowed to spend with the girls. They fantasised that when Julia and Lisa came of age, they would all live together again.

Walter kept up a voluminous correspondence with his daughters to compensate for the little time they spent together. Julia still carries one of these letters with her to this day. 'I have a letter from my daddy that he wrote to me on 6 July 1977. It's the only letter I managed not to lose as a child. If anybody ever took that away from me, I would just be destroyed. It doesn't mean anything to anybody else, yet I can read that letter ten times a day and it moves me in a different way every time,' she has said.

During the summer of 1977 when Walter got his fortnight with the girls, he took them to New York to visit Eric, whose acting career was taking off with amazing speed. Eric proudly showed off his new stomping grounds to the country bumpkins from Georgia. Julia was only ten at the time, but it planted in her mind the desire to one day share the excitement of the theatre capital and join her brother there.

The summer of 1977 that began so happily for Walter ended in unthinkable tragedy in September. Eileen and Walter decided to spend a weekend on Lake Lanier at Georgia's Six Mile Creek resort and rented a houseboat. In from New York, Eric would join them on the getaway. Before departing, the holidaymakers visited Eileen's aunt, Vivien McKinley. 'They stopped by my office and Eileen was really excited because she was going to study to be a court reporter and had bought her machine the night before. I always remember her saying to me, "Do you think I'm finally on my way?" because she really hadn't found what she wanted to do. But after working for lawyers, she'd really gotten interested in being a court stenographer,' McKinley told Aileen Joyce in 1993. 'Anyway, I could see out the front door into the parking lot and Eileen's green Maverick was out there with a canoe strapped on top of it. Since I knew she couldn't swim I said, "Now, Eileen, don't you get in that boat. You know how easily those things tip over and you can't swim." And she said, "Oh, don't worry, I've got a life jacket."'

On Sunday, 18 September, Eric and Eileen decided to leave the houseboat, which was anchored in a cove, and take the canoe out on the lake. Walter stayed behind. As Eric and his stepmother ventured into ever deeper water, a speedboat appeared out of nowhere and created a huge wake which almost capsized the smaller craft. As the canoe rocked violently from side to side, Eileen, who wasn't wearing a life jacket because of the heat, fell overboard. As Eric screamed, Eileen disappeared into the opaque water and never resurfaced. Eric dived into the lake repeatedly, but his rescue efforts were fruitless. 'She slipped away,' he said in the police report. The lake was dredged, and Eileen's body was found two hours after the accident. Walter had deeply loved the quiet, unassuming Eileen, and her sudden death devastated him. A few days after the tragedy, he called Eileen's aunt, but hung up quickly, unable to speak as he dissolved into uncontrollable weeping.

Eileen's death wasn't the only problem Walter had at this time. With a nagging cough and difficulty swallowing, he hadn't been feeling well for months. His doctor thought these symptoms might be a psychosomatic reaction to the sudden loss of his wife and recommended that he see a psychiatrist. Walter also went to Emory University's hospital for tests. He went into the hospital and never came out.

His illness hadn't been psychosomatic after all, because three months after Eileen died, Walter followed her to the grave. The coughing and the swallowing problems had been signs of advanced throat cancer, and he died on 3 December 1977.

The funeral, which Eric managed to arrange despite being devastated by his father's loss, was as theatrical as Walter's life had been. A friend who attended the memorial said, 'It was more a celebration of Walter's life than a funeral. People he'd known stood up and told anecdotes about him. And the music was lovely. I remember they played one of Walter's favourites, the theme song from *Romeo and Juliet*. He would have loved it because it was theatrical, not at all your typical funeral.'

Despite their ugly divorce and custody battle, Betty showed up for the service, bringing Julia and Lisa with her. The ceremony became a turning point in the young Julia's life, marking an end as well as a beginning.

'My childhood was real weird to me. I feel like I grew up twice. Once till I was about ten. After that it was completely different. My father died around then, which probably changed me a lot more than I realised. I don't think I'd be what I am today if that hadn't happened. It was just a rough time.

'I miss my dad. I don't feel that boundless injustice over his death any more, which is good, because that's not a fun bag to carry. It was just something that happened to me. It's funny that I said that because his death happened to a lot of people. But when I was ten years old, it felt like this was done to me. Now I look at it as I can talk to him whenever I want. He's everywhere I go,' she told *GQ* magazine in 1991.

Still, memories can never replace the real thing, as Julia said in 1994: 'I guess my life would be completely different if I had had a father. I miss my father and would give anything to have him here.'

More than one reporter acting as armchair analyst has speculated that Julia has spent her adult life searching for her lost father with one failed romantic liaison after another. The dissolution of her family, first by divorce and then by Eileen's and Walter's untimely deaths, has led her to recreate a substitute family on her movie sets, with cast and crew standing in for real-life relatives. Tragically, the movie-set experience in a way recreates the loss of her family when the production ends and her 'relatives' move on to the next project.

Or, as a New York psychotherapist told *Redbook* magazine in 1994, 'I suspect she unconsciously associates acting with happy family life and intimacy.'

Without accepting that theory, Julia has admitted the profound effect her father's death had on her. 'His death changed the course of my life, and at some point or other has altered every philosophy of life I've ever had,' she said in a 1991 interview with the *Ladies Home Journal*.

Chapter Four

FAMILY FAIRYTALES

Nineteen-seventy-seven was a year of endings and beginnings for Julia Roberts. That year her half-sister Nancy was born, and the Motes family moved into a spacious three-bedroom ranch house on Maner Road in a rural area just outside the Smyrna city limits.

Julia also found herself something of an heiress at this time. Two days before he died, Walter had signed a will leaving everything to his three children, with Eric as guardian and trustee. The luckless Walter didn't have much to leave of his own, but it turned out that their late step-mother possessed a small fortune, which Walter had inherited upon her death. Eileen's $20,000 estate came from her mother, who had died only a year and a half before her daughter.

Legal battles began almost immediately, recreating the nightmarish atmosphere for Julia and Lisa of their parents' divorce and custody struggles. In keeping with his father's dying wish, Eric, only twenty-two at the time, filed papers in Cobb County court, seeking to be named guardian and executor of his sisters' estate. Betty sued to have her son's petition overturned. In court papers that still sound cruel more than two decades after they were filed in 1978, Betty maintained, 'Eric Anthony Roberts is not a fit and proper person to serve as guardian and trustee. He is a New York City actor with no regular income and caveators [Lisa and Julia] fear the waste of their inheritance.'

The court battles over Eileen's estate and custody of the girls dragged on for a year and a half. During this time, it was discovered that Eileen's estate was worth nearly $100,000, not the original $20,000 mentioned in Walter's will. Eileen, it turned out, had inherited part interest in an office building in downtown Atlanta. One of her relatives countersued and laid claim to Eileen's fortune. The case went all the way to the Georgia Supreme Court. Finally, Julia, Lisa and Eric were named their stepmother's heirs. After court costs, their inheritance came to $90,000, which was split evenly among them.

During the messy legal battle, and perhaps to form a united front against Eileen's litigious relative, Eric and Betty had a reconciliation of sorts. They agreed to have attorney C.R. Vaughn serve as Lisa and Julia's guardians, while Eric would remain executor of the estate. The money was placed in a trust fund, and at the age of twelve Julia found herself a little heiress worth almost $25,000.

His legal and fraternal duties fulfilled, Eric moved back to New York and almost immediately landed a starring role in a big-budget film, *King of the Gypsies*. He was living his father's wildest fantasy, and yet sadly Eric couldn't share his success with Walter. More importantly, Eric's return to the big city led to a three-year separation from his sisters, who remained in Smyrna. He did return for brief visits, but the three siblings would never again enjoy the close-knit family life presided over by their father.

In her 1993 biography of Julia, Aileen Joyce claims the separation was more than merely geographical: 'despite his decades-old dream of being reunited as a family, the truth is that, with almost a dozen years of age difference between them, Eric and his two sisters . . . grew up as virtual strangers.' In the ensuing years, various emotional, legal and substance-abuse problems would turn these strangers into, if not enemies, feuding siblings. Their parents' battles would be replayed by the children.

Compounding these problems was the fact that Eric detested his mother, while Julia and Lisa treated her more like an adored confidante than a parent.

Julia's relationship with her stepfather was another matter. If she was estranged from her brother, her feelings toward Michael Motes could be best described as active dislike, even loathing, mixed with fear. Eric, it turned out, wasn't the only one in the family who didn't get along with his testy, often unemployed stepfather. Motes, friends of the family have said, never showed his stepdaughters any affection and was either hyper-critical or simply ignored them.

As an adult and a movie star whose childhood has been picked over by journalists serving as amateur psychologists, Julia has basically repressed memories of her troubled relationship with Michael Motes. Or maybe she is just being diplomatic. To the press, she has presented an upbringing from which the warts have been surgically removed. The family may have been of slender means, but it enjoyed a hefty sense of togetherness, or so she claims. 'I come from a real touchy family,' she said on the cusp of stardom in 1991, when *Rolling Stone* magazine came knocking on her door. 'A lotta hugging, a lotta kissing, a lotta love. "You're going to the market? See you later, I love you!"'

In all fairness, she was no doubt accurately describing her tight-knit relationship with Lisa and Betty, but the angry, insulting Michael Motes never appears as the ogre in Roberts' retelling of this *faux* family fairytale. Although they lived together for eleven years, Motes has never even been identified as her stepfather by Julia in the hundreds of interviews she has given since becoming a movie star. Julia simply cut him out of the picture, a ruthless efficiency she would later employ in adult relation-ships, whether professional or romantic.

Julia was not only emotionally close to her sister and remains so to this day, but growing up in straightened circumstances also forced upon the sisters a physical closeness. For much of their childhood, Julia and Lisa not only shared a bedroom, they slept in the same bed. 'Lisa has this celestial thing. I would wait until she was asleep and touch her, to tap into this safe place so I wouldn't be scared at night,' Julia has recalled.

Despite or maybe because of the physical and emotional proximity, typical sibling rivalry and fights erupted between the two sisters. They argued over everything and nothing, doing the dishes, setting the table, folding the laundry. The arguments sometimes became physical, and Julia would pull Lisa's hair with all her might, using both hands. When they saw a report on the TV news that two squabbling sisters had stabbed each other in the kitchen, they decided to stop fighting – at least in the kitchen. 'We never fought in there again,' Julia later said with a laugh.

Looking at the two girls, no one would have thought they were related, their physical traits were so different. Like Eric, Julia took after her father, whose dark good looks perhaps came from his Cherokee heritage. Julia is also a strapping five foot, nine inches tall. Lisa barely reached five three, sharing her Scandinavian mother's diminutive stature and blonde hair.

Although Julia resembles her father, perhaps it was her closeness to her mother that led her to duplicate Betty's mannerisms, which include a penchant for waving her hands in the air and a love of hats. The hand-waving is practically a family heirloom, since Betty's mother also made dramatic gestures. 'My father used to kid us both about that. He'd say if they ever tied our hands behind our backs, we wouldn't be able to talk,' Julia said.

Reams of newsprint have been devoted to Julia's thousand-watt smile, which lights up movie screens and fills box-office coffers. Her perfect smile, however, is the product of dental work she had at the age of eight. An inveterate thumbsucker, she sported a yawning gap between her front teeth, which was closed by her dentist, Dr Ted Aspes. 'The gap was so big between my front teeth you could shove a Popsicle stick between them,' Julia once said.

She graduated from Fitzhugh Lee Elementary School on West Atlanta Road when she was twelve and enrolled at Griffin Middle School on King Spring Road. At about this time, Betty left her job at the Archdiocese's *Georgia Bulletin* and took a position at the Ridgeview Institute, a private psychiatric hospital which specialised in the treatment of substance abuse. After almost a decade at Ridgeview, Betty went back to work for the Archdiocese in its legal department.

While at Fitzhugh, Julia had her first encounter with racism, which made her sensitive to the issue for the rest of her life. When she encountered it years later on a movie location, her condemnation made national news. In the sixth grade, classmates called her names and vandalised her locker after she entered a dance contest with a black youth as her partner. This incident may explain why she still has mixed feelings about her hometown, which she has described as 'nice' but disappointing because of its inertia. 'I go back and see that there's been no movement in time.

I'm so easily enraged by the flailing ignorance, which is tossed about as if it's God's words.'

Julia had already developed into a striking beauty when she enrolled at Campbell High School on Ward Street. She didn't believe it herself, though; her mouth, in particular, made her feel unattractive. 'There was a time in high school when I felt a little grief because I had an unusual mouth, unlike the other girls who had perfect mouths with little heart-top lips. But I never have done anything to accentuate my mouth,' she said years later, when her huge smile was the subject of so much attention in the press. Her mouth, she added, is 'crooked and I have a couple of little scars. I never wear lipstick. In fact, I'm really bad at putting it on. Every time I've put it on, I've taken if off before I went out.'

Julia described herself as mediocre during these years. 'In high school, I was like everybody else,' she says. 'I had my girlfriends. I did sports. I wasn't really great at anything, just middle of the road, a basic kid. I was never a cheerleader, none of those really glorious high-school things.'

But school records and her peers contradict Julia's claim. 'Although Julia is always talking about how she was Miss Nobody in high school because she wasn't a cheerleader, that's not really true,' Joan Raley, a classmate, told biographer Aileen Joyce. Julia did enjoy some of 'those really glorious high-school things'. She was one of twelve finalists in her high school beauty contest, which she described as 'thrilling. It was that kind of feeling of "Oh, my God, I can't believe they picked me!".'

She was also an avid, almost obsessive participant in extra-curricular activities. She served on the student council every year at Campbell High. During her sophomore and junior years, she won the Parliamentary Award and was elected class treasurer both years as well. In one campaign speech, this self-alleged mediocrity touted her qualifications for the office: 'I see myself as a person who can communicate ideas from students to the administration.'

As her high-school yearbooks show, Julia was a whirlwind of student activities. She may not have made the cheerleader squad, but a list of her other affiliations sounds exhausting: the Allied Medical Club during her freshman year, the Spanish Club the following year. She also found time to play on the tennis team for three years.

Betty proudly recalled her daughter's steely determination to make the tennis team despite poor eyesight and her mother's own misgivings. 'She wouldn't give up when they said her left eye wasn't good enough. She made the team. She had too much determination to listen to me,' Betty has said.

Julia loathed maths and simply stopped attending algebra class. But in high school, she began a lifelong love affair with literature. To this day, Julia keeps a voluminous journal and writes reams of poetry. Her daily diary, which she takes everywhere with her, has been archly titled 'All the Makings of Insanity', and records her musings and most intimate thoughts. If someone ever got a hold of this work in progress, she has joked, 'they would crucify me'. The diary also contains her essays and poems, which she self-deprecatingly dismisses, saying, 'Actually, it's mostly fucking hearts-and-flowers poetry.'

Even so, Julia would like to publish her work, but if she does, her mother says it would be under a pseudonym so her literary efforts would be judged on their own merits.

The epiphany that turned her into an avid diarist and poet occurred in the school library, where she was hiding out while skipping maths.

'I started reading more when I started failing algebra class because I stopped going to it – there wasn't any point. So I started going to the library, and one day I came across this huge book called *Leaves of Grass* by Walt Whitman, and I spent the rest of the semester reading that book.'

Julia's love affair with literature began on her own, but it was nurtured by one special teacher, who also inadvertently steered her towards her future career. 'I started reading more poetry, and then I was lucky enough to have a wonderful English teacher, who had us reading *The Canterbury Tales*. In that same class we watched *Becket* [the 1964 film about the English martyr starring Richard Burton and Peter O'Toole], and I found my first real affection for movies. The school had a handful of really great teachers, it turned out, and I started getting more and more interested in writing, with some encouragement.'

David Boyd and Keith Gossett both taught Julia English at Campbell High. They were her favourite teachers, and when she returns to visit her family in Smyrna, she often drops by the school to see the men who kindled her love of literature.

Boyd taught Julia during her sophomore year and gave her A-minus/B-plus grades. 'She was a fairly typical high-school student. She enjoyed watching a lot of sports teams. She enjoyed basketball . . . She enjoyed supporting the teams,' recalled Boyd, who also coached the boys' basketball and baseball teams.

Julia's dramatic flair and intense identification with acting roles were already evident in high school. Boyd recalled, 'When we read *Julius Caesar*, I remember she was a very emotional Brutus. She really put a lot into it. In a sense, I guess, her success doesn't surprise me because she was the type of individual who was unafraid of risk, who could leave Smyrna and go for it.'

Her other English teacher, Keith Gossett, remembered Julia's enthusiasm for trying new things, which contrasted with that of her less adventurous peers. 'In my composition class, I'd say we were going to do something different, and a lot of times the students would be very negative. But Julia was always open to different things. It was like she was always watching and thinking about things. She was a very conscientious student.'

Ironically, although Campbell High produced the number-one box-office actress in the world, the school didn't have a drama department when Julia was a student there. She never had the chance to perform in school plays. Since then, however, the school has instituted acting classes and named an acting award in her honour, bestowed on the student who shows the most promise.

Because Julia never got to flex her dramatic muscle during these years, classmate Joan Raley assumed her career would take a literary turn: 'Most of us really thought she was going to be a writer because she always said she wanted to write and she always was writing. She wrote wonderful poetry. I still have a poem she wrote for me about a guy I was going out with.'

Although Julia claims she kept a low profile and wasn't particularly popular, almost everybody at Campbell High recalls her presence there and has mostly nice things to say about the pretty teenager. But they tend to contradict each other when it comes to determining whether their classmate was a loner or Miss Congeniality.

'She used to dress real preppie and always had nice clothes,' said one classmate who graduated with Julia in 1985. 'The only guy she seemed to hang around with was Maddox Kilgore, although I heard she dated Joe Thompson, the school's star basketball player, for a while. She was a little heavier than she is now. She's really slimmed down.'

Another former pupil agrees with Julia's own claim that she was not a big star on campus. 'Julia was real quiet, not much of an outgoing personality. She seemed like a nice person. She wasn't a cheerleader, didn't run with the most popular crowd. She was sweet, quiet, and from the way she dressed, seemed to have a little bit of money.' Eileen's inheritance, no doubt, provided an ample wardrobe budget. 'Other than that, she blended in. She never stood out,' the classmate added.

Her signature laugh, which would punctuate so many of her movies, had already developed at this time, along with the cascading mane that helped make her one of cinema's most beautiful stars. Another classmate recalled, 'She was always well groomed. Her hair was feathered back and she wore her hair more shoulder-length. I remember her laughing a lot. I remember it echoing down the halls. It was a loud laugh.' Years later, directors would complain that Julia's laughter off-camera spoiled takes. One of Julia's best friends at the time, Maddox Kilgore, described her laugh as 'hyena-like'.

'We took an SAT [college entrance exam] preparation course in our senior year and she sat behind me. I'd say something that tickled her and she'd break into this howling laugh. The whole class would stop to let her get it out of her system.'

Although Campbell lacked a drama department, Julia found other avenues to vent her flair for the dramatic. Joan Raley recalled, 'When we got bored in class, Julia could be very creative. She could muster up tears in a second to get out of homeroom and, of course, I'd have to follow her out to help her.'

The only acting Julia did at Campbell had her playing Elizabeth Dole in the school's annual mock-election campaign. Julia didn't consider it acting. Or, as she told *Vanity Fair* in 1993, 'That wasn't really a role. That was in my high-school civics class. We did a mock convention so people could really understand the process. A certain few of us were the candidates who ran for president and, yes, I was Elizabeth Dole. This is how crazy my high school was; when all was said and done, my friend Kevin Hester, who was George Bush, was elected president, and I, as Elizabeth Dole, was vice-president.' As the real Elizabeth Dole's campaign for president gears up, it seems like that long-ago civics class was a case of life imitating art.

Classmate Kelly Jones said that Julia was 'very nice, very outgoing at school and at parties. She always had a lot of girlfriends. She always wanted to have fun. Julia was very easy going, and I have really fond memories of her. She always said my hair was perfect, and she'd run her hands through it, saying, "Oh, I feel so much better now." She was always joking.'

Julia's inheritance, which was mostly invested in high-yielding bonds, didn't turn her into a spoilt and idle rich girl. She had a series of after-school jobs, which included waitressing at the Pizza Inn on South Cobb Drive in Smyrna. It was a popular hangout after Friday-night football games. Although she was working, the job allowed her to spend time with friends – and get paid for it.

Other jobs included a stint as a shop assistant at the Cumberland Mall and as a cashier at the Piggly Wiggly supermarket. She spent the entire summer of 1984 making popcorn and selling sweets at the Galleria Mall Cineplex's snack bar. Her uniform consisted of decidedly unglamorous black trousers, white blouse, red vest and bow tie. She earned the minimum wage of $3.35 an hour. All the junk food she could eat was free.

When Julia wasn't working at the mall, she was often hanging out there and acting like, well, a girl her age. 'I heard she was pretty wild, you know, nutty, crazy in the malls, laughing, joking, playing practical jokes, but she was always nice to everyone. She'd always say, "Hey!" and smile,' one classmate recalled.

'She wasn't shy, but I don't recall her being loud or boisterous,' Jeff Feasal, the Cineplex's assistant manager at the time, has recalled. 'She seemed to fit in with the rest of the kids, but she was not someone who would stand out. I was surprised when I saw her in *Mystic Pizza*. She'd slimmed down and had lost her girlish look.'

Just three inches short of six foot, Julia towered over her girlfriends. She also weighed more then she does today, when her extreme thinness has led to rumours of drug use and anorexia. She tended to carry her weight back then around her hips. Indeed, when I interviewed her in 1990 at a press junket for *Flatliners*, I was struck by the broadness of her hips, which contrasted with the rest of her extremely thin body. A classmate described her as a 'big-boned person with wide hips'. Her transformation from slightly overweight duckling to svelte swan occurred around the time she graduated from high school. 'My body went through a drastic change at eighteen or nineteen. I was kind of not getting taller but still growing, starting not to be a girl any more, but a woman,' Julia said.

The consensus of classmates and teachers seems to be that the teenager was a mixture of shyness and boisterousness, alternating between the two extremes as the mood struck her. She was no wild woman, but not the geek she sometimes claims she was.

This balanced assessment changed, however, once she became famous, and the tabloids needed to concoct a scandalous early life for their readers' titillation. In 1991, after *Pretty Woman*'s $450 million gross made her an international star, the *National Enquirer* ran a story which claimed she had been the school slut at Campbell High, with a special yen for jocks. An unnamed (of course!) classmate told the tabloid, 'When baseball season came around, we had batting practice and Julia was always hanging around. It was the same in football and basketball seasons. Julia always chased the sports stars. It made her the butt of locker-room jokes, where the guys nicknamed her "Hot Pants Roberts".'

Julia claimed these stories were fabricated by people with little if any connection to her past. 'I'll tell you something – not long after *Pretty Woman* came out, suddenly everyone who ever passed through Smyrna's city limits went to high school with me and was my best friend. I was suddenly reading accounts of my would-be life based on people I had barely known in school. I find it more amusing than anything else,' she shrugged.

Eventually, Julia decided to ignore the fiction printed about her. 'It's out of my control. I can either spend the rest of my life being upset and disturbed and annoyed and bothered by things that are inaccurate, or just live my life. So I've detached myself from all that. People will write what they choose to write regardless of how you try to explain to them who you are and what you're about.'

Her successful career took a lot of the sting out of these published lies. In 1999, at the top of the box-office heap, she said, 'Every day of my life is just the greatest revenge, isn't it?'

Former classmates who had known her back then also rallied to her defence and insisted the *Enquirer* had grotesquely distorted her behaviour in high school. Before stardom provided an analgesic, Julia admitted that stories like the *Enquirer's* did sting. Eventually, though, she learned to develop a thick skin and ignore the fiction published by the tabloids. 'I've been really hurt by the press. I've had some really terrible things said about me. But I've learned to laugh, ignore it, and forget it.'

Far from being boy-crazy at school, classmates insist Julia had only one serious boyfriend. One acquaintance believed she graduated a virgin. 'Nearly all the other girls were having sex with the football team,' said Jeff Hardigree, who, as the star of the team, should know. 'But not Julia. She'd go so far, but never all the way. She used to love talking about sex. She was very interested in it, but she seemed to have a problem when it came to doing it. I'm pretty sure she was still a virgin when she left school.'

Less kindly, another student speculated that Julia's virginity remained intact because she was not the great beauty she would later become. 'She wasn't that spectacular to look at in those days,' claimed Tom Acres. 'There were prettier girls around. Everyone liked her, and she was great fun at parties, but she wasn't popular as a date. Guys loved to talk to Julia, but when the lights dimmed and the music slowed, they'd drift off and she'd be on her own.'

In fact, according to Acres, Julia was something of a sad sack and suffered from unrequited puppy love. 'I don't really believe she was interested in anyone other than Joe Thompson. Even when he made it obvious he wasn't interested, she couldn't let go.'

Thompson's best friend at the time, Cal Boyd, recalled, 'Julia had a massive crush on him and connived to get a date with him. But they only went out a few times before Joe dropped her.'

Her obsession with Thompson seems to have been the talk of the school because even years later, several schoolmates still remember the teenage crush. Julia's friend, Holly Aguirre, recalled, 'She chased Joe relentlessly for months and she thought about him day and night.'

Julia felt her crush was less obsessive than her peers' recollections. 'I've never had the "I'll do anything" philosophy, but I had a crush on a boy [Thompson] in high school who took me on one date but then couldn't have cared less. Well, he's living his own life now, isn't he? Some magazine called his mom, and said, "Julia Roberts said she had a big crush on your son," and she was, like, "My son has moved to Vermont and made a good life for himself and he wouldn't want to have a life with some *starlet* from Hollywood,"' she recalled at the height of her stardom in 1997.

It's easy to understand Julia's attraction to the dashing athlete. Joe Thompson was an aristocrat, while Julia's mother and stepfather had trouble making ends meet. Thompson's father was a Georgia state senator and his grandfather had been a legendary football coach at Georgia Tech. Joe was a year older than Julia, and after graduation he enrolled at West Point. At least Julia's senior year was free of her obsession with Thompson, who was no longer around to turbocharge those adolescent hormones.

The summer before her senior year, Julia finally found someone to take her mind off the departing Thompson. In 1984, she began dating Bill Knight, who worked with her at the Cineplex. Within a few months, however, the romance had ended. Years later, when every aspect of the actress's life was picked over by the media, Knight was interviewed by *People* magazine, and he described the short-lived fling. 'It was an infatuation, and it lasted as long as infatuations last.' The break-up wasn't acrimonious, though, and they remained good enough friends that the following spring Julia asked Knight to the senior prom. Ironically, the future screen goddess would end up with a platonic date on the big night.

Knight, a junior at Atlanta's Lovett School at the time, recalled his date. 'She looked charming – she had her hair all done up nicely. She was a lot of fun to hang out with.' The evening ended early for the couple. Knight had to take a college entrance exam the next day, so he drove her home while the other teens continued their revels at post-prom parties. Knight remembered giving Julia a platonic kiss goodnight. In 1996, he found himself chuckling about his brush with the future movie star, telling *People* magazine, 'It's turned out to be a little amusing. You don't think of your friends being in the movies.'

*

Julia's high-school years coincided with the deterioration of her mother's marriage to Michael Motes. Financial troubles had made Betty's first marriage difficult; they made her second a nightmare. Julia and her sisters grew up with the sound of the couple constantly fighting about money.

In 1980 Betty's credit union sued for repayment of a $500 loan she had taken out seven years earlier. Three weeks later, a medical collection agency went after her husband. Two months after that, an Atlanta photographer sued Motes for hundreds of dollars. In 1981 a department store sued the couple for failing to make payments on household furniture they had bought two years earlier.

In 1983, Julia's sophomore year, her mother finally sued Michael Motes for divorce. Within a few months, however, the couple had reunited. Aileen Joyce has speculated that Betty may have reconciled with her difficult husband because she wanted to become executor of her daughters' estate. At the time, the position was still held by the attorney C.R. Vaughn. Betty may have felt that a married woman rather than a divorcee would stand a better chance at becoming her daughters' financial guardian. For whatever reasons, Vaughn voluntarily relinquished his role as guardian, and Betty took on the role. As part of her duties, she disbursed funds to the girls from their stepmother's estate. It's testament to the healthy nature of Betty's relationships with her daughters that her control over their fortune never soured their love for one another.

The same could not be said of her ongoing difficulties with Michael Motes. Betty filed for divorce again, and the messy legal battle dragged on for two years. At one point, opposing attorneys for the couple almost broke into a fistfight in the courtroom.

An unnamed source characterised the split as 'an extremely bitter divorce. They fought about everything, right down to the pots and pans. It was, in my opinion, a very dysfunctional family.' In one of the court documents dividing up the commual property, there was an intriguing order from the judge, which remains unexplained to this day. Both Michael and Betty were forbidden to take Julia's half-sister Nancy to Narcotics Anonymous meetings. Nowhere else in the exhaustive accounts of Julia's formative years has there been a mention of drug abuse in the family.

When Lisa turned eighteen in May 1984, Betty did her duty as executor and turned over the remainder of her daughter's share of the estate by writing Lisa a cheque for $37,000. Lisa was by now a struggling actress in New York, and the windfall must have come in handy.

A year later, on her eighteenth birthday, Julia received a cheque for $28,000 from her mother. The reason for the disparity in her daughter's inheritance had to do with the fact that before turning eighteen, Julia had dipped into her trust fund, with Betty's permission, to finance holidays during summer breaks in high school. One was spent at Camp Birchwood, others visiting Eric and Lisa in New York. Interestingly, Julia made these trips without her mother. She wanted to get away from the constant bickering which by then had made the house on Maner Road an unpleasant place to live in.

In fact, even after Betty and Michael Motes split, home must have held unpleasant memories of years of parental strife. As soon as she got the chance, Julia escaped. 'I had convinced myself that I had three choices: I could get married, I could go to college, or I could move to New York. Nobody was asking me to get married, and I didn't want to go away to school, so I moved,' she said.

Only three days after graduation, she threw all her belongings into her car, an extravagant gift from her brother, and drove to New York, where she joined Eric and Lisa. Like Julia, Lisa had left for New York immediately after her graduation, in 1983. When Julia arrived, Eric was already an established actor; Lisa a struggling one. Their sister would pursue the same dream, only with much greater success and achieve stardom much more quickly than her brother had.

Chapter Five

BIG APPLE, BIG BREAK

Julia's move to New York was made easier by the presence of her siblings, and she later admitted that it didn't take much courage to relocate to what was basically the same home only in a different city. 'It wasn't exactly some heroic move on my part. I wasn't up in Manhattan braving the elements alone. I moved in with my sister Lisa, and it was the same as being at home – except Mom wasn't there, and, if we started wrestling, we didn't get yelled at!'

Although Julia was happy to get away from her troubled home in Smyrna, she moved to New York with some trepidation. She had never really wanted to be an actress. Indeed, her love of animals led her to think of pursuing a career as a vet. So she arrived in New York with profound second thoughts about why she was there. 'I didn't want it to seem like I was doing it just because the others were,' she said, referring to Eric and Lisa. 'But there comes a time when you have to own up to what's pulling you.'

The move to New York wasn't particularly disorientating for Julia. She had been spending summers there for years. Shortly before her father's death, he had taken his daughters to Manhattan to visit Eric, who was delighted that the family was reunited, if only temporarily.

Eric's burgeoning stardom made Julia's visits to New York even more exciting because his social set included even bigger stars. 'I started going up at thirteen,' she said of her summer trips to the Big Apple. 'Everybody else would go to Fort Lauderdale for spring break and come back with this great tan. I'd come back pale, having been in New York where it was freezing. So I was always a little different from everybody else. It was also funny because I would come back from New York, and I would have met somebody [famous] and nobody would believe me. I felt kinda stupid talking about it because they're all talking about these great parties, talking about people we all knew, and I would sit there and say, "Well, Robin Williams said to me that, uh . . ."'

Years later, her high-school classmates would admit they had been sceptical of Julia's alleged encounters with the rich and famous. 'Julia would say "I was in New York this weekend, and I hung out with Billy Idol or Carrie Fisher and . . ." I'm not saying we didn't believe her, but it was pretty unbelievable,' her high-school buddy, Maddox Kilgore, said.

Eric was a terrific big brother, and not just because he shared his celebrity friends with his starstruck kid sister. In the spring of 1984, Julia flew to Australia, where he was filming *The Coca-Cola Kid*. When she returned to Smyrna, she was driving the new car Eric had given her.

When she moved to New York a year later, Eric was living the high life of an actor, an established star with major movie credits like *Star 80* (1983) and the cult classic, *The Pope of Greenwich Village* (1984). His lavish lifestyle included a penthouse apartment at 45 West 73rd Street, a block from Central Park on the swank Upper West Side.

Despite the generosity he displayed in giving her a new car, Eric didn't invite his kid sister to move in with him, which would have seriously cut into his swinging bachelor lifestyle. Instead, Lisa welcomed her younger sister to her tiny apartment at 306 West 18th Street, in the funky neighbourhood of Chelsea, near Greenwich Village. Her apartment was near the Neighborhood Playhouse, where Lisa took acting lessons.

Julia has remained grateful to her sister for making New York a less forbidding place to live. 'Lisa really cushioned a lot of things for me. I always considered her fearless. When we were kids I always thought she would protect me if I was scared,' Julia said, even though she towered over her sister. When she moved to New York, Julia still felt protected by Lisa. 'At seventeen, in New York, it was the same thing.'

Although they are still so close that Julia calls her mother long distance for cooking tips while she's making dinner, Betty seems to have been mis-informed about her daughter's career goals at this time. Betty withdrew $4,500 from Julia's trust fund to pay for tuition fees at Wesleyan Univer-sity in Connecticut, where she was under the illusion her daughter planned to study journalism.

According to Julia, however, college was never on the cards. 'The minute I got out of Smyrna and stopped hot-rolling my hair, all of these ideas of what I wanted to do were dropping in the street like wet sponges. I knew if I stayed in Smyrna I'd have to go to the University of Georgia or get married. And I gotta tell you, higher education wasn't for me. I couldn't see bolting out of bed at 8 a.m. to be ten minutes late for some fucking class with some fucking guy who's just gonna stick it to me again,' she has said, without explaining who 'stuck it to her' originally.

When Julia finally informed her mother that she wouldn't be going to college, Betty took the news in her stride, since she had always suspected her daughter would join her siblings in the family business. 'She was just reluctant to say so because she was uncomfortable about it,' Betty said.

New York seems to have liberated Julia sexually. The girl who had had only one boyfriend in high school quickly began to make up for lost time. A friend from her early days in the Big Apple claimed: 'I don't know how she is now, but in those days Julia was very outgoing, very much a party girl, and had a lot of friends, especially boyfriends. She was very flirta-tious, even with guys who didn't really interest her. She had a lot of flings, at least four that I personally know of in New York. From what I've heard, she didn't change her lifestyle on movie sets, either. She operated the same way.'

In contrast to the fierce independence she would later demonstrate when it came to romantic relationships, Julia tended to defer to her man of the moment, although even then she had trouble maintaining those relationships. 'It's been interesting to read about her different romances over the last few years,' another New York acquaintance said, 'because when I knew Julia, whoever she was involved with ran her life. They dominated her. At least that's the impression I got. But they only domi-nated her briefly because she always got rid of them.'

The Big Apple also introduced her to the big grape. A sober-minded student at Campbell High, Julia quickly got into the hard stuff when she moved north. Another friend from this time said her alcohol of choice was tequila or beer. 'She drank straight out of the bottle. She was wild, very free-spirited, always up for a good time, a real party girl.'

Sex and booze weren't the only new lifestyle changes. With money from her trust fund, Julia had always dressed expensively and tastefully in high school. In New York, she began her 'bag lady' phase, which continues to this day and has landed her on many Worst Dressed lists. Julia favoured baggy jackets several sizes too big. She also wore second-hand jeans with holes in the knees before the 'distressed look' became fashionable. A friend recalled, 'She wore no makeup yet she was beautiful. [She was] a fun-loving kid, short of money a lot of the time, but always busy, always running around doing something.'

Although Julia lived in run-down Chelsea, she liked to hang out in her brother's pricier neighbourhood, where she might bump into Oliver Stone, Robert DeNiro or Tom Cruise at her favourite restaurants, the Empire Grill and the Columbus Restaurant.

This would have a crucial effect on her career. Less than a month after arriving in New York, while walking down Columbus Avenue near Eric's apartment, Julia caught the professional eye of agent Mary Sames and casting director Glenn Daniels.

Sames recalled her first impression of the gangly seventeen-year-old who dressed like a homeless person. 'Glenn and I were walking down Columbus Avenue, and I saw this girl coming towards us.' Sames said to her colleague, 'Glenn, look at that beautiful child!'

As it turned out, Glenn Daniels and Julia had already met a month earlier. Eric, ever the helpful brother, had asked the casting director to take a meeting with his kid sister.

Unlike Sames, Daniels was not impressed with the shabbily dressed teenager. 'I met with her, and frankly, I was underwhelmed,' Daniels admitted ruefully years later. 'I really don't remember too much about the interview, except that she had a very strong southern drawl, and I told her she had to do something about her accent.'

Sames, however, didn't share Daniels' indifference. She handed Julia her card and invited her to come in for an interview.

At their second meeting, Sames was even more taken with the young woman's transcendent beauty, despite the distraction of the Georgia twang which Daniels had found so problematic. 'When she came into the office a couple of days later, she had the thickest southern accent I've ever heard – and I'm from Texas myself. She sat in a chair across from my desk with her legs crossed, her arms folded and, truthfully, she was breathtakingly beautiful,' Sames recalled.

Julia was curiously unprepared for what could have been her big break – a meeting with a powerful talent agent. At this time, needless to say, she didn't have representation. She didn't even have a portfolio of 8 by 10 glossies, every aspiring actor's bible of self-promotion, despite the fact that Betty had given her $850 for photos and modelling school.

Sames' impression of Julia at seventeen doesn't sound all that much different from the actress's public image today. 'She seemed so innocent, so completely without guile, and yet at the same time so guarded, so wary, that I was fascinated by what I perceived to be a unique personality. I mean, here was this free spirit, this breathtakingly beautiful young girl who was nevertheless shy and awkward and gave off the vibes of a fragile, wounded bird.'

Even so, despite Julia's riveting good looks – or maybe it was that country bumpkin accent – Sames declined to take Julia on as a client. Instead, she referred her to a personal manager who was also just starting out on his career, Bob McGowan.

In 1991, after *Pretty Woman* had turned Roberts into a major movie star, Sames was able to laugh at herself for passing up the opportunity to represent the pretty teenager. 'Don't think I haven't taken a lot of teasing over the last six years about having turned her down. But I just didn't know whether I'd have the time, the energy, to work with her. I was very stressed out, the office was in total chaos, and I realised instantly that this demure, shy, waif-like girl sitting across from me needed somebody special and kind-hearted to take care of her, that she was going to need twenty-four-hour-a-day nurturing. And, frankly, I just didn't have it in me at the time.'

While Julia was still in her office, Sames got McGowan on the phone and said, 'I have someone I think you should be interested in. She's too new for me, but I know you're developing young people . . .'

McGowan was happy to take a look and set up an interview two days later. Julia's incandescent presence seemed to have had the same effect on him as it had on Sames, only more so. 'As soon as she walked in she lit up the room. I mean, there were a bunch of adults in there and she came in and kind of took over the whole conversation. She was only seventeen, but she had a presence even then. She was seventeen going on forty. She looked like a kid, but mentally she was much older,' he said.

McGowan's awe was mixed with pity, and both those emotions led him to make a decision that would be pivotal in Julia's career. Not knowing about her trust fund and thinking her bag-lady apparel represented severe financial distress, he decided to represent her despite what he considered a major handicap, her accent. 'This young raggedy thing with a thick southern accent – I thought I'd give her a chance because I felt sorry for her. She didn't have a dime.'

Not exactly. According to author Aileen Joyce, Julia still had almost thirty grand left of Eileen's inheritance, which she received in a lump sum on her eighteenth birthday in 1985.

McGowan turned out to be a soft touch, and although Julia didn't need the money, her manager found himself constantly bailing her out with small and not-so-small loans that were repaid with commissions he received when he found her work. 'I never got involved in her personal life, and we never talked about her childhood, so I didn't know about any inheritance. But I can tell you she was broke when she was around nineteen or twenty,' McGowan still insists, despite evidence to the contrary. 'She was always borrowing money from me, always a couple hundred there, a couple hundred there . . . I remember one day she called me up and said she needed $3,000 right away. I said, "Okay, I'll give you a cheque." And she said, "No, it has to be cash."'

Eventually, Julia made good on all these debts as her career picked up steam. 'One thing about Julia, she was always fair and honest with me. She always paid me back. She was very good that way. I always got my commissions. There was never any problem,' McGowan recalls.

McGowan and his young client had an unusual relationship in which Julia seems to have kept him at arm's length, but close enough to keep her hands in his pocket. During the four years McGowan represented her, he paid her rent several times, even though he never found out where she actually lived. 'I was never at her apartment, and never asked her. Besides, she was always moving around . . . with her sister, then not with her sister, then back with her sister . . . who could keep track?' he said.

Just as Eric had helped Julia jumpstart her career, she tried to do the same with her sister, but failed. Julia asked McGowan to meet Lisa and become her manager as well, but McGowan dropped her after a few abortive attempts to get her representation. 'It's not a good idea to manage sisters. Lisa was very nice, very bright, and she'd done a lot of theatre, so I sent her to a couple of agents, but I don't think anything much came of it,' McGowan said.

Besides their physical dissimilarities, the sisters had contrasting personalities as well. Lisa, according to McGowan, was bossy, upfront and all business. Julia, at least during the early years of her career, was more laid back. McGowan recalled, 'Julia would come into the office and lie on the couch or the floor. She was just a free spirit. I think Julia looked out for her sister a lot, but Lisa also looked out for Julia, too, letting her live with her and everything, but I know Julia paid the rent a lot of the time.' Except, of course, when McGowan was paying it!

Julia had a mesmerising presence, but she was totally untrained as an actress. Then there was that accent that would have typecast her forever as a Southern belle (call it Sissy Spacek Syndrome). McGowan urged Julia to take acting lessons and work with a vocal coach to develop a more neutral accent. Julia grudgingly obliged, but dropped out after only three acting classes, which were taught by Sally Johnson.

Years later, on the set of *Hook*, Julia would explain why she quickly abandoned formal training and decided to rely on her instincts and on-the-job training, which in retrospect turned out to be a successful combination. 'I went to acting classes a few times, but it never seemed very conducive to what I wanted to do, somehow. I never really decided, "I'll go to school, I won't go to school." Things just sort of happened. Basically, I've learned on the job. It's an instinctive thing with me. I don't quite know what I'll be doing until it's done. Sometimes people seem kind of disappointed by that because they want to hear about all the gruelling years. But I'd never done it before. So I thought what I did must be pretty much what everyone does.'

Her instincts, she shrewdly realised, wouldn't help change her speech, and losing her accent required the help of a professional, whom she found in the person of voice coach Sam Chwat. Part of her vocal exercises consisted of repeatedly saying 'cat', 'dog' and 'I'm going to a restaurant', without dragging out the vowels.

Julia admitted she was tone deaf when it came to unlearning her accent. She thought she sounded like every other New Yorker. 'I couldn't hear my accent. I used to go to these auditions and say, "Hello, I'm Julia Roberts." And I never understood why the first thing out of their mouths was "Where are you from?". After a while I began replying "Connecticut",' she said, but no one was fooled.

Julia spent her first two years in New York unemployed as an actress. The statuesque beauty couldn't even find work as a model, despite the enthusiasm for her looks that had overwhelmed agent Mary Sames. During these years in the wilderness, McGowan recalled, 'I couldn't even get agents to respond to her, you know. She tried to do commercials. She went on a lot of commercial calls, but she couldn't get anything. I sent her over to the Click Modelling Agency, but they turned her down.'

As friends from her high-school days had also commented, Julia was a bit plump. Years later, McGowan diplomatically said, 'She's a lot thinner now. Back then they said she was too heavy.'

Julia paid her dues – and the rent when McGowan wasn't paying it – working a series of typical struggling-actor's jobs. There were stints at an ice-cream parlour and a shoe shop called Athlete's Foot.

Although she never invited Bob McGowan over to her place, she spent a lot of time at his. When she wasn't at one of her minimum-wage jobs, you could usually find her at McGowan's office, using his phone or getting tips from other actors on upcoming auditions.

McGowan described a future star on the make: 'She was extremely ambitious. She had a burning ambition to make it. She would even go on calls and auditions that were other clients' callbacks. She would bug me, or my secretary, to find out where the auditions were, and then she would just show up. She can do anything she makes her mind up to do.

'You see, when I first started, none of my clients had agents. So I would get [information on auditions] and do the work myself. I had a bunch of clients the same age and I'd submit them myself and a lot of times if I couldn't get Julia an appointment, she'd go with someone who had the appointment and crash it. She did a lot of auditions for someone who didn't have an agent,' McGowan said.

Although she never landed the role, during these years she got enough reinforcement simply from being asked to return for a second audition, known as 'callbacks' in the business, although even these were few and far between.

'I auditioned for commercials, TV shows, anything, but I don't think I really impressed anyone,' Julia conceded years later. 'I didn't get called back a lot, just enough to keep going. I really didn't know what else I could do. I'd go to all these auditions, and I remember getting so excited about getting a callback or just meeting the director.'

Her mother believed Julia's ability to derive encouragement from very little contributed to her ultimate success. While others would have given up in the face of so much rejection, Julia could always find some tiny mote of approval to fuel her energy and stifle her disappointment.

'I've always admired Julia because she always finds something positive in the experience – if somebody said just one nice thing to her, that's what she'd latch on to,' Betty said.

After two years of pounding the mean streets of New York and subsisting on kernels of praise from casting directors, Julia finally got her break. It would be wrong to call it a 'big break', but it was a beginning. Who helped her on her way? That remains a topic of debate and speaks volumes of the troubled relationships that still plague her family.

Chapter Six

BROTHERLY LOVE AND NEPOTISM

In 1986 Eric Roberts' career was in a slump. Actually, his entire career had been what in the theatre is known as a *succès d'estime*. He received rave reviews, but his films didn't do well at the box office. Just the year before, he had received an Oscar nomination for his over-the-top performance as an escaped con in *Runaway Train*, but the film itself had been a commercial disappointment. Film historian Leonard Maltin has described Eric's choice of roles as 'erratic at best', which would explain why only a year after starring in a big-budget studio film like *Runaway Train*, he would agree to appear in a no-budget western called *Blood Red*, which *GQ* magazine labelled a 'straight-to-video embarrassment'.

Although the western never even made it into movie theatres, it has an honoured place in trivia books as Julia Roberts' film début. How she got the role, typecast as her brother's sister, depends on who's telling the story. Every magazine article that even bothers to mention the minor movie says Eric twisted a few arms to get the job for an actress who didn't have a single credit on her resumé.

Betty, who remains estranged from her son ever since he stomped out of the house after one too many run-ins with his stepfather, refuses to give Eric credit for opening the door for his sister. Betty insists that Eric's manager, Bill Trevsch, got Julia the job. 'They were discussing the tiny role of Eric's sister in the film because they were having trouble finding an actress who looked enough like Eric to play his sister. So the manager

[Trevsch] laughed, pulled out a photo of Julia, and said, "How about this girl?" The producers and the director looked at the picture and said, "My God, she does look like Eric!" And Julia got the role,' according to Betty.

Eric has never even bothered to contradict his mother publicly about Julia's first break, but friends give him credit, not his manager. Eric's close friend, the screenwriter Eddie Bunker, insisted that Eric pulled strings to land Julia the role.

Bunker recalled, 'It was Eric who went to the director and said, "I've got this sister. Is it okay if she plays my sister?" It was Eric who introduced her to contacts in New York and who kicked open doors for her in Los Angeles. How else do you get into Hollywood? There's a thousand girls out here as pretty as she is, and she was not even a trained actress. The hardest thing was getting through the door.'

Blood Red's director, Peter Masterson, backed up Eddie Bunker's story, saying, 'Eric said she was good.'

During interviews early in her career, Julia credited Eric with helping her break into the business. But, over the years, due to family conflicts which will be discussed later, she has engaged in a bit of revisionist history as to just how helpful Eric was.

'For as many people I meet who love Eric Roberts, I meet just as many who think he's a jerk,' she has said. Her connection to her brother she later claimed was neutral in terms of finding her work. 'It doesn't help, it doesn't hurt. Eric has given me advice and, of course, my first movie role,' she did concede, 'but the biggest help has just been watching him, how wonderful he is, and the choices he's made.'

But she later even dismissed his helpfulness as an exemplar of good acting. Eric, it seems, is methodical to the point of being obsessive when it comes to preparing for a role. Julia found her brother's method, if not madness, at least maddening.

'The one time Eric directly helped me with an audition, he nearly drove me crazy. He'd taken me out to dinner and we'd talked about this audition I had for [the TV series] *Spencer for Hire*, and then we'd read this scene over and over. He wouldn't give up. And I got bored because I just wanted to have dinner. I'm not much on just rehearsing and rehearsing, anyway,' she said.

A man with no axe to grind in the Roberts family feud came down on the side of Eric. Julia's manager, Bob McGowan, explained the sequence of events that led to her casting in *Blood Red*. 'It probably was Eric who got her the role because I remember getting a phone call from the producer and then sending them a photo of Julia.' McGowan, at least, didn't take credit for Julia's first job.

The bad blood between Eric and Julia may have already started when her casting made the pages of the *New York Daily News* on 17 August 1986. Contradicting later interviews, Julia told the tabloid that her brother had no knowledge of the casting, an unlikely situation which wouldn't explain how an unknown with no acting credits had been hired. 'He didn't even know I tried out for the part and that I got it,' she told the newspaper columnist. 'When he got back from Cannes a couple of days ago, I told him and he really flipped. It's my first role and I'm only eighteen, and I'm planning to go to college, but that's off for now. I want to ride this lucky break to the fullest.'

Maybe it wasn't the beginning of the family feud that continues to this day but rather an attempt by a fledgling actress to avoid accusations of nepotism. Perhaps she needed to believe it was her talent alone, and not a family connection, that had led to landing the role.

Blood Red must not have seemed like much of a break at the time. The script had been burning in development hell for a decade before it finally began principal photography in the autumn of 1985. Apart from the Roberts siblings, the cast included Dennis Hopper, Burt Young, Aldo Ray, Susan Anspach, Charles Dierkop and Horton Foote, Jr. The melodrama told the story of Sicilian winegrowers oppressed by an evil railroad tycoon and was set in Northern California during the 1880s.

Working on the film made Julia realise once again how different her spontaneous approach to acting was from her brother's style, based on his formal training. '*Blood Red* was real interesting for Eric and me, because we realised that even though we're related, even though we may look alike and be in the same profession, we don't go about the process of acting in the same way at all. We're really different. He went to the Royal Academy of Dramatic Arts in London. I'm a kamikaze actress,' she told a reporter from *Rolling Stone* in 1989.

Blood Red finished principal photography in November 1986 and lay on the shelf for almost four years. During this time, the filmmakers scrambled for a distributor and didn't find one until 1990, when it was released in a handful of cinemas, before quickly ending up in video stores.

Daily Variety panned the film for its 'predictable script, flat direction and miscasting'. Another critic, however, had the prescience to comment on one minor bit of casting, and predict big things for the actress cast in the role. 'Eric Roberts is more subdued than usual, but his scenes with real-life sister Julia are intriguing because of the visual match. She doesn't get much chance to emote, but that nascent star quality already is evident.'

Julia chiefly remembered the turkey because she had to be confined in a corset throughout filming. But her career had finally taken off. Only a month after completing work on *Blood Red*, she landed a supporting role in an episode of the NBC TV series *Crime Story* which was shown on 13 February 1987.

Although the episode appeared in early 1987, almost a year later, when Julia returned to spend Christmas with her mother in Smyrna, she got a tiny taste of the effects of stardom. 'My friend Paige was home from Iowa and we were walking around and I realised people were staring at me. At first I thought it was just my imagination. But Paige noticed it, too. "Why are people looking at you?" she said. Then a couple of people came up because they recognised me from that small role in *Crime Story*. But it was weird, because they didn't really know who I was. They'd just kinda go, "Are you . . .?" And I'd say, "Nah, you're in Cumberland Mall."'

One wonders whether, if Julia had known how oppressive her international stardom would one day become in comparison to this gentle recognition in a suburban mall, she would have had second thoughts about continuing her career. As she became more and more famous, simply denying her identity wouldn't suffice, and she'd have to resort to wearing big wigs, sunglasses and tent-sized dresses.

Julia's small TV roles fed on one another. Bonnie Timmerman, who had cast her in the episode of *Crime Story*, hired her for a guest spot on the hugely successful detective series *Miami Vice*. The episode, 'Mirror Image', was shown on 25 October 1988.

Her manager, Bob McGowan, capitalised on his client's growing resumé and pitched her to every casting agent for every project he learned of. One was a low-budget feature called *Satisfaction* about an all-girl band. Julia couldn't play a musical instrument to save her life, but that didn't stop her industrious manager from pitching her to the project's casting director, Johanna Ray. Calling her in Los Angeles, McGowan pleaded over the phone, 'Listen, Johanna, I've got the perfect girl for this.' Ray asked if his client could play a musical instrument. Thinking quickly, McGowan said, 'I'm not sure. Let me ask her, and I'll get back to you.' After spending almost two years with his client hanging out at his office, McGowan knew Julia didn't play an instrument, but he quickly found a way round this minor handicap.

'I picked the drums because I figured it was the easiest instrument to learn,' McGowan explained, so Julia began an intensive course in drum lessons. Then he called Ray back in Los Angeles and told her his client was an expert on the drums. It turned out his subterfuge was unnecessary. So were the drum lessons. Julia did land a role in *Satisfaction*, but as a bass guitar player.

One of the fringe benefits of appearing in *Satisfaction* was that the film earned Julia her Screen Actors Guild card, the equivalent of the British Equity card. That presented a minor problem, however. Although she had been born Julia Fiona Roberts, throughout her childhood and early adulthood friends and family alike had called her Julie. But there already was an actress registered with the Guild under the name 'Julie Roberts', and the Guild doesn't allow the duplication of names.

Julia called her mother and asked if she should change her professional name to Julia or Fiona, her middle name. Betty felt that Fiona would be too confusing, and Julia agreed. So, unlike so many other actors who shed their birth names for the sake of a SAG card, Julia found herself reverting to her real name. But to this day, those closest to her still call her 'Julie'.

With her new old name and SAG card, all Julia needed was an agent, since by law managers are not allowed to negotiate contracts for their clients. McGowan had always had a good relationship with Risa Shapiro, an agent at William Morris, whom he had been begging unsuccessfully to represent Julia for years.

Maybe the prospect of a feature film would finally change Shapiro's mind, McGowan thought. No such luck. 'I used to call up Risa all the time, asking her to try and get Julia an audition for this film, that film. But she'd always tell me the same thing, which was, "Bob, I just can't do that." Every now and then, though, they'd send her on something idiotic, like an industrial [training film] or some bullshit like that. This time I told her, "Look, this is what's happening. Julia's probably going to get something like $50,000 and you guys can do the deal,"' McGowan recalled.

Julia's manager was, of course, grasping at straws. For a powerhouse agency like William Morris, a 10 per cent commission on $50,000 was lunch money at the Russian Tea Room.

Although it was a low-budget teen-oriented film, *Satisfaction* had one element that McGowan used as his trump card in winning Shapiro's services. The feature film division of Aaron Spelling's TV company was producing the film, and Spelling in the 1980s was the king of prime time with hits like *Dynasty* and *The Love Boat*. McGowan finally sold Shapiro on Julia when he mentioned that a clause in her contract would cast her in a spin-off TV series of the feature if it was a hit at the box office. With visions of million-dollar residuals dancing in the agent's head, Shapiro finally signed Julia.

'I practically had to beg Risa to take her. I told her, "Look, put this on a personal level. Take a shot with her for one year. I'm throwing you the deal." And they did. The Morris agency signed her,' McGowan said. But none of the firm's top agents wanted to handle Julia, and she ended up being co-represented by the second-tier Shapiro and Elaine Goldsmith, whom McGowan said originally balked at taking Julia on. In fact, neither agent wanted to represent her, although Goldsmith remains Julia's agent to this day.

To prepare for her first major film role, Julia spent four weeks trying to learn to play the bass guitar, but she seemed to be all thumbs. 'There's nothing more frustrating than having this great instrument and a great song and not being able to put them together,' she has recalled. But she kept at it, with one-on-one lessons in the morning and group classes in the afternoon. By the time principal photography began, Julia was a passable guitar player. 'We all knew the quicker we learned, the quicker it would be fun,' she said in reference to her eight-hour-a-day jam sessions. 'And that's what happened. We got it up fast and we had a good time.'

Julia would have an even better time once the cameras started to roll and she met her handsome co-star.

Chapter Seven

DATING ON LOCATION

───⟪∿⟫───

With the original title *Sweet Little Rock'n'Rollers* and a minuscule budget, the film that eventually came to be known as *Satisfaction* was shot on a back-breaking TV-movie schedule of only thirty-five days in May and June of 1987, with two primary locations: Charleston, South Carolina, and Baltimore, Maryland.

If it weren't for the participation of a future superstar, *Satisfaction* would still make it into the trivia books as the feature-film début of Justine Bateman, the star of the hugely successful TV series *Family Ties*. Indeed, Bateman was the biggest star on the project, although it also boasted the services of Blondie's Deborah Harry as the girlfriend of a burnt-out songwriter from the '60s.

For Julia, the most significant thing about this forgotten film is that it began a pattern that would continue for much of her career – falling in love with a co-star on the set. The lucky man in this case was Liam Neeson, who played Deborah Harry's boyfriend. Off camera, Neeson and Julia soon became an item.

Now best known as the star of George Lucas's latest entry in the *Star Wars* saga, *The Phantom Menace*, Neeson's career at this time wasn't much further along than Julia's.

Their relationship may have been a case of opposites attracting. Both in temperament and geography, the two actors couldn't have been further apart. Neeson was thirty-four at the time, fourteen years Julia's senior. Born in 1953 in the working-class town of Ballymena in Northern Ireland, Neeson was raised a Catholic in a Protestant neighbourhood. His father was a school janitor and his mother a cook. He grew up fast and tough, and Neeson turned the need to use his fists into a short-lived career as a boxer. He also had a stint as a forklift operator. His speech was laced with profanity from on-the-job training. Despite a gentler upbringing, Julia matched her new boyfriend profanity for profanity.

Neeson grew up in a household filled with sisters. He felt comfortable around women and had the reputation of being a ladies' man. 'I love women!' he once said. 'Every shape, size and colour created. They are the better sex. Men have a lot of ground to make up as regards to emotions and their place in society.'

By the time *Satisfaction* wrapped, the unlikely couple was sharing a modest apartment three blocks from the beach in a scruffy section of Venice, California. When the film came out in February 1988, Neeson was so put off by the teen-themed film he refused to attend the première or see it at the cinema.

Satisfaction was Julia's first starring role, however, and curiosity if nothing else compelled her to attend the première, with Eric as her date. After the screening, Julia wished she had stayed at home with her boyfriend. She dismissed her role as a 'boy-crazy peacock' and worried about being typecast as a pretty bimbo. Eric tried to cheer his sister up.

Julia recalled, 'Eric laughed, but when it was over, we talked and he made it seem not so bad. But the film taught me a lot about what I hope to never do again in a movie.' She failed to specify the lesson she had learned. Never try to fake playing a musical instrument, perhaps? 'There's only one scene I was embarrassed about that I was supposedly in. But I had the day off, so it was actually kind of funny. In the film, there's a scene where I'm supposedly in the van with my boyfriend, and the van is rocking, and a great amount of time passes, as if we've been going at it for quite a long time. Well, actually, it was an empty van and there were a couple of grips behind it pushing it back and forth. I was at the beach all day.'

Besides landing her an agent and introducing her to Neeson, *Satisfaction* played another important role in Julia's career, regardless of the quality of the finished product. It was produced by Alan Greisman, who was married to Sally Field at the time. Over the years, Field would go from being Julia's mentor to cheerleader for the top film actress in the world. Field would play a pivotal role in several career-making projects for her young protégée.

For Field, it was a case of mother love at first sight. 'The minute I met her I wanted to wrap my arms around her,' the actress told *Redbook* magazine in July 1994.

Julia now took a step backward in her career, agreeing to play a small role in a cable movie after having starred in a feature film. The movie, which ran on America's HBO pay channel, was called *Baja Oklahoma*, and she played Lesley Ann Warren's rebellious daughter.

As she would on so many other sets, Julia turned the cast and crew into a surrogate family, once again compensating for the unstable life of her formative years. She cracked jokes and played ping-pong with the grips and gaffers – ingratiating herself with everyone.

One crew member had happy memories of the time he spent working with the young actress: 'Julia was one of the nicest people I've ever met on a set. There was no attitude from her. She didn't have the barracuda mentality that often affects actors. She wasn't obsessed with acting. She was very natural. She had an interesting mix of being very real, very focused. She knew what she wanted and where she wanted to go in terms of her career, and she felt confident it was going to happen at her pace.'

By now, Julia seemed to be working non-stop. Returning to New York after *Baja Oklahoma* finished filming, she almost immediately auditioned for a role that would firmly set her on the route to stardom. The low-budget feature, *Mystic Pizza*, was to be shot on location in Mystic, Connecticut, home of the movie's fictional pizza parlour, which employed three waitresses at a seaside resort. All three characters, Jojo, Kat and Daisy, were marvellously written, and any one of them could propel to stardom the lucky actress who landed it. But despite her growing resumé, Julia would have to compete with almost a hundred other actresses for one of the three roles. Ironically, when she went to the audition, she didn't know which part she'd be reading for. Insecure about her looks, she didn't suspect she was being considered for the part of the drop-dead gorgeous waitress, Daisy.

'They'd sent me a script and I read it, but I actually didn't know what part I was up for. I just assumed that I was Jojo, who was described as cute, earthy and unable to commit to marriage to her boyfriend – because Kat was too young, and Daisy was too voluptuous or something.'

Julia underestimated her charms because the casting director, Jane Jenkins, thought Julia was certainly 'voluptuous or something' enough to try out for the role of Daisy. As it turned out, Julia was beautiful enough but ethnically incorrect. Daisy was Portuguese, and the WASPy Roberts, despite her exotic facial features, didn't look Hispanic.

The audition, Julia later recalled, 'went fine, but the casting director told me I just didn't look very Portuguese.' Julia's reading, however, so impressed the casting director that she urged the producer, Mark Levinson, and director, Donald Petrie, to meet Julia the next day.

Referring to the producer and director, she told her manager, 'Bob, when I see these guys, I'm gonna blow them away.' For her second audition, Julia raided her manager's wardrobe, looking for a man's suit which she felt would define the spunky waitress. McGowan said, 'That's when she started wearing men's suits. I thought it was quite sexy, to tell you the truth. She'd wear the trousers and the jacket, nothing else. I thought it looked hot,' he recalled. Thus, sartorial history is made.

Although a mannish suit helped flesh out her role, it didn't make her look Portuguese. Julia bought a can of black hairspray, but even that failed to darken her dark blonde hair enough. Desperate, she resorted to black shoe polish thinned with mousse. It took hours to apply the gelatinous glop, but she finally got the midnight-black hue she was looking for. She described the final effect as 'grotesque' and spent all night achieving it, showing up for the audition without having slept – not that she could have anyway since she was so pumped for her second attempt.

Julia returned to the casting office with jet black hair, wearing McGowan's suit and no shirt. She also wore earphones and a Walkman, which blared Jimi Hendrix. That was how she prepared for the role. The room was filled with other potential Daisys, preparing in the more traditional way, poring over the script and running lines past each other.

Julia surveyed the competition. Instead of being intimidated by the assembled beauties, any one of whom could have snatched the career-making role away from her, she concentrated on psyching them out. 'I remember thinking, "What is going to give me the edge over these girls?"' Julia recalled years later. It certainly wasn't her shoe-polished hair, which was beginning to drip on her face. 'I had my Walkman on. I was listening to Jimi Hendrix live at Monterey, singing "Wild Thing". I played it over and over again, and the more I played it, the more cocky I got. And the more attention I got from the women in the room. And the more they stopped reading their pages and started watching me, the more sure I became that I was going to get the role.'

Her second reading almost turned into a disaster, saved only by the director's and the producer's sense of humour. At one point, the actor reading opposite her ran his hands through her hair, and they got covered with shoe polish. Everyone started laughing, and Julia got the job.

As it turned out, Julia brought more than shoe polish to the audition. Her reading helped the filmmakers, who were still uncertain of Daisy's personality and motivations, to understand the character. Producer Levinson recalled, 'Julia walked in and she was very much like a light at the end of the tunnel. There was no doubt that she would be Daisy the minute she walked in the room. She made it a lot clearer for us how to get to that character.'

Director Petrie also became a charter member of the Julia Roberts fan club after her second reading: 'Julia was real smart to put that rinse in her hair and make it jet black, like the colour of the Portuguese character she played in the film. It worked. It made her look exotic and perfect for the part. She was exactly what I needed for the role . . . unpredictable, and willing to take chances, fiery, spirited, and yet very real.'

The movie began principal photography in the fall of 1987 with Lili Taylor, Annabeth Gish and Julia as the waitresses, and co-starring Adam Storke, William R. Moses and Vincent Phillip D'Onofrio. Julia was Daisy Araujo, a tart-talking girl from the wrong side of the tracks who falls in love with the son of a wealthy family summering at the resort.

Julia's co-star Annabeth Gish described the story as a distaff *Diner*, a buddy movie that just happened to star girls instead of boys. Julia agreed.

'Our characters and our generation are a little more independent and open about the philosophy of friendship,' she said. There were no catfights in the story. The girls were allies, not rivals.

She added, 'If women didn't play the kind of women that they wouldn't hang out with, there would be fewer of those roles. We wouldn't see so many surface cheese puffs.

'I like to see movies that are real. Things with heart and soul, not ones that are just about sex or silly surface feelings. *Mystic Pizza* isn't *Apocalypse Now*, but we have a little heart and soul. All our characters are honest.'

Ironically, Julia had been rejected for acting and modelling jobs in the past because of a minor weight problem that had plagued her since high school. Now, apparently, she had become so slim that she had to stuff herself to 'flesh out' her character, since the script described Daisy as someone with 'all the right curves and all the right moves to drive men crazy . . . the kind of girl men would kill for'. While Julia binged, she also had to endure the good-natured jibes of crew members who would shout, 'There's that girl men are going to kill for today.' Julia confessed that she had a lot of trouble living up to the script's expectations – not to mention the crew's.

In terms of ethnicity and career-aspirations, Daisy the waitress in a dead-end job couldn't have been more unlike Julia. But both enjoyed swearing. And the role allowed her to engage in a Charles Bronson-like fantasy on screen: demolishing her rich boyfriend's Porsche in a fit of rage.

'Daisy was somebody I might have been if I had been different, if that makes any sense. I could relate to her in a lot of ways, but at the same time she had a lot of gusto, a lot of chutzpah that I never had,' Julia said. 'It was a little scary being Daisy, though, because she's kind of like ten feet tall and I'm happy being five foot eight,' she added, deducting an inch from her actual height.

If they had held an election or taken a poll, Julia would have been voted most popular by her co-workers. Once again, she turned the cast and crew into a surrogate family. One member of the production said, 'She really interacts with the crew. She's not the kind of star who hangs out in her trailer and never talks to anybody. She really makes you feel she's part of the team.'

Once, Julia's behaviour did cause a bit of a problem during shooting, but it wasn't a case of a temperamental star. Director Petrie had to reshoot a scene that didn't involve Julia after high-pitched laughter coming from her rented home spoiled a take. When the director dispatched a gofer to tell Julia to be quiet, the crew member found her surrounded by fifteen adoring production people. 'She had them eating out of her hand,' the director's emissary said. 'They were just cracking up.'

Julia turned twenty while shooting *Mystic Pizza*, but she hadn't told anyone about her birthday and began to feel lonely, missing her mother and her boyfriend, Liam Neeson, who was back home in Venice. Suddenly, late in the day, a huge birthday cake in the shape of a pizza appeared, compliments of her adoring colleagues. Julia was so overwhelmed with emotion that she ran away from the crowd, returning after she regained her composure. 'I'm shy and I'm an extrovert. So everyone seems to get a kick out of the fact that I blush very easily. But I do. Certain things kind of make me go, "Well, I've got to run, see you later . . ."'

Unlike her brother, who drove her crazy when he helped her audition for a TV role, Julia doesn't like to do numerous takes. Her style of preparation – or lack thereof – perfectly complemented the director's style of filmmaking. In fact, Petrie almost asked her not to rehearse her scenes so her first take would be as fresh and spontaneous as an audition. 'She has a wonderful spontaneity on screen that really makes her light up. Most actors have that in their eyes, but Julia has it in her eyes, her face, everywhere. She's the kind of actress you want to film without a rehearsal because she's so quirky you never know what you'll get!' Petrie said.

With a minuscule budget of $3.5 million, *Mystic Pizza* more than recovered its costs with a final gross of $14 million after opening in October 1988. Critics gave the film mixed reviews, but Julia earned raves. Michael Wilmington of the *Los Angeles Times* called her performance 'a minor triumph . . . generating smoky tension: the livid fire of a small-town belle, blazing up high against the possibility of inevitable small-town entropy or eclipse'.

Just as her quickie appearance on a TV show had people recognising her at the Smyrna mall, *Mystic Pizza*'s much wider audience gave her a taste of the kind of attention that would grow until it eventually became smothering.

'Every day for a week' after the film opened, she recalled, 'people came up to me and said, "I thought you were six foot tall."' On screen, Julia's statuesque figure and gangly limbs made her look even taller than she was. But before she could let this attention go to her head, one moviegoer quickly deflated her minor stardom by asking, 'So where's the fox from *Mystic Pizza*?'

At this point, Julia was beginning to get a taste of the bizarre permutations stardom can take and the fans it can attract. Back home in Smyrna, she was using the ladies room at a cinema when a woman in the cubicle next to her said, 'Uh, excuse me? Were you in *Mystic Pizza*?' Taking the bizarre question in her stride, Julia owned up to her identity. Then the woman asked, 'Can I have your autograph?', and slid a piece of paper under the partition. Julia declined, explaining with great understatement, 'I don't think right now is the time.'

To capitalise on the positive word-of-mouth her client had received from *Mystic Pizza*'s cult status success, Julia's agent, Risa Shapiro, sent out dozens of copies of Julia's photo-spread in *Esquire* magazine, which featured the new star in a skin-tight minidress. The outfit seemed even tighter because Julia had been sprayed with water. The photos landed on the desk of every important movie executive in Hollywood, and Shapiro was swamped with calls from them, all inviting Julia to drop in when she was in Los Angeles.

A month after *Mystic Pizza* finished filming, Julia followed Liam Neeson to Los Angeles, where he had moved a year earlier. Julia wanted to be closer to the man in her life, but relocating also represented a shrewd career move. After moving to the heart of the movie industry in 1987, Neeson had seen his career take a quantum leap. Julia hoped changing coasts would have a similar effect on her career. She underestimated the importance of the move.

By March 1988 the handsome couple were living together in a modest apartment in a three-storey stucco building on 26th Avenue in Venice, a stone's throw away from the Pacific Ocean.

Julia loved the Los Angeles climate and, as an avid swimmer, often took advantage of her proximity to the beach. But her love of the water almost killed her when in March she contracted a near fatal bout of spinal meningitis. Although it was never proven, she suspected the notoriously polluted waters of the Santa Monica Bay had exposed her to the deadly virus. Initially, the symptoms didn't seem particularly serious and Julia attributed her aches and pains to the rigours of making three movies without a break. But, as her condition worsened, Neeson begged her to see a doctor. It wasn't until he called Betty, however, that the stoic young woman finally agreed to check into the hospital for tests. By now she was seriously ill, semi-conscious and with a high fever. Julia was so ill she remained in the hospital for several weeks, during which time her mother, alarmed by her daughter's rapid decline, flew in from Smyrna. Eventually, the entire Roberts family – Eric, Lisa and their baby sister Nancy – converged on Los Angeles because Julia's condition was so grave.

The family hadn't been together in the same place in sixteen years, and a friend immortalised the gathering with a snapshot. Julia loved the grainy photo so much she later had it enlarged and hung on the wall of her apartment.

Julia realised how close she had come to death. 'I thought I was going to die, and so did everyone else. So I was forced to face it and found that I wasn't scared to die, that it wasn't a scary thing. Not that I want to die – I want to live forever. It's just that having been there, I found out it wasn't such a bad thing,' she said.

Julia's close call with the Grim Reaper was a weird blessing in a way, since it provided her with the emotional 'research' to interpret her next film role.

Chapter Eight

OSCAR GOLD MAGNOLIA

———◆———

In 1988, up-and-coming actress Meg Ryan found herself with an embarrassment of riches. She was offered two meaty roles, one a drama entitled *Steel Magnolias*, the other a romantic comedy, *When Harry Met Sally*. Ryan chose the latter, and her decision inadvertently propelled Julia Roberts' career, already chugging along nicely, to even greater heights.

The role Ryan turned down was that of a young diabetic, based on the real life of the sister of Broadway playwright Robert Harling. After Ryan bowed out, Julia's agent, Risa Shapiro, went after the role with the tenacity of a pitbull, but found the director of the film unwilling to play fetch.

Director Herb Ross at first refused to even meet with Julia or take a look at her previous work. Bob McGowan remembered the director's resistance. 'Herb did not even want to look at the tape of *Mystic Pizza*. What happened was there was someone else in *Mystic Pizza* who was after the role, and their agent talked him into looking at it.'

Julia's foul-mouthed, mini-skirted waitress in *Mystic Pizza* was not exactly a good calling card for the role of the saintly diabetic Shelby Eatenton-Lacherie in *Steel Magnolias*. Thick-skinned Daisy Araujo of *Mystic Pizza* was a tart-talking northerner. Fragile Shelby was the quintessential good ol' southern gal.

The film was based on Harling's hit Broadway play, and every actress within spitting distance of Shelby's age knew how powerful the role was and clamoured for an audition. Ross still refused to see Julia until Sally Field, who happened to be Ross's friend, begged the director to meet Julia.

Seventy-five actresses were up for the role. In the face of such fierce competition, Julia didn't think she had a snowball's chance in mid-summer Atlanta of landing the part, so she went to the audition with an 'I don't give a fuck' attitude, hoping that if nothing else Ross might consider her for a future role.

'When I got the call to audition for the movie I asked who was in it. And I was told Sally Field, Shirley MacLaine, Dolly Parton, Olympia Dukakis and Daryl Hannah,' Julia said, describing a veritable *Who's Who* of Hollywood's respected actresses that ran the gamut of ages from ingenue to old battle-axe. 'I felt like, "Yeah, right". I went to the audition with the intention of not getting it – it was too perfect. I would go do the reading and do the best I could to try to impress somebody for a future role.'

Despite her pessimism, Julia threw herself into the ordeal of a five-day audition, reading and rereading for the part every single day. Julia's other agent, Elaine Goldsmith, suspected her client's pessimism was a sham because she pursued the part as though she felt she would get it. 'When Julia wants something, she goes after it. Julia's got passion. She's very focused,' Goldsmith said with understatement.

After three auditions, Julia got to read with Sally Field, who would play Shelby's mother. Field had fallen in love with Julia's talent on the set of her husband's production, *Satisfaction*, and the steel-willed Oscar-winner mounted a full-scale assault on the reluctant Ross that yielded surprisingly quick results.

Three hours after her final audition, Field broke the news to her protégée that Julia would be playing her daughter. As happy as she was with the news, another emotion immediately overwhelmed the neophyte actress: fear. She'd be acting opposite Oscar-winners who had been in the business for more years than Julia had been on the planet. But her biggest fear involved Ross, who still had misgivings about her ability to play the role. (The outspoken director would continue to express his doubts even after the movie was released. In an interview, Ross revealed he suggested she take in a few acting classes now that the film was finished and she had time on her hands.)

Ross immediately decided to play Pygmalion to what he obviously considered a lump of human clay in desperate need of remoulding. He told her to lose weight, change her hair colour to a less 'threatening' dishwater blonde and even ordered her to pluck her eyebrows.

Julia drowned her terror in drink. To celebrate this potentially career-making role, Bob McGowan, Risa Shapiro, Elaine Goldsmith and Julia toasted themselves into a stupour with champagne during an all-nighter at the Beverly Hills Hotel's Polo Lounge.

A few days later, she flew to the production location, Natchitoches, Louisiana, for rehearsals. Sally was already on the set, ready to continue the nurturing of her favourite ingenue. Betty was grateful for the interest the accomplished actress took in her daughter, who was still on her way up. 'Sally knew Julia and liked her and really worked with her. She really wanted Julia to get the part. She's that kind of person and that kind of actress. I can't imagine her not being gracious or helpful with anyone she works with,' Betty said.

Roberts' biographer, Aileen Joyce, has suggested that Julia knew just who to schmooze to further her career. Although Joyce called her subject's ability 'instinctive', the fact that Julia always picked the right person to charm hints that calculation rather than instinct guided Julia's behaviour at critical points in her career.

When Sally met Julia, it was bonding at first sight. Julia's apparent vulnerability was like a beacon to the daughterless Field.

A former friend, however, suspected that Julia's vulnerability was a façade hiding, well, a steel magnolia of a human being: 'Julia's manipulative in that if she wanted something and she thought somebody could help her get it, she would zero in on them. Anybody who could help her she'd work on and make them like her,' the friend was quoted as saying in Aileen Joyce's 1993 biography.

The movie crew of *Steel Magnolias* was not the first the tiny town of Natchitoches (pop. 17,000) had played host to. Back in 1959, John Wayne had filmed *The Horse Soldiers* there. But a movie star hadn't set foot in the sleepy hollow since then, and the arrival of major actresses like Shirley MacLaine and Sally Field created a Mardi Gras atmosphere in the otherwise somnolent backwater. Every location where the cameras set up shop was mobbed by starstruck locals. Some citizens hung out at restaurants where they hoped to catch a glimpse of the stars during a break in shooting. Others sold T-shirts with the actors' faces emblazoned on them. The cast had virtually no privacy during the entire shoot, their every step and forkful being followed by the locals.

Even Dolly Parton, something of an expert at crowd control since her days as a concert diva, felt her space had been invaded. 'Everybody knows every move you make,' the normally sweet-natured southerner said in a rare moment of pique. To provide an emotional buffer of sorts between her and the locals, Dolly invited all eleven members of her immediate family to stay at her rented home in Natchitoches. When she wasn't on the set, Dolly could usually be found in the kitchen preparing her favourites, home fries and corn bread, for her family and co-stars.

But it wasn't just Dolly's stuffing her colleagues with carbohydrates that kept these divas calm and untemperamental. Parton suspected that the actresses started a mutual admiration society instead of catfights because no one received special treatment. 'I think the reason we all became such good friends is because we all had the same exact Winnebagos, we didn't have beautiful clothes to fight over, and there were no available men in the cast.' In the latter situation, Parton was speaking of herself. There were no available men in her age group to romance, but more on that later.

Daryl Hannah literally moved out of town to keep enquiring eyes as far away as possible, renting a farm outside the city limits. Hannah spent her free time riding horses and jumping on a trampoline in her backyard. Although there was potential for rivalry between her and Julia since both actresses were of the same age, Hannah's career was much more established after hits like 1984's *Splash!*, and the beautiful blonde emulated Sally Field by taking an instant liking to Julia. The two women could often be seen riding Hannah's horses through the backwoods of Natchitoches. Julia loved Hannah's offbeat personality, especially since they shared so many personality traits. Julia could have been describing herself when she said of her equestrian pardner, 'One minute Daryl can be this big-eyed puppy and then the next she can get wild and silly, pinning clothespegs to everyone's shirts just for kicks.'

Sally Field played Julia's mother on screen, and many observers felt the older actress continued the role even after the cameras stopped rolling. Field pled guilty to serving as surrogate mother. 'Something about Julia makes you care for her. And it goes beyond her looks. The part of Shelby didn't call for a great beauty, which was fortunate because no one, including Julia, agreed with me that she [Julia] was one. She grew up as kind of an ugly duckling, not a "pretty woman", and the impression we form of ourselves in early adolescence always remains,' Field said.

The older actress looked after her adopted daughter professionally and personally. When filming for the day ended, Field often invited Julia over to her rented home to rehearse the next day's scenes. After rehearsal, Field would make Julia dinner.

On the set one day, Julia seemed especially tense, and the strong-willed Field shut down production for ten minutes while she gave Julia a pep talk and went over her lines. 'Sally's inexhaustible support staggered me. It got so I didn't call my real mother for three months,' Julia said, no doubt exaggerating, since her reliance on Betty is legendary. Instead, she claimed, 'I would call Sally and say, "Momma", and she would just answer me back.' During a visit to the set, Julia's mother recalled with a chuckle the time all three women ended up in an elevator together and Julia said, 'Mom . . .' Both Field and Betty said, 'Yes?'

Julia took full advantage of Field's maternal instincts, while the older actress found herself envying Julia's spontaneity, which the tightly wound Field felt was something she lacked.

'I think we were a good combination. I took on the mother role for her and I think she felt she was able to lean on my steadiness and my experience, while I was able to use my delight and affection for her,' Field said. 'Julia is much more independent than I ever was. She's a real free spirit and that's one thing I've never been or ever will be. I've often wished I was, but I'm always sort of grounded, which is why I think I get a kick out of the Julias of the world. I'm delighted by them.'

Despite Field's best efforts, Julia still needed her real mother, and Betty was there to offer comfort. 'I spent some time there, especially towards the beginning of the movie, because Julia was feeling a little overwhelmed. And it was really amazing. I've never seen such harmony,' Betty said, describing the cast.

Field loved to do needlepoint to get rid of tension, so she taught the rest of the cast the craft. The actresses became such enthusiasts it began to interfere with shooting, and director Ross banished all needles from the set.

In the beginning, Julia had a strained relationship with another co-star, the notoriously skittish Shirley MacLaine. But eventually, Julia's emotional neediness ended up turning MacLaine into a member of her surrogate on-set family.

Julia described the evolution of her relationship with MacLaine: 'The first time we met I felt she was looking right through me. It was my most tense moment, which is very funny to me now. I went over to her house one day and we got into this intense conversation in which I talked non-stop for an hour and a half about feelings and family and ideas and goals.

'And when I finished, this amazing woman dissected everything I'd said, starting from the beginning. I was absolutely blown away by her extraordinary gift of really listening to a person.'

While Sally made her home-cooked meals, MacLaine treated Julia and their colleagues to barbecues at the lakefront house she rented in Natchitoches. Although Julia was MacLaine's next-door neighbour, they never bonded anywhere near as tightly as she had with Field.

Julia did become very friendly with Dolly Parton, who was everyone's favourite on the set, but not for the reason Julia and Sally had bonded. Dolly and Julia discovered they both loved telling dirty jokes.

Although filming began on 12 July 1988, the cast had assembled in Natchitoches two weeks earlier for rehearsals. They had a picnic on 4 July and often got together during filming at a local bar called The Bodacious Club. Dolly Parton loved the place and called it 'just a lil' ol' beer joint out on the edge of town'. Occasionally, Parton and family members joined the club's band on stage and performed country-and-western numbers.

Olympia Dukakis gave a weird dinner party for her co-stars at which she only served leftovers. She claimed she had been too busy to cook because she was working on the presidential campaign of her cousin, Michael Dukakis.

Julia not only had a substitute family, her 'relatives' were all A-list actresses. 'It's one thing to watch them act, but it's another thing to work with them and see at first-hand that they're not just really great actors but also really great people.'

Herb Ross, unfortunately, spoiled this family tableau. Directors often function as father figures, treating their charges like children to coax the best performance possible out of them. As far as Julia was concerned, the imperious Ross was more like a wicked stepfather. In a strange cosmic way, Ross was perhaps playing the Michael Motes role.

The director and the actress had strong opinions about Shelby's character, and their ideas often clashed. Choosing her words carefully, Julia described what are often euphemistically called 'artistic differences'.

'Herbert has his ideas of action and result, and I have mine, and they didn't always receive each other perfectly,' she said. 'But you have that relationship and that's one you deal with every day and you do what you have to do to get the result you feel is most true.'

Ross admitted he wasn't a touchy-feely type when it came to handling delicate young actresses. 'I am a taskmaster. I never spoke privately to anyone. If I had criticism or advice, I would say it in front of the other women. But Julia worked hard. She stayed in bed for the coma scenes eight, twelve hours a day, until she was ill and dizzy.'

Sally Field tried to serve as a buffer between the two camps, but she made it clear whose side she was ultimately on. 'Herb is a good director, but in some ways he was extremely hard on Julia. We all felt it was uncalled for, but she's a warrior.'

Exacerbating the tension she felt with Ross was the nerve-racking role of Shelby itself. None of Julia's previous films had required her to dig so deeply within herself to find a character. She may have been a warrior, but she got wounded a lot during the battle of the steel magnolias.

'It was a really difficult part. In terms of the friends I made on the set, it was tremendous. In terms of the things I've received from the outcome of it, it was tremendous. But it was not an easy road to travel. Challenge-wise, it was like sitting exams every day.'

Fortunately, Julia got along much better with the writer than the director. Robert Harling based his play, which was adapted for the screen, on the death from diabetes of his sister Susan only three years earlier. Harling's emotions were still raw, and Julia tapped into them. The writer and the actress became inseparable as he poured out his feelings. Cynics might say Julia cozied up to the author so she could give a better performance, but Harling would disagree. 'Julia became like a member of my family. She'd come over and we'd have hamburgers and look through albums and talk to Mom and Dad. They got very close. She's very important to my family,' Harling said.

Julia had found a way to create yet another surrogate family, this time with an even stronger bond than simply sharing a movie location.

In an eerie way, Julia even bonded with Susan to the point that she refused to look at Harling's snapshots of his sister. 'I thought if I ever looked into her eyes I would lose control. When I finally did see them, I was a mess. I was just a puddle.'

Julia's connection with Susan sometimes bordered on the paranormal. During dinner in one of the houses used as a set, Harling told Julia, 'You know, Susan used to babysit in this house.'

Julia recalled, 'Suddenly, I had a feeling she'd been sitting in the chair I was sitting in. It was very odd and uncomfortable.'

Finally, for her own emotional health, Julia had to put some distance between herself and the deceased woman. 'I had a lot of conversations with Robert, and I felt an obligation to a truth, to explain to the people who would see this movie, "This is true; this is what happened." I felt I had a mission to be just to the woman that she was; yet, as the same time, I had to understand that I was not her, that I didn't look like her, that my clothes weren't the clothes she wore, that this wasn't a documentary, that I was playing Shelby Eatenton, not Susan Harling.'

The most dramatic scene in the film, where Shelby suffers a diabetic fit, was shot on the first day. Julia hadn't yet learned the knack of separating herself from the role and almost found herself being swallowed up by the emotions of the scene.

'I was concentrating so hard on what it would be like inside myself – the way my heart looked, the rate it was pumping, all the blood racing through my veins – I got so far down inside my body that as we were coming to the end of the scene a panic went through me. I had gotten stuck down there and didn't want anybody to know. I thought, "I'm never going to get out of here!" I finally did, but I sobbed hysterically after it was over. It was the first day and things got too close to what had really happened. Bobby [Harling] flipped out – he had to leave.'

For the writer, it did seem as though Julia were starring in a documentary of his sister's life, and witnessing Julia/Susan's attack dredged up recent memories so painful he ran out of the room.

'Julia would take herself so far down it was scary. She had this magnificent control. She came as close to death as you can while you're still alive. After every take, they'd have to pick her up and help her back to her trailer. I had been through those sorts of things with my sister, and I just wanted to go over and hug her, and tell Herbert, "Okay, stop it. Let's not do this any more."'

If the diabetic fit scene was hard to watch, Julia's death scene was even more painful, and not just for the real-life relative of the dead woman Julia portrayed. Crew members who had never met the writer's sister began to feel emotionally connected to her when they arrived on location. Pretending to be unconscious and hooked up to IV tubes on the hospital set, Julia scared people without even acting. After all, she was just lying there. One grip recalled, 'She wouldn't sit up and talk or have a coke. She'd just stay there, and that created an eerie feeling. You really felt there was a life hovering in the balance, even though you knew it was just a set built in a gymnasium. There was an incredible power in her stillness.'

While the crew admired Julia the actress, whose dramatic talent was so intense it gave them the creeps, some members of the production team were not big fans of Julia the human being. In her 1993 biography of the star, Aileen Joyce reported that Julia didn't charm the hair and makeup people the way she had endeared herself to her co-stars. In fact, these crew members called her 'The Troll' behind her back, according to Joyce's sources.

'She was a monster,' said one observer. 'She couldn't sit still. She was always late getting to the set, which meant everyone had to hurry to get her ready so that shooting wouldn't be held up, and she was never happy with her hair or her makeup. She was always in a bad mood, throwing

fits, throwing brushes and combs at people. It was absolutely horren-
dous.' Maybe the pent-up emotions from her dramatic scenes found an
unhealthy outlet in acts of petty tyranny. Her fidgeting may have erupted
after having to lie still for hours during her comatose hospital scenes.

Julia's party-hearty lifestyle seemed to have followed her from New
York to Natchitoches, and it diminished her usual professionalism. 'Julia
was a wild, fun, party girl. She'd stay out all night. That's why she was
always late for her call. Dolly Parton wasn't kidding when she said that
Julia was "a sleepyhead",' another member of the crew said.

Julia may have appeared to be a 'sleepyhead' not because of late-night
carousing but because of her exhausting work schedule, which she
compared to a marathon run at sprint speed. 'It was kind of like being in
a race and [her co-stars] were all people on my team. They would start
running faster and they'd be like, "C'mon, just run a little faster. You can
do it." So I'd start running faster. They were great support, and they left
it so if I did feel lost, got dizzy, didn't know what was happening, then I
could just go up and say, "What's happening? Could somebody tell me?"
They would definitely clue me in.'

Steel Magnolias would have a profound effect on her career, boosting
her closer to the top of the heap of Hollywood actresses. But the production would also make a dramatic change in her romantic life as well. Her
feature début *Satisfaction* found her a boyfriend, co-star Liam Neeson. On
the set of *Steel Magnolias*, it was, in Yogi Berra's much-quoted phrase, '*déjà
vu* all over again'.

Within days of landing in Natchitoches, Julia once again found her
real life imitating her on-screen life. Studly Dylan McDermott, a twenty-
five-year-old actor who played her husband in the film, soon began
playing her boyfriend off screen. As for the boyfriend back in southern
California, Liam Neeson, it was a case of out of state, out of mind. The
stoic Irishman has remained tight-lipped and never commented on their
split, but his defenders couldn't keep their mouths shut. One buddy said,
'Liam was one of the nicest people you'll ever meet in your life. When
Julia was in hospital with spinal meningitis, he called the hospital all the
time. He was very worried about her, very concerned.'

Years later, during a press conference, when asked about his relationship with Julia and a later romance with Barbra Streisand, Neeson, who is now married to Vanessa Redgrave's daughter, the actress Natasha Richardson, displayed a rare moment of pique. Tellingly, he also used a morbid image to end the discussion: 'Is this what it's going to say on my tombstone? "He dated Julia Roberts and Barbra Streisand."' He then refused to say anything more about either woman. A gentleman of the old school, Neeson kissed but didn't tell.

Julia's romance with McDermott survived the shoot and grew more intense. A few weeks after leaving the set, they announced their engagement in September 1988. Like Neeson, McDermott declined to discuss his lovelife. In fact, he didn't describe his relationship with his new fiancée beyond 'hanging out'. On the set, he said tersely, 'We all hung out together. It was the kind of movie where everyone really hung out.'

As one door opened in her life, two doors were shutting. Neeson was out . . . and so was her manager, Bob McGowan. With an efficiency remarkable for its ruthlessness in one so young, Julia decided she had outgrown the man who had believed in her and her inevitable stardom long before anyone else did. They met in McGowan's office in New York to discuss her contract, which was due to expire. McGowan didn't mince words. He didn't grovel either, asking her bluntly, 'Julia, what's going on with you? Are we going to work together or not?' At that, Julia got out of her chair and gave McGowan, the man who had often paid her rent and literally gave her the clothes if not off his back at least from his closet, a big hug of gratitude. 'Bob,' she said, 'you started all this. I want you in my life forever.' It was an Oscar-worthy performance – if the Academy gave out statuettes for deception.

Less than two weeks later, McGowan was on the phone with Elaine Goldsmith, who had signed on as Julia's agent – along with Risa Shapiro – while the actress was in Natchitoches. Goldsmith and McGowan had never met so maybe their lack of a prior 'history' made Goldsmith's news easier to deliver. 'Julia doesn't want you as her manager any more,' Goldsmith told McGowan, who had had no inkling of Julia's plans until that fateful phone call. That was the end of their two-year relationship. Julia didn't bother to call to say goodbye. Maybe she was too embarrassed after having said she wanted him in her life forever only a fortnight before.

As shocked as McGowan was by his cavalier dismissal by a third party, this would turn out to be Julia's signature *modus operandi*. Whether she was dismissing a professional or a romantic partner, when the axe fell, it cut with surgical precision and instantly. A former friend said, 'When Julia is through with someone, she is through. She puts the same kind of determination into that as she does if she wants something. She has that killer instinct, and she'll zero in on whatever she wants.'

That kind of angst-free dispatch makes a wonderful career tool, but it's a killer when applied to personal relationships.

Julia didn't consider the split ruthless or a sign of ingratitude after McGowan's all-encompassing promotion of her career. Her professional life was getting too complicated, and getting rid of one of her loyal retainers would simplify it.

McGowan's dismissal, she said, 'was the first completely difficult decision I had to make in my life. Bob had gone to bat for me, but I felt I had to be honest. We'd outgrown each other. There were too many people around me making decisions, and I wanted a clearer line between me and the work.'

'Outgrowing' McGowan was a kind way of saying that he was a B-list manager, while her agents Goldsmith and Shapiro belonged to the A-Team, William Morris.

McGowan tried to put a positive spin on the split, although a bit of resentment showed when he recalled their parting: 'Julia didn't like confronting things, even with me. Plus I think we did sort of outgrow each other. It's like the boyfriend/girlfriend thing. After a couple of years of me telling her what to do and how to do it, someone else comes along and tells her the same thing, and it's all new and exciting. I have no hard feelings about it,' McGowan insisted. 'Julia did a lot for my career. She helped put me on the map . . . The only thing that bothered me,' he said of his dismissal via Ma Bell, 'was the way it was done . . .'

*

Julia didn't get much breathing space after her arduous work on *Steel Magnolias*. A month after leaving Natchitoches, *Mystic Pizza* opened in cinemas and trouper Julia went on the road to publicise the picture that would give her career such an important boost.

When the press tour hit Atlanta, Julia took the opportunity to buy her half-sister Nancy an unusual birthday present, paying for her sister's expensive orthodontia.

Mystic Pizza's gala première in her hometown was a special treat, as she was surrounded by family, especially her proud mother Betty, who was her 'date' for the event, which was held at the same shopping mall where not too long ago Julia had hustled popcorn. 'It's nice to be able to come back home with a triumph to lay at your mama's feet. That's a really neat feeling. I think there's something to be said for the humility of coming from a small place, remembering where you came from and what it was like to have your feet stained with clay all summer long. I think coming back semi-frequently is a good, consistent grounding thing for me,' she told a reporter covering the première.

After her publicity tour ended, Julia returned to Los Angeles, but not to Neeson's apartment near the beach. With boyfriend and manager surgically excised, she could devote all her energies to her career and the important decision of what project to do next. *Mystic Pizza* had marvellously announced her arrival as a major new talent in the acting world, and *Steel Magnolias*, with its A-list cast, added her name to that list.

Her next project would be critical. At this point in her career, type-casting was not a worry. Each of her film roles had displayed a different facet of her versatility. Her WASPy bubble-gum band member in *Satisfaction* bore little resemblance to *Mystic Pizza*'s saucy Latina, and a dying diabetic in *Steel Magnolias* was even farther away from either of those characters.

As word of mouth about her star-making turn in *Steel Magnolias* spread even before the film's release, Julia found herself being offered meaty roles in classy productions.

Her choices at this time suggested a sort of idiot-savant's knack for making the right decisions for the wrong reasons. Perhaps the meatiest offer was playing a concentration camp inmate in *Triumph of the Spirit*. Julia said no, which turned out to be a wise move, since the film was critically mauled and failed at the box office. But the reasons she gave for rejecting the role suggested this was no Method actress willing to sacrifice herself for the sake of the work: Julia loved the script, hated the haircut.

'I was really vacillating,' she said. *Triumph of the Spirit* 'was a very good script, and [co-star Willem Dafoe] is a great actor, but they wanted me to shave my head. It may seem superficial to say I can't shave my head, but it would have been five years before I looked like myself again. Willem said it would give me the opportunity to kill the stereotype I have as a glamour girl, but I told him I'm not tired of it yet.'

Julia was no Vanessa Redgrave, who went under the barber's knife to play an Auschwitz survivor in a TV movie. Not for her Demi Moore's buzzcut to play the first female Navy SEAL in *GI Jane.*

On the other hand, while *Playing for Time* burnished Redgrave's resumé, a TV movie seemed unlikely to do much for her feature-film career, which remains doldrum-stuck. And poor Demi had to sport a crewcut for a movie that flopped.

Even more importantly, if Julia had cropped her curls, she would have been ineligible for her next role, which would turn the up-and-coming young actress into one who had arrived – at the top.

Chapter Nine

CINDERELLA GOES SHOPPING

While Julia was saying no to disfiguring A-list projects, her savvy agent, Elaine Goldsmith, was informing B-list producers of her client's new standing in the pecking order.

Before the release of *Steel Magnolias*, which would earn her an Oscar nomination, Julia wanted to star with William Baldwin in the courtroom drama *Beyond a Reasonable Doubt*. The film company producing the movie turned her down because it felt she wasn't a big enough star. 'They didn't believe Julia Roberts could carry a film,' said Phyllis Carlyle, the film's producer. 'It's not unusual. In this business, a studio gets behind someone once they're established. By the time things came together, the ship had sailed,' Carlyle explained. A more accurate metaphor would be that Julia's star had skyrocketed after the release of the critically acclaimed *Steel Magnolias*.

By then, the company producing *Beyond a Reasonable Doubt* was begging for Julia's services in the courtroom drama, and Elaine Goldsmith had the delectable 'I told you so' pleasure of rejecting the offer. It was only one of many projects Julia turned her nose up at during this heady time in her career. 'I turned down more movies that year than I ever thought I'd turn down in my whole life,' she recalled.

The young actress finally found a script she wanted to be her next vehicle. Called *3,000* and written by J.F. Lawton, it was a sad tale of a drug-addicted streetwalker in Hollywood. A wealthy business executive offers her $3,000 (hence the film's title) to spend a week with him. During this time, he introduces her to a world of luxury, and dreams come true. At the end of the week, he drops her off at the same corner where he picked her up and she returns to her sordid life.

Vestron, the film company which owned the rights to the script, went bankrupt and sold the project to Disney, which immediately turned it into, well, a Disney movie. The grim drama was transformed into a light-hearted fairytale in which a business tycoon transforms a happy hooker into his fair lady and marries her. It was *Pygmalion* relocated to Hollywood Boulevard and Rodeo Drive.

'The script changed a lot,' Julia said with understatement. 'It was not a happy or funny story in the beginning. Then they took it on this journey and turned it into a delightful, funny, extremely different story.' It's interesting that Julia was happy to play either incarnation of the role – happy hooker or junkie prostitute.

Garry Marshall, the creator of the TV series *Laverne & Shirley*, signed on as director of what was now a feel-good comedy rather than a slice-of-life look at Hollywood's mean streets.

For the original version of the script, Vestron had wanted Michelle Pfeiffer to play Vivian, the hooker. When she turned it down, Vestron agreed to Julia. The company offered the role of the corporate raider to Sting, Sean Connery and Al Pacino, all of whom passed, as well as Richard Gere. 'It just was not the kind of movie that I do,' Gere wryly commented. 'In this film the wild exotic flower was the girl. Usually, I'm the exotic flower.'

After Disney had dumped the original script, it wanted to dump the actress who had been attached to it. Garry Marshall wasn't bullish on Julia either. Disney wanted a big star in its high-concept project. *Steel Magnolias* hadn't been released yet, and Julia wasn't even a minor star.

Julia began laying siege to Marshall, who was always polite – and always put her off. 'Garry told me later that half the people at Disney were concerned that you couldn't dress me up – that I could have on jeans and look sort of dirty or whatever but you couldn't dress me up – and the other half were saying the opposite. So Garry was saying, "So I don't know" – meaning I absolutely wasn't right for the role no matter what I was gonna do.' Julia's habit of wearing shabby, torn clothes didn't help change the mind of the Disney people who felt this sow's ear couldn't be turned into a silk purse.

Elaine Goldsmith really earned her commission when she took on the big guys. She arranged for screenings of *Mystic Pizza* and *Steel Magnolias* for Disney's chairman, Michael Eisner, and its president, David Hoberman. And for a little emotional arm-twisting, Goldsmith asked Julia's biggest fan, Sally Field, to call her good friend Eisner to plead her client's case.

Julia subjected herself to numerous auditions and a screen test. 'No one had seen *Steel Magnolias* so no one really cared that I was in it. I could've been Waitress No. 3. I chased that role down like a dog,' she said.

Goldsmith was just as tenacious as her client. Disney president David Hoberman recalled, 'Elaine was like a dog tugging at your cuff who wouldn't let go. She was dogged in her pursuit of the role, getting us to believe Julia was right for it.'

Goldsmith didn't deny this or her willingness to gamble everything on an ultimatum. 'Julia was not an automatic choice. Disney tested her for the part – and she had to wait until the eleventh hour before she got it. The studio was reticent about casting her until they'd cast the male lead. Finally, we told them she would take another movie, so they eventually agreed and signed her.'

Julia hadn't worked for a year when she landed *Pretty Woman*. As soon as she learned she finally had the job, she called her mother in Smyrna to tell her the good news. Then Julia realised her mother might not think playing a prostitute was such a blessing. Julia decided to be a bit less than forthcoming with her mother when they spoke. 'My mom works for the Catholic Archdiocese of Atlanta. I mean, my mom's boss baptised me. So I called her at work, and it was like, "Hi, Mom. I got a job." She said, "You did? What'd you get?" And I said, "Oh, it's a Disney movie! I gotta go, Mom. I'll talk to you later."'

Richard Gere had already rejected the role of the corporate raider when *Pretty Woman* was a pretty ugly script about the harsh reality of prostitution. He was even less interested in the new, happy-face, Disney version. But Garry Marshall, a director noted for his boundless charm and ability to work with difficult stars, wanted Gere for the part. Marshall explained that he wanted the male lead to be as gorgeous as the female star. Or as Marshall put it, he wanted 'two one-hundred per cent beautiful people'.

Gere's agent rejected repeated offers, but finally agreed to meet the affable Marshall. 'We got along great, but we didn't talk about comedy at all. Somehow it was about the Dalai Lama and Dostoyevski.'

Marshall set his trap for Gere using Julia as the beautiful bait. The director urged him to take a look at *Mystic Pizza* on tape. Gere was charmed but still not sold. Marshall visited the actor in New York, with Julia in tow.

'We sat around my office and read the script, which was not very well written at the time and didn't take advantage of possibilities,' Gere recalled, 'so we carefully talked about a lot of ideas. My character, for instance, was very underwritten, while Julia's character had all the energy. That was one of my problems.' Ironically, critics of the finished product – and they were legion – would later cavil that both characters remained underwritten fantasy figures in a not-so-Grimm fairytale.

To placate Gere, Marshall agreed to beef up the role of Edward, the tycoon who takes on Vivian. 'We did a little rewriting to make it more substantial,' Marshall said, but the deal-maker was Julia. 'I think Richard saw she wasn't just some crazy girl, some starlet. She could act and that impressed him,' the director added. A few weeks after his meeting with Julia, Gere finally signed on to the project.

Meanwhile, Julia attacked her role like a terrier with a new bone. As a once-sheltered Catholic from the Deep South, Julia had no idea what made Vivian tick, so she decided to find out by doing some primary research, interviewing real prostitutes. She came away from the experience saddened but with her role enriched by what she had learned.

Despite Julia's effective charm, the girls didn't bond immediately. 'A couple came on kind of strong and tough at first, but once I sprang for lunch and took them to Del Taco, they seemed to be nice and talkative. I met enough of them to get a sense that a hooker is not what the average person imagines one to be. She could be the girl you're sitting next to on the bus. It's real sad because these are girls not unlike me. They look like your average girl, talk like your average girl, and they have wonderful hopes for the future. But they're in this situation, and they don't really acknowledge it that much. They cry a lot, but their common goal is a real focus for the future. One girl wanted to be a makeup artist for Jane Seymour; she was very specific. One girl wanted to be a psychologist. That was amazing to me.'

Julia's fastidious research led her to strip clubs, which made her even more depressed. 'It was sad, too, because you realised that the girl who took off the most clothes on stage got the most money. They have a view of men – and life – that no one should have to live with.'

This may explain why Julia eventually had a no-nudity clause written into all her contracts, although she once offered a more sardonic reason: 'I just don't feel that my algebra teacher should ever know what my butt looks like.'

During pre-production, Disney employed a battalion of rewrite men whose job was to make the fantasy even happier. Julia met the writers and claimed they incorporated her research and ideas into Vivian's character, which seems unlikely, since Julia found the real-life prostitutes anything but cheerful. 'It made me feel I was part of bringing this person to life,' Julia said about her alleged input.

After being verbally mugged by Herb Ross on the set of *Steel Magnolias*, the *mensch*-like Garry Marshall was a pleasant change and turned out to be Julia's off-screen Pygmalion. The director, who had found himself playing peacemaker between his own sister, Penny Marshall, and her co-star Cindy Williams, during their epic battles on the set of *Laverne & Shirley*, had plenty of work experience in the care and feeding of actors' egos.

Marshall said, 'Julia needs a lot of holding and hugging, particularly in the scenes where there's meanness. She performs well when loved, which is why Richard Gere and I took great pains to make her feel comfortable, make her feel loved and make it a pleasant experience – not because we're such nice people, but because we felt that was the best thing for the project.'

Pretty Woman began filming in Los Angeles on 24 July 1989. The horror-story-turned-fairytale would take the crew from sleazy alleys near

Hollywood Boulevard to the gilded showrooms of Rodeo Drive. The film's depiction of luxury took place on soundstages carefully reconstructed to resemble the Beverly Wilshire Hotel, where Vivian and Edward seal their Faustian pact. As a nod to inflation and the fairytale element, the original script's three grand jumped to $4,000 for their week of pleasure. Despite all the other fantasy elements, Marshall strangely declined to create a *faux* Hollywood Boulevard for the film. Instead, he dragged his twenty-year-old star, along with the crew, to the most run-down areas of the real thing.

To her horror, Julia found herself wearing the regulation streetwalker uniform – mini-skirt, halter top, stiletto heels and really big hair – in the middle of Los Angeles' red-light district. 'I took so much shit for that outfit. In fact, at one point there were so many catcalls directed at me I went back to my trailer. I felt hideous and just wanted to hide. I know how to deal with any kind of attention somebody's going to give Julia Roberts, but the attention that Julia got as Vivian standing on Hollywood Boulevard in that outfit was not the kind of attention I'm used to or prepared to deal with. Vivian's clothes were a thousand times more provocative than anything I'd have in my closet. Vivian, of course, would simply say, "Fuck you! Blow it out your ass!" But I turn red and get hives,' she said, describing her physical reaction to the catcalls and whistles from passers-by who thought she was the real thing. Research at Del Taco may have helped her understand Vivian, but it didn't provide her with Vivian's thick skin.

Rude whistling wasn't the only thing that caused an allergic reaction in Julia. She had had no experience with on-screen nudity, and even appearing in bra and pants for the first time on the set made her break out in a rash. Julia wasn't a star yet, so she didn't have the clout to keep her clothes on. But ever since *Pretty Woman* gave her the power, she has tried to keep as fully clothed as possible on film. 'I'm really against nudity in movies. When you act with your clothes on, it's a performance. When you act with your clothes off, it's a documentary. I don't do documentaries.'

Both Marshall and Gere helped Julia feel comfortable with the 'documentary' portions of this fairytale. Marshall recalled, 'We went slowly and Richard was very, very helpful. She blushed when we first did the screen test. She wasn't used to being that scantily clad.'

For a bathtub scene in which Julia wore only bubbles, Marshall cleared the set of everyone – including the cameraman! The director simply left the camera running as Julia emerged – alone on the soundstage – from the tub.

At first Julia refused to do the scene in the nude, but Marshall's view prevailed. 'Garry convinced me, thanks to a trick! He instructed me to get into the bathtub with a swimming costume on, then the film crew left the scene, but left the cameras rolling. I took off my swimsuit and walked out of the bathtub quite naturally without the least feeling of shame, because there was nothing in front of me except for a camera lens . . . It was quite funny,' she said of a scene that could have been a nightmare for the shy actress who was and remains anything but an exhibitionist.

Julia was flummoxed but also relieved that she hadn't had to appear nude in front of a crew which Marshall archly described as consisting of 'guys with tattoos'. The director's act of kindness and consideration set the tone for the rest of the shoot. When Julia emerged from the bath and found no prying eyes, 'she was startled and then she laughed and got the idea we were going to do this lightly,' Marshall said.

The director thought of other ways to relax his skittish leading lady. One incident, which was intended to become an outtake for a gag reel of the production's bloomers, ended up not only in the movie, but used in numerous trailers. Early in their relationship, Edward gives Vivian a box containing a lavish diamond necklace. As originally and predictably written, Vivian takes the choker and puts it on. After a few takes, Marshall decided to play a prank on Julia and use her reaction in the gag reel. The director told Gere to snap the box shut just as Julia reaches for the bauble. It wasn't in the script, and Julia, startled once again as she had been in her solitary bathing routine, let out one of her signature whoops of laughter. Her reaction played so well that Marshall kept her scream in the final cut. The studio's marketing people apparently liked the ad lib as well, because the jewellery box scene became the centrepiece of the movie's ad campaign of thirty-second trailers on television.

Marshall clearly fell a little bit in love with his star, platonically of

JULIA ROBERTS

course, as his comments about their collaboration suggest. He told one reporter, 'A girl who looks like that, with a man like that, who can still laugh that bottomless laugh – well, that is a girl you can love.'

The director wasn't the only person Julia managed to charm. The rest of the crew also fell for the beautiful young woman who didn't put on movie-star airs or hide in her trailer between takes. Like any grip or gaffer, Julia hung out on the set and used her free time to add to her collection of jokes. 'She tells a good joke. She likes to hear a good story and after that she turns them into her own. She's very creative that way,' Marshall said.

In the middle of the shoot, Julia adopted a stray dog, which became her constant companion on the set. Her pet became as popular as its new owner. Sometimes Julia would stop filming to feed the dog. Even when the animal ruined a few takes by barking, Marshall didn't complain and simply reshot the scene after the pet shut up. Love Julia, love her dog.

Veteran character actor Hector Elizondo, who played the hotel manager who gives Vivian tips on how to behave on Rodeo Drive, also fell under the spell of a young woman whom he found more serious-minded than the wise-cracking crew did. Both actors discovered that they shared a love of poetry and spent hours sifting through the 'library' Julia had turned her trailer into. 'I was impressed by the fact that there were actual books in the trailer, and by her interest in literature. She had poetry, a book of essays, and she was reading a novel. And they were well thumbed,' Elizondo said, as though amazed to find someone who actually read in Los Angeles.

Elizondo was only slightly less impressed that such a young woman already had a well-developed sense of self. He praised her ability to 'concentrate and really listen. She had a sense of privacy – a sense of being self-contained and belonging to herself as opposed to wishing to please other people all the time. I had a feeling she was serious about her work but not solemn about the way she did it. I liked her a lot.'

The director also considered Julia a rare fauna, and photographed her as cinema's most famous faun, Bambi. 'We try to shoot each performer differently. And the approach for Julia, quite honestly, was that we shot her like Bambi. She moves around, Julia. She never quite stands still. You just kinda see her, and that's the way we shot her. She's there, she's beautiful – bam, she's gone. We kidded about it: "All right, we're doing Bambi in the penthouse today."'

Unlike Disney's more famous animated Bambi, this Bambi got knocked around on the set a lot. In one scene, Edward gives her a tongue-lashing. In another, a would-be rapist throws her to the ground. After hours and hours of this verbal and physical abuse, the line between reality and fantasy began to blur. Even after the director yelled, 'Cut,' Julia more often than not found herself holding on to the painful emotion of the scene.

Marshall said, 'The dramatic moments where she was going to be very vulnerable were very hard for her too. You're with Richard Gere for six or seven weeks, and suddenly you do this scene where he screams in your face and yells at you. It hurt her. Richard is used to that, but she was devastated by the scene. After each take she was crying, and we'd have to hold her a moment to make sure she was all right.

'In the scenes where she got verbally beaten up by Edward's lawyer and Edward screamed at her, she was playing the vulnerability off camera so she could play against it on camera. So off camera, I had a sobbing mess on my hands. But on camera she fought against it, and I think that worked.'

When a reporter kidded Julia about Marshall's delicate treatment of her, the actress was not amused and defended her staying in character between takes. Asked why she needed so much hand-holding, Julia asked the reporter from *Time Out*, 'Well, wouldn't you think so? You know, some guy comes in and basically says, "I'm gonna fuck you whether you like it or not," and then throws you down on the floor and jumps on top of you, and you're screaming – I think you might feel a little fragile. Garry is a great hugger, a great supporter, he's really right on, but I got thrown on the floor a lot, and it didn't feel so good. I'm not going to pretend like I'm all brave and it's all really easy. I mean, it's fake up to a point, but at some point you're going to get pushed the wrong way, you're going to get hurt.'

Gere found an ingenious way of providing Julia with emotional support, even when his character was abusing her on screen. Like the weeping actress, Gere stayed in character between takes, but unlike the director, he didn't do any hand-holding with his co-star. On days when Edward had been particularly brutal toward Vivian, Julia would often return to her hotel room to find a message on her answering machine from Gere, saying, 'You did good work. And I'll see you tomorrow.'

On another occasion, however, the mercurial actress claimed that the more established star aggravated her self-doubts as a novice. 'There were moments I doubted if I could be an actress. For example, during the filming of *Pretty Woman* when Richard Gere was complaining that I wasn't reacting the way he wanted me to. I felt he was blaming me for his shortcomings, but I wasn't capable of protesting against such a sacred idol.'

For his part, Gere had nothing but praise for his leading lady. 'I've worked with actresses who have been really difficult, and Julia's not one of them. She's a very real, very decent person, and she's not caught up in the actress thing.'

Julia's mother visited the set and saw only happy faces, none of the wailing and backbiting that Julia apparently engaged in when Betty wasn't present. 'The set of *Pretty Woman* was really a happy place,' she said. 'It was a happy movie to make. I was out there when they had to reshoot a scene and I watched Julia and Garry Marshall and he was really like Big Daddy. He's one of those very, very nice people and obviously was a real father figure for Julia,' she recalled, reinforcing the theory that Julia uses movie sets to create a temporary family. Her father had died when she was ten, but here was Garry Marshall stepping in, however briefly, to play Walter II. It was an unusual surrogate father–daughter relationship, however, or as Marshall joked with Betty, 'I'm the one who made your daughter take off all her clothes.'

'It was a very close group, even the crew,' Betty said. 'When it came time to film the love scene, the crew were shaking like a leaf because they knew how she felt.'

The crew might have been shaking, but Julia was literally throwing up. She later recalled that she was so nervous about her first love scene with Gere that she became nauseous. 'I felt like I was twelve years old and had never been kissed. Then I called my mom, and then I did throw up; and then I called my mom again. But it went very smoothly.'

Julia had mixed feelings about her co-star, and they extended beyond the set. Aileen Joyce, Julia's biographer, has claimed that the actress would have been happy to fall in love with her leading man once again, but Gere rebuffed her because of his long-term relationship with super-model Cindy Crawford, his future wife. But rumours of an on-the-set affair, according to Joyce, were enough to destroy Julia's relationship with her last leading man, Dylan McDermott.

Although McDermott was halfway around the world on a movie set in Morocco, the rumours of his girlfriend's 'affair' managed to reach him there. When he phoned Julia, she denied having anything but a professional relationship with her new leading man. McDermott apparently didn't believe her because he soon left Morocco and showed up on the set of *Pretty Woman*.

A friend of the couple recalled, 'Julia was supposed to come visit him while he was [in Morocco], but she didn't, which is when he knew something was up. Then Dylan began getting gossip from Hollywood about the sexy bed scenes between Julia and Richard Gere, and he got really upset. He was getting so frustrated, he finally got the producers to change his shooting schedule so that he could take a week off. He flew to Los Angeles, went to the set, and saw the chemistry between Julia and Gere, and he didn't like the look of it.'

Although Julia definitely did not drop McDermott for Gere, she did end their relationship during his visit to Los Angeles. A friend said, 'She dumped him, and he was devastated, terribly upset. She broke his heart.'

Back in Morocco, McDermott confided in his co-workers. 'It's over. I'm going to have to get over it.' The split, however, upset him so much that the hunky actor reportedly lost a stone. A year later, after his wounds had healed a little, he called Julia during a stop in Los Angeles, and she invited him to drop by for a visit. A friend said, 'He thought perhaps they could, at least, be friends.'

An obsessively fastidious type, McDermott was appalled at his former girlfriend's living conditions. She had recently won a Golden Globe award for *Pretty Woman*, and the gleaming statuette dramatically contrasted with its inelegant setting, which McDermott later described to a friend: 'There was dog shit on the carpet and the bedroom door was open, and the sheets had rolled off the bed onto the floor. The Golden Globe was sitting on the dressing-room table surrounded by clutter,' the friend quoted McDermott as saying. 'I felt like a toilet seat,' the actor allegedly said of his visit.

Julia was already beginning to display her love-'em-and-leave-'em attitude which would become so dramatic that her behaviour eventually made international headlines. But at this stage in her career, there were no dramatic abandonments at the altar, just the chiding of gossip columnists like Liz Smith, who chronicled Julia's lovelife at age twenty-three. Julia and McDermott 'started having a wild affair and seemed to be very, very much in love. Julia was very sweet to him, very into him. Then all of a sudden she dumped him. Her time limit seems to be twelve to eighteen months. As soon as the romance gets serious she can't handle it. She can't seem to handle the reality of commitment,' Smith wrote.

*

Long before *Pretty Woman* was released – indeed, while it was still filming – the buzz began to spread that Disney had both a major hit and a major new star on its hands. The press began treating Julia like a megastar before the movie which would make her one hit the cinema screens. *Harper's* magazine proclaimed Julia a 'contemporary beauty' and placed her on its 'Ten Most Beautiful Women in America' list, just the first of such lists she would grace for the rest of the decade.

Garry Marshall couldn't resist deflating Julia's new status just a bit. Maybe he was afraid he'd end up with a prima donna who would need a lot more than hand-holding and hugging. The day after *Harper's* came out, he appeared on the set and shouted, 'I see we have a contemporary beauty in our midst.'

At this stage in her career, Julia found the press attention flattering, rather than maddening, as it would later become. She was especially happy about *Harper's* acknowledgement since the Campbell High School library subscribed to the fashion magazine, and Julia relished the thought that 'all the teachers who flunked me will see it!'.

Playboy magazine soon added its praise to the emerging star, hailing her as the 'Lips of the '90s'. Julia was surprised to find herself so honoured since she considered that part of her face flawed. 'They've never gotten in the way,' she said of her famous pout. 'When they're your own lips, you don't really think about them. But there was a time in high school when I felt a little grief because I had an unusual mouth, unlike the other girls who had perfect mouths with little heart-top lips. But I never have done anything to accentuate my mouth. In fact, I'm really bad at putting [lipstick] on. Every time I've put it on, I've taken it off before I've gone out.'

Despite the praise from *Harper's* and *Playboy*, the makeup artist for *Pretty Woman*, Bob Mills, described the effort he had to put into compensating for her facial flaws. Mills said, 'The hollows in Ms Roberts' cheeks were filled with highlights, as were the eyesockets. The jawline was also highlighted to broaden it. Shadows were added to slim the nose and contour the forehead. The cheekbone line was lowered to produce a fuller effect. Hidden liners to thicken the lashes were applied, the lips were corrected to soften the very generous quality of her own.'

Another magazine, *GQ*, also reflected at the time on Julia's less-than-perfect parts, but felt the total was much more beautiful than the sum of her allegedly flawed features. 'She is made up of fascinating features that seem sometimes in harmony and sometimes not,' wrote Alan Richman. 'Those wide-screen eyebrows. The florid Señor Wences mouth. That nose she called "the apparatus". Plus all that wild stuff atop her head, her "bed hair". She thinks it looks the same whether she combs it after getting out of bed or not. She's a kaleidoscope of body parts.'

When Julia read the article, she took the combination of praise and criticism in stride. 'My God,' she exclaimed. 'I've got to call my mom and tell her that genetically I'm great for conversation!'

While her body provided fodder for enchanted journalists to rhapsodise about, the people in charge of marketing the film wanted perfection. No amount of makeup or turgid magazine prose could hide the fact that Julia's body just wasn't, well, pretty enough for *Pretty Woman*. As Vivian gets dressed in the opening sequence of the film, the camera examines every inch of her body, except her face. The reason is that the body belonged to someone else. In the posters used to advertise the movie, the body belonged to Shelley Michelle, whose head was chopped off and replaced with Julia's.

When principal photography on the film ended, Marshall gave Julia a necklace with a diamond heart. The gift came with a card that said, 'For my schlumpy girl. Wear this wherever you go and know there's someone who loves you.'

In an interview, Marshall clarified the sentiments expressed in his card: 'Even when Julia is being schlumpy, she's schlumpy with elegance.'

Julia broke down when she read the director's unusual Valentine. Or as she said, 'I was a puddle.'

*

No one knew it at the time, but the little fairytale called *Pretty Woman* would become such an important part of Hollywood lore that when *Newsweek* devoted an entire issue to important events of the twentieth century in 1999, it ran an entire column to Marshall's recollections of the event. In the magazine's special 'Voices of the Century' issue, Marshall provided this oral history on the making of the film: 'Steven Reuther, a producer attached to the script, suggested Julia. I didn't know her at all. We met, we talked, I saw *Mystic Pizza*. Talked about the character, Vivian. We're such geniuses, we said, "Let's screen-test her!" I remember she never sat in a chair. Kept sitting on the edges and arms of things. I put that right into the movie. She never sits on anything until the opera; there she sits like a lady. I called the head of the studio, Jeffrey Katzenberg, and said, "It doesn't matter who's the guy, I've found the girl. She can carry this picture."'

Ironically, Marshall was engaging in a bit of revisionist history, his vision distorted perhaps because he recalled the making of the film through rose-tinted glasses. At the time, Marshall admitted in an interview that he had insisted on pairing Julia with somebody as physically attractive as she was.

But in 1999, Marshall continued his saga in *Newsweek*: 'A lot of times I would give her the lines and tell her what I wanted her to say. Then I'd ask her how she would say that. She was twenty-one and I was a hundred and twelve. I don't know the young way of saying things. She didn't know why I liked what she said. She was very brave to try it like that. She had that Audrey Hepburn thing, but she was also Lucy. But she had to believe she could be funny. That thing we did with the jewellery case

LEFT: Julia graduated in 1985 from Campbell High School in Smyrna, Georgia, where she was an A-minus student; BELOW: 'Oh my God, I can't believe they picked me!' said Julia when she was chosen as one of twelve finalists in Campbell High's beauty contest (photos courtesy of Seth Poppel Yearbook Archives)

RIGHT: For her first starring role Julia took a crash course in guitar lessons to play a member of an all-girl rock band in *Satisfaction* (1987); BELOW: nice-guy director Garry Marshall cleared the set and left the camera running so Julia would be alone when she emerged naked from her bath in *Pretty Woman* (1990) (photos courtesy of Larry Edmunds)

LEFT: Julia fell in love with co-star Kiefer Sutherland on the set of the supernatural thriller *Flatliners* (1990) (photo courtesy of Columbia Pictures); BELOW: with Patrick Bergin, who played her abusive husband in *Sleeping with the Enemy* (1991) (photo courtesy of Twentieth Century Fox)

TOP: Sally Field became such a big fan of Julia when they were filming *Steel Magnolias* (1989) she bought the rights to *Dying Young* (1991) and produced the film as a showcase for her protégée; ABOVE: audiences wanted their Pretty Woman in fairytales, not a soap opera about a young man (Campbell Scott) with a terminal illness, and *Dying Young* died at the box office in the summer of 1991; RIGHT: Joel Schumacher, who directed Julia in *Flatliners* and *Dying Young*, said he was 'mesmerised' when he first saw her and they became 'instant best friends' (photos courtesy of Twentieth Century Fox)

LEFT: In *Michael Collins* (1996), Julia took a minor role as part of a love triangle (opposite real-life ex Liam Neeson) in a historical epic about the Irish freedom fighter (photo courtesy of Geffen Pictures/Warner Bros); BELOW: good friends in real life, Susan Sarandon and Julia Roberts played rivals in *Stepmom* (1998) who become allies when Sarandon's character develops a terminal illness; the two actresses served as executive producers of the film and rewrote the script together (photo courtesy of Columbia Pictures)

RIGHT: With Cameron Diaz, one of her co-stars in the hit comedy *My Best Friend's Wedding* (1997); BELOW: the devious character Julia played used her gay friend (Rupert Everett, right) to make her ex-boyfriend (Dermot Mulroney) jealous; BOTTOM: in one of the film's most amusing scenes, Cameron Diaz is compelled to perform at a karaoke bar, much to the delight of Mulroney and Roberts (photos courtesy of TriStar Pictures)

TOP: As a petulant American movie star who falls in love with Hugh Grant in *Notting Hill* (1999), Julia insisted she wasn't playing herself; ABOVE: a much more relaxed director Roger Michell confessed he was terrified when he first met Julia to discuss her appearance in *Notting Hill*; LEFT: audiences love Julia Roberts in romantic comedies, and *Notting Hill* became her sixth film to gross more than $100 million and the highest grossing British film of all time. (photos courtesy of Polygram Filmed Entertainment)

LEFT: Julia hated every script Richard Gere sent her until she read *Runaway Bride*, in which he played a journalist who wrote a nasty article about a woman (Julia) who keeps dumping her bridegrooms at the altar; BELOW: *Pretty Woman* director Garry Marshall and stars Julia Roberts and Richard Gere spent nine years trying to find a project they all wanted to make, *Runaway Bride* (1999) (photos courtesy of Paramount Pictures and Touchstone Pictures)

snapping her fingers was for the gag reel. But when she broke into laughter, we put it in the movie. She is just so honest and free. Her "entourage" was a dog she found. She fed the dog, then herself. When you have an entourage, you eat better – someone goes for the food. One night she fainted. I asked her when she last had a snack. She hadn't eaten all day. Once we gave her my tuna-fish sandwich, she was fine. Now she has people who make sure she eats.'

*

Three weeks after *Pretty Woman* completed principal photography in 1989, Julia had become a star when she returned to her hometown for the première of *Steel Magnolias*. The $150-a-ticket gala raised funds for the Juvenile Diabetes Fund, as a tribute to the screenwriter's sister, Julia's character in the film, who succumbed to the disease. Apart from Dolly Parton, who had to cancel at the last minute because of an illness in the family, the rest of the star-studded cast turned out for the première, which was held at the Phipps Plaza Cineplex. The screening was followed by a banquet and dance at the Ritz Carlton Hotel. Julia's date for the evening was her half-sister, Nancy Motes.

A month later, *Steel Magnolias* opened nationwide and received scathing reviews. 'Herbert Ross's *Steel Magnolias* runs for 118 minutes, but seems even longer than *Intolerance*,' wrote Vincent Canby of the *New York Times*, referring to D.W. Griffith's interminable 1916 silent epic. Canby oddly criticised Julia's performance, saying, she 'plays a beautiful young woman, who happens to be diabetic, with the kind of mega-intensity the camera cannot always absorb'. And yet he also hailed her performance as the 'brightest screen début since Audrey Hepburn', unaware that *Steel Magnolias* was not her first film.

The most important 'reviews', of course, came from the public, which turned *Steel Magnolias* into a sleeper hit, with a worldwide box-office gross of $83 million.

Despite the bad press, Julia received both a Golden Globe award and an Oscar nomination for best supporting actress. Significantly, out of a cast of much more established and respected actresses, Julia was the only one so honoured. The young actress refused to be overwhelmed by her good fortune, since she felt she had been working toward her present status for some time. She was by no means an overnight success. 'My girlfriend said it's like a wine bottle filled with beads and you shake it, and none of the beads come out. But you know that if two little beads would move, they'd all come out. I feel a bit like that. It's starting, but it's not too fast,' she said.

In a nod to her co-stars who did not receive acting awards, Julia praised them for teaching her by example. 'I've worked with some really great actors and I hear them talking about structure, and I listen. But mostly I watch. I learned so much from those five tremendous women in *Steel Magnolias*, by watching them do what they do perfectly. I owe them a lot more than I could ever articulate.'

Julia refused to take herself seriously, and self-deprecatingly described her appearance at the Golden Globes ceremony: 'I have to say the Golden Globes was the most shocking night of my life. I was so unprepared. I heard a recording of my acceptance speech later and I had to laugh. I was such an idiot.'

Chapter Ten

SLEEPING WITH THE CO-STAR

—◁▥▮◊▥▷—

As it turned out, Julia's troubled relationship with director Herb Ross would be the exception, not the rule, in almost all her future projects. The mutual admiration society she enjoyed with Garry Marshall was more typical. And with her next collaborator, the admiration would turn into something close to adoration.

Director Joel Schumacher had been keeping track of Julia since he first saw her in *Satisfaction*. While he was in pre-production on the film *Flatliners*, Julia read the script and asked to meet him. The superhot director, who specialised in Brat Pack movies like *St Elmo's Fire*, happily agreed. Even though she was just one of the girls in the band in *Satisfaction*, 'there was just something about her that was so sexy and infectious,' he said, 'I decided to keep an eye on her. Then, when I saw her again in *Mystic Pizza*, well, that was it. That's all I had to see. When I decided to do *Flatliners* she was my first choice.'

Although Schumacher liked what he had seen on film, when she showed up at his door he was even more impressed, despite the fact that Julia had strangely dressed down for the occasion, wearing cut-off jeans, a man's T-shirt and no shoes. Her 'bed hair' was haphazardly piled on top of her head.

While others might have seen Garry Marshall's 'schlumpy girl', Schumacher saw an object of fascination he couldn't take his eyes off. 'I watched her for two hours while she told me why she had to do this film, and I was just mesmerised by her. I kept thinking, "Where has she been?" '

Schumacher later said the two became 'instant good friends'. Julia's agent, Elaine Goldsmith, got word of the director's infatuation with her client and used this information as leverage in demanding half a million dollars for *Flatliners* – double what she got for *Pretty Woman*.

A movie executive said, 'Elaine was smart, very smart. Not only did she almost double Julia's fee, but the film was an ensemble piece, which meant it was a no-lose situation for Julia. If it failed, she was one of ten people. If it worked, it was because she was in it. In that way, it was a bulletproof idea.'

By now, Julia was turning into a workaholic. Less than a week after finishing up on *Pretty Woman*, she was on a plane to Chicago, where *Flatliners* began shooting on 23 October 1989. The script had an intriguing concept. A group of medical students, among them Julia's character, decide to find out what it's like to have a near-death experience by inducing comas in one another and so find out what it's like to pass to the other side. They are all revived at the last minute before their passing becomes final. With a seemingly impossible role to research short of killing herself, Julia found a healthier substitute by immersing herself in the *Tibetan Book of the Dead* and a real page-turner entitled *The Tao of Pooh*. Her crazy co-conspirator/med students included Kiefer Sutherland, Kevin Bacon and William Baldwin.

Flatliners will probably best be remembered for introducing her to Kiefer Sutherland, whom she had not met until her arrival in Chicago. 'We just started shooting, and I didn't know anybody,' Julia said. 'We were shooting at night, and it was real cold. I had this one easy thing to do, just run up these stairs, looking for the character played by Kiefer. I started talking to Joel, and I'm asking him, "How did I get here, did I take the bus?" "No," he said, "you ran." I thought about how long it would have taken to run there, and all of a sudden, I realised how panicked a situation this was. I'm running and I have to get there for about ten reasons, the biggest of which is to save Kiefer's life, and the least is to tell him it's all right and he's my friend. So I get into this place in my mind where I'm breathing really hard, and I say to Joel, "Is Kiefer here?" "Yeah, he's in his trailer." So I say I really need to see him, and Kiefer comes out.

He doesn't know what I'm doing, he doesn't even know who I am. He came out and I just flailed my preparation at him, tugged at his shirt, and I didn't need him to say anything. I just needed him to be there, to be a person. I remember the three of us standing in the cold, and me feeling the support from Kiefer and Joel. That's why you make a movie, for the support, to be like a family. You can't ask for more than nights like that – amazing nights.'

Once again, the movie set provided Julia with a ready-made family, and it would soon provide another boyfriend as well. The cast and crew adored her, and when the low-budget film had to save money by shooting through the Thanksgiving and Christmas holidays without a break, Julia didn't complain. She was, after all, spending the holidays with 'family'.

Because of the holidays, many of the crew members brought their real families to the set, and Julia promptly adopted all of them. She played den mother and best friend to the children, who hung out in her Winnebago.

Schumacher said, 'She had all the kids in her trailer all the time. There was always a line of kids in and out of Julia's trailer. She was feeding them, mothering them. And, you know, that's unique. A lot of people in Hollywood aren't nice to the parents, let alone their children!'

While the director approved of her maternal behaviour between takes, it was while the camera was rolling that he truly fell in love with his new Galatea. 'She does her emotional homework before she comes in,' Schumacher said. 'If she has to do a highly emotional scene, she's figured out what she's going to use from her own life and feelings to get there. And she would always let me know, either deliberately or in a more covert way, what the trigger would be from her life. For instance, her father is dead in this film as well as in real life, and my father is dead, and we'd have that to relate to between takes if she came over to me for help staying in the moment.'

The director and the actress found their professional relationship developing into something much more personal. Indeed, the fifty-year-old director and the twenty-one-year-old actress became confidants despite their age difference. Schumacher described their connection as 'poignant and personal'. Their bond was further strengthened by Julia's intelligence and wisdom, which he noticed the first time he met her. 'She was twenty-one, and I thought I was talking to someone my own age. It's nice to know there's someone like her on the planet. She's brilliant. She's talented. She gets the jokes. She's raunchy. She's the perfect lady.'

A friend who knew her when she was a struggling actress in New York also noticed Julia's chameleon-like ability to take on her interlocutor's colouring. 'Julia always had a great personality. She could sit and talk to anybody about almost any topic. And if she didn't know about the topic, the person she was talking to didn't know she didn't know about the topic.'

As a director, Schumacher pointed his actors in the right direction and then let them explore the role on their own. Julia flourished under this kind of *laissez-faire* direction, which must have made filming *Flatliners* seem like a holiday after the martinet Ross and *Steel Magnolias*.

Julia described Schumacher's light touch: 'Joel was just so intense and articulate. When we did small scenes, he would give us something basic and then not say anything, but when he did say something, it was succinct and exactly right. And he'll lead you to things so that, in the end, the ideas he has become your ideas as well. He created a really happy set, which makes that eleventh and twelfth hour of work worth it.'

It wasn't just the director – his camera seems to have fallen in love with Roberts as well. 'She's quite mesmerising in person. When the camera hits her, it just gets enhanced to a point where it's dazzling. She's really in a class by herself. I've worked with a lot of other extraordinary women, but Julia is just not interchangeable with anyone,' he said.

At this stage in her career, Julia was still finding her way, and criticism could paralyse her in front of the camera. Realising this intuitively, Schumacher heaped on the praise – and not just when he was speaking for public consumption to the press.

Some people find praise makes them uncomfortable. Julia couldn't get enough of it. 'Some directors, they give you support, but they're essentially cool with their flattery because they don't want to give an actor a big head, which I think is poppycock. Half the time I'm thinking I'm delivering the biggest pile of garbage, and all I need is this one kind word that's going to save me from myself.' Schumacher was always there with the life-saving word. 'On *Flatliners* we would do a scene, and when it was over Joel would hoot, "I can't wait for dailies! [footage filmed that day]" He would just start screaming and make you feel good,' she said.

Julia's bawdy sense of humour and famously foul mouth also made Schumacher hoot. 'She can be funny, sexy, even raunchy, and she's a master at telling dirty jokes. But she never seems to come off vulgar in any way, shape or form,' he said.

Julia's special treatment of Schumacher was not because he was the director and could help her career. She seems to have lavished as much attention on the guy who drove the honeywagon (portable toilets) as she did the guy who 'drove' the film, the director. The actress was anything but a snob, Schumacher said. 'Like most truly intelligent and enlightened people, she has no class system with her. People are people and she doesn't treat the high-rollers any differently from the blue-collar people. It's a very enlightened way to live. She adds a great deal of nurturing and support to the communal situation, which is always welcome.'

Julia wasn't quite as democratic with her affections as Schumacher insisted. She did play favourites, but only when it came to affairs of the heart.

Kiefer Sutherland played one of the medical students who engage in dangerous, heart-stopping behaviour to simulate death and explore the hereafter. When he arrived on the set in Chicago, he hadn't even heard of his co-star, despite her Oscar nomination and Golden Globe fame. He didn't bring any baggage or preconceived notions with him when the two first met. 'I had no reason to like or dislike this person. There was no outside input except for my agent saying, "Oh, I'm so glad Julia Roberts is doing this film." And I was going, "Julia who?" and thinking, "Okay, here's this novice." Then she comes into rehearsal and she had a really incredible presence just as a person, which made me sit back and take a look.'

Kiefer fell in love with Julia's talent before he fell in love with the actress herself. He described the evolution of the relationship: 'We started working together and then I got really excited because she was one of the best actors I'd ever worked with. I mean, she was incredibly giving, incredibly open, and she had qualities you can't even articulate when you're watching her work.

'I thought that I had been the only one to see this and that I'd made this great find, until friends of mine who had seen *Steel Magnolias* said, "Everybody knows that, Kiefer. Grow up!"'

The first mention of the Sutherland–Roberts romance, which would eventually make headlines around the world, occurred as a blind item in an interview Julia did with *Vogue*, which came out while *Flatliners* was still in production. The high-fashion magazine couldn't help but point out that Julia dressed like a bag lady instead of a movie star, although it more politely described her lack of fashion sense as belonging to 'a poetry major rather than a budding sex symbol'. The author of the article speculated that her wardrobe made sense since she liked to hang out in coffeehouses rather than nightclubs: 'She's a free spirit who likes to roam around barefoot, has memorised the entire Elvis Costello songbook, enjoys her privacy and talks endlessly about her boyfriend, although she never reveals his name.'

The *Vogue* piece is also memorable because it hinted at what would eventually become her full-blown disillusionment with Hollywood and the obnoxious trappings of fame – a paparazzo lurking behind every bush, an annoying fan demanding an autograph in the ladies' room.

'There are times when Hollywood is very unattractive to me,' she told *Vogue*, 'but there was a time in New York when I had nothing but time on my hands. So, when Hollywood has no charm and everyone just wants you, you have to be grateful and remember the times you were sitting in your apartment with nothing to do.'

In 1989 Julia was grateful for the work but very tired because there was so much of it. After *Flatliners* completed filming, she promised herself she would take a well-deserved vacation, having made six films in three years. 'I just want to go in a field somewhere and pick flowers,' she told *Vogue*.

It was while filming *Flatliners* that Julia realised her modest career was turning into a major one, and she wouldn't be collecting wildflowers any time in the near future. News hit the Chicago set that she had been nominated for a Golden Globe for *Steel Magnolias*, which she called 'quite shocking and really a surprise. I was on location and the phone in my trailer kept ringing. I'd had a bad day, and I kept picking it up and hanging it back up. Then I got a bouquet of flowers with a note that said, "Congratulations on your nomination". A short time later, my agent called and said I'd been nominated.

'I was really excited and I wanted to tell somebody. It was not embarrassing, but you don't want to be overly bold.' She decided to confide in her favourite confidant, Schumacher. She felt she could rely on his discretion. As her biggest fan, Schumacher, however, wasn't going to hide his leading lady's light under a bushel. The director assembled the cast and crew and announced, 'We have somebody here who is a Golden Globe nominee.' To her mortification, for several days thereafter, colleagues referred to her as 'Miss Golden Globe'.

Flatliners completed principal photography on a freezing Chicago day, 23 January 1990. Escaping the cold of the Windy City, Julia fled to Tucson, Arizona. Adding extra warmth was her new boyfriend, Kiefer Sutherland, who accompanied her there. Their idyll lasted only a few months because, despite her plan to take time off, Julia had somehow agreed to start another film in April, *Sleeping with the Enemy*.

Things just seemed to keep getting better for the young actress. She had a new love, a sunny holiday spot and a Golden Globe nomination. While she was in Tucson, she got wind of another accolade when Elaine Goldsmith called with even better news. The Academy of Motion Picture Art and Sciences had also nominated her in the Best Supporting Actress category for *Steel Magnolias*.

'The day I got nominated was Valentine's Day, and I was with a friend of mine,' she recalled. 'I got a call about it at five in the morning. I was too excited to go to sleep and too tired to get excited. So it was about two in the afternoon and we'd known since early in the morning, but it just hadn't registered with me. Then, I'm watching MTV and all of a sudden I started giggling, and I just couldn't stop laughing.'

The Oscar nomination definitely topped being named a finalist in her high school beauty contest, but the emotions it raised reminded her of the earlier honour. 'It was that same kind of feeling of, "Oh, my God. I can't believe they picked me!" It was that feeling but on an adult scale.'

Still, as she confided to a reporter from her hometown newspaper, the

Atlanta Constitution, the nomination didn't make her all that happy. You can hear a hint of the pessimism that would eventually overwhelm her as acting accolades accompanied box-office triumphs. The Oscar nomination, she said, was 'not something that makes me happy all the time. It comes in waves. I had pretty much blocked it out of my mind because you can only find disappointment in an expectant mind, right?' she asked with a riddle that might have stumped the Sphinx. 'And then the call came in and, well, I didn't even make the cheerleading squad at Campbell High, now I'm nominated for an Academy Award? Of course, it scares me and thrills me.

'It feels like it does when you're walking around on a hot summer day and all of a sudden it starts to rain really hard. It's cold, and it feels good, and it makes you want to dance around. Then it stops, and you keep on walking. I don't really sit around and constantly think of myself as an Oscar nominee. I mean, what's the point?'

She definitely didn't think of herself as an Oscar winner, since killjoy Las Vegas bookmakers listed her chances of winning as only one in three, trailing *My Left Foot*'s Brenda Fricker (who did in fact win the statuette) and previous Oscar-winner Anjelica Huston for *Enemies: A Love Story*.

A month after the Oscar announcement, Julia finally got to take some time off and spend it with the man she loved. Kiefer was filming *Young Guns II* in Cerillos, New Mexico, and Julia was happy to decompress and play house-girlfriend while her lover worked twelve-hour days. It was during this period that they exchanged rings, which the press immediately claimed were engagement rings. The couple called the tokens 'friendship rings'. On her twenty-second birthday, Julia gave Kiefer a more permanent gift, which she couldn't remove as easily as a ring. She went out and got a tattoo of a red heart inside a black Chinese character which translated loosely as 'strength of heart'. 'My love for Kiefer will last as long as this tattoo,' she told friends.

Julia made her first major purchase at this time. A woman who cared little for clothes or jewellery had been living in a modest apartment in New York. Now, as her career kept her in Los Angeles for longer periods of time, she decided to splurge on a $1.5 million, three-bedroom home in Nichols Canyon, just north of Hollywood. The house's location was perfect for a star who needed privacy. The only part of the place you could see from the street was the garage. A portico surrounded the house and kept intruders out. The balustrade gave the place the look of a Tuscan villa. Modest by California's rich standards, Julia's new home had only a tiny patch of grass for a garden. The place did boast some luxuries, though. The outdoor Jacuzzi included a fountain with spotlights. The master bedroom had a breathtaking 360-degree view of the Hollywood Hills and the Los Angeles basin. And parked outside was her brand new BMW.

Julia told a visitor to her new place, 'My boyfriend is gonna die when he hears I've bought a house. He keeps telling me I've got to own things. So first I bought this car. And then he told me I oughtta get a house. I remember telling him, "Why do I need a house?" And he said, "Well, you gotta have a place to park the car!"'

Eventually, her new home would turn into a white elephant she rarely used for anything more than storage space. Because of her heavy work schedule, Julia rarely spent more than a few days a month there.

Although everyone on the set of *Flatliners* became aware of the growing romance between the two stars, the couple tried to keep a low profile. When *Newsweek* named them as an item in March 1990, Julia was furious. And it wasn't the case of a temperamental actress demanding privacy: Julia was involved with a married man. Kiefer was still married to Camelia Kath, a Puerto Rican actress with whom he had had a daughter in 1988 after their marriage a year earlier. Julia wasn't a homewrecker, however. Even friends of Camelia conceded that the couple had already become estranged by the time Julia entered the picture, literally, on the set of *Flatliners*. And Sutherland moved quickly to formalise the dissolution of his marriage by filing for divorce in February 1990, shortly before Julia and he took off for their R&R in Tucson and New Mexico.

Kiefer and Julia had a lot in common. Both their fathers were actors, although Walter Roberts never achieved anywhere near the success of Kiefer's father, Donald Sutherland, who had starred in classics like *Klute* and *Ordinary People*. Like Julia, Kiefer came from a broken home. His parents split when he was four, the same age as Julia when her parents divorced. Also like Julia, Kiefer tended to turn co-workers on movie sets into surrogate family members.

Julia loved living on movie sets. 'I've always thought of going on location like going to an island and all you have is one another, so a lot of bonding goes on.' A soundstage was also a refuge for Kiefer, who reinforced the family analogy when he said, 'It's soothing and relaxing and you're guaranteed a hundred friends every day. It's a family, a little cocoon.'

The two were so evenly matched, they even liked to drink the same thing, tequila. Significantly, however, Kiefer drank to excess, while Julia was a sip-one-drink-all-night kind of girl. And, perhaps most importantly, alcohol made Julia even more outgoing. Friends said that Kiefer was not fun to be around after he had been drinking.

Two years before they met, Kiefer had bought a piece of land in Whitefish, Montana. With his new love, he began to build a ranch where they could spend rare time together when they weren't separated by movie locations.

Slowly, Julia decided to go public about her affair. After Kiefer filed for divorce, she didn't feel the need to be so secretive. But, always publicity-shy, she teased the public with snippets of information about her new love. During her acceptance speech at the Golden Globes ceremony in March 1990, she coyly said, 'I want to thank my beautiful, blue-eyed, green-eyed boy, who supports me through everything and brings so much happiness to my life.' She hadn't brought the mystery boy to the event, however, and refused to identify him at the press conference after the ceremony.

Three weeks later, at the Oscars, Julia finally unveiled her new beau. They made a particularly striking couple since both wore identical Giorgio Armani double-breasted suits. Julia didn't win the Oscar that night, but she must have felt a winner twice over. Not only did she have a man she was crazy about, but just three days before the Academy Awards ceremony, on 23 March, *Pretty Woman* opened at number one at the box office. It would earn $150 million less than a month after its début and go on to gross $450 million worldwide, making it Disney's most successful film ever.

Director Garry Marshall couldn't resist commenting on the irony that a movie about prostitution would become the squeaky-clean studio's biggest moneymaker. 'Walt is somewhere in his grave saying, "Pinocchio, no, a nice duck, no, it has to be a hooker as my highest-grossing picture."'

Unlike the critical reception for *Steel Magnolias*, this time the press was nice. 'Roberts has wit and warmth, and she suggests that a new Rosalind Russell or Kay Kendall may be on the way. Whereas most hookers might steal your wallet, Roberts' character steals the picture,' the trade industry paper *Screen International* said.

The all-important *New York Times* review was even more supportive. Janet Maslin wrote, 'Julia Roberts is so enchantingly beautiful, so funny, so natural, and such an absolute delight, it's hard to hold anything against the movie. This performance will make her a star.'

The only sour note was sounded by *Time* magazine's Richard Schickel, who wrote, 'Without taking anything away from Julia Roberts, there were doubtless twenty-five other actresses who could have played the role and played it fine. It wasn't exactly a stretch. There was nothing inherent in what she or Richard Gere did that pushed the film over the $150 million mark. It took off because the public wanted to plug in to the fantasy.' (Less than a year later, the same critic would be hailing Julia as the 'designated heroine of our redemptive fairytales'.)

Although Julia would grow to loathe the press for invading her privacy, she never let criticism of her professional life get her down. 'If you take the good reviews seriously then you have to take the bad reviews seriously,' she said.

Julia was on top of the world with a man she loved and with a film at the top of the charts. But it was now that she began to reveal a touch of the melancholic nature that would eventually turn her into a recluse, hiding from the press and fans. Just before *Pretty Woman* opened, she told a reporter she was suffering from 'a case of the "mean reds". That's when you're blue and you don't know why.'

What made a woman who seemed to have everything so blue – or red? Columnists and interviewers would be asking themselves that question for the next decade as her increasingly successful career and disastrous personal life made her an object of morbid fascination and an enigma no one seemed able to understand.

Chapter Eleven

STRIPPING WITH THE ENEMY

—◄◄◄∫▶▶▶—

After the commercial success of *Pretty Woman*, Julia could have demanded to star in a musical based on the telephone directory, and every studio in Hollywood would have begged for the privilege of financing the project.

But before *Pretty Woman* and even after *Steel Magnolias* showed she was an up-and-coming star, Julia didn't always get what Julia wanted.

In 1990, what she wanted was the female lead in a courtroom drama called *Class Action*. Julia hoped to play a crusading attorney who finds herself facing her father in a legal battle. When Twentieth Century Fox turned her agent down, the relatively unknown actress had the chutzpah to call the head of the studio and ask for the job.

Fox's chairman, Joe Roth, said, 'I turned her down because she was too young, and she got mad at me. Two weeks later I offered her *Sleeping with the Enemy* and we became good friends.' Roth marvelled at the nerve of this twenty-two-year-old. No other actor or actress had ever had the nerve to call him directly and beg for a part.

Sleeping with the Enemy offered an even juicier role for a young actress than *Class Action*. It was a melodrama about a horrifically abused wife who finally kills her husband. Kim Basinger had already landed the lead when Julia phoned Roth to badger him about *Class Action*. Shortly after Julia's phone call, however, Basinger dropped out of the project to star in *The Marrying Man* with the new love of her life, Alec Baldwin.

Roth immediately thought of the brazen Julia as the perfect person to play a woman capable of stabbing her husband to death.

Julia was lucky she had the affable Roth in her corner. The film's producer, Leonard Goldberg, had some misgivings – not because he doubted Julia's talent but because she lacked marquee power. 'We thought we might be in real trouble when Kim decided not to do it. Kim was just coming off *Batman* and was on every magazine cover. *Steel Magnolias* was just coming out, and Julia was basically no more than an up-and-coming actress. We were trading maximum star power to work with a near unknown. But Julia seemed really right for the role, and we figured we'd end up with a better film, if not a more marketable one. Now, of course, we look like geniuses,' Goldberg said after *Pretty Woman* had opened.

Julia would continue her lucky run with directors who adored her when she met *Sleeping with the Enemy*'s Joseph Ruben. 'I remember this shy, but dazzling smile, and her body language,' he said. 'It was a shyness, but there was something coming out of her smile. That's the part of what makes her so fascinating on screen – all the contradictions, being both very shy, but very much out there at the same time. She's both very sexual and very innocent, too. But she's very vulnerable and there's a private side to Julia. There's an incredibly warm aspect to her, but she can be very cold when she's angry,' Ruben said, only touching the tip of the iceberg Julia would become when her career and lovelife began to unravel a few years later.

A friend who had known her for years described this duality, saying, 'She can go from Bambi to bitch in two seconds.' A colleague compared her to a steel magnolia, soft and pretty on the outside, but unalloyed iron inside. 'Yes, I'd say she's a steel magnolia. She never got angry with me, at least she never got angry in front of me, but I saw her get angry at other people. You can always tell when Julia's really mad because her eyes narrow down and her chin juts out. Believe me, if she's angry, you know it,' this colleague, who had known her since she was seventeen, told Aileen Joyce in her biography of the star.

Sleeping with the Enemy turned out to be a difficult film for Julia in both emotional and physical terms. In *Steel Magnolias*, all she had to do was die. In *Sleeping with the Enemy*, she had to spend two hours getting knocked around by the husband from hell. Julia even came down with a nasty case of ringworm while making the film.

As always, the dedicated actress threw herself into the part, but during the shooting of one scene, even she admitted her pursuit of realism had gone too far. British actor Patrick Bergin played her abusive husband, a financial tycoon who is so controlling he beats his wife if she doesn't have the towels in the bathroom neatly lined up. After one housekeeping *faux pas*, he knocks her down and she hits her head on the marble floor in the living-room. The scene was shot in close-up, and Julia couldn't use a stunt double, although she probably should have taken some stunt lessons to prepare her for the gag.

The crew had placed a cushion on the ground to break her fall, but on the first take Julia flinched before hitting the floor, ruining the take. The second time she overcompensated for her original hesitation by hurling herself to the ground. Instead of breaking her fall with her hands, she made contact with the floor head first, missing the cushion altogether. 'I really fell, and my head bounced like a basketball on the marble floor, and I can't tell you how much it hurt – I'm hysterical with pain, I'm crying. It's gone too far.

'I cracked the floor so hard I had a black eye, but that's what made the take really exciting, cracking my head like that.'

It would go further. After knocking her down, her husband kicks her. Bergin may have also needed to take some stunt lessons in pulling punches and kicks. A sand bag had been placed out of camera range near Julia, and Bergin was supposed to kick that and make it look as though he were kicking Julia.

'Anyway, I'm in pain, and lying there, when Patrick comes to kick me, and misses the sandbag and kicks me right on the bottom. It can't get any worse. By now I'm just a blithering idiot. I can't even see straight.

'When the take was over, the director came up to me and said, "I wanted to call 'cut' when I saw what happened." And I said, "If you'd called 'cut', I would've wrung your neck – 'cause I'm not gonna do that scene again!" '

Bergin recalled having a good working relationship with Julia that included chatting and joking during breaks from the filmed abuse. 'There was nothing we weren't able to do, from love scenes to violence. It was never a question of mistrust.'

After Bergin missed the sandbag and kicked Julia in the bum, trust wasn't exactly the word she would have used to describe their off-screen relationship. As their on-screen marriage deteriorated, she found herself holding on to the resentment when the scene ended. 'I mean, when you come to work and somebody kicks the shit out of you for three hours, you don't really feel like finding out where he is and saying goodnight,' Julia said dryly.

When a reporter from *GQ* mentioned that Bergin was attacking her character, not her, Julia said, 'Yeah, right.'

Regardless of how she felt about her co-star, Julia did a lot of improvisation with Bergin to get in the mood before the cameras rolled. These warm-up exercises were even more violent than the abuse called for in the script. The director would watch Bergin knocking Julia about and even though he knew they were only play-acting, the intensity of the violence scared him. 'They knew they were in control, but I didn't,' Ruben said.

Julia found her role as an abused wife the hardest part she had played to date in terms of both emotional and physical capital spent. 'Every emotion that you see in the movie, that you feel or think about from one moment to the next, I probably went through drastically. It was physically exhausting. By virtue of size, it was the biggest part I've ever played, as far as hours spent working. And I did get hurt,' she said.

Fans who loved the fairytale ending of *Pretty Woman* might be turned off by the less-than-fairytale existence her character in *Sleeping with the Enemy* endured, but in interviews Julia begged fans not to boycott the film, promising an end to her misery by the film's end. 'Somebody who doesn't want to see me get beaten up should stay past those scenes, because I get out of it. The purpose of this movie is not: here she got beat up, her life's horrible, now go home with that. It's to show, as desperate as it may be, the prevailing of an individual,' Julia said.

As usual, the actress turned the crew into her family, and some of these 'family members' began to feel sorry for her as she endured fourteen-hour days of on-screen abuse for weeks at a time. At the end of one day's filming, Julia left the set in tears. A grip came up to her and squeezed her hand. Julia melted. 'It was worth fourteen hours of what I did just for that because it told me I had done something, you know?'

Like any 'family', this one also had problems that resulted in crew members walking off the set. Their angry exit resulted from Julia's demand that they strip down to their underwear. .

In a tale that has acquired the flavour of legend, Julia found herself one night shivering in the cold, wearing only bra and pants, soaked head to toe after her character has tried to escape the abusive relationship by faking her death in a drowning accident.

Julia had spent most of the night shooting the scene. 'It was absolutely freezing. I said to the crew, "I think we need a little group support here. So drop your trousers. If you're not going to take your pants off, you can't stay in the house."'

The director, who by now had clearly fallen for his actress like so many of his predecessors, was charmed rather than irritated by this flash of temperamental star power. 'It made a kind of perverse sense,' Ruben insisted. Later, the director, who was actually the one who had to deliver Julia's order to strip, felt he may have abdicated some of his authority. In retrospect, he wished he had told her to shut up and get on with her work. 'But I was at a low ebb, and Julia was so cold, and having such a hard time, and somehow her request did not seem unreasonable,' Ruben recalled. 'With the benefit of hindsight, I think it was very unreasonable.'

So did half the crew, who stomped off the set – with their clothes on. The others were as amused as the director and seemed to take a, well, 'perverse' joy in getting nekkid with their leading lady. And at least she didn't insist they also douse themselves with water for more 'bonding' and empathy for her predicament.

Roberts immortalised the incident with her Instamatic. She took pictures of the men in their undies. The snapshots show the lighting men crouched in the corner in their shorts. Another crew member wasn't wearing underwear that day, so he appears in the picture with a towel wrapped around his waist. A nerdy camera assistant shocked everybody when it was revealed he had bright purple shorts with the words 'bam', 'whap' and 'zap' on them.

The director also stripped down to his boxers. One wonders how *Steel Magnolias*' Herb Ross would have reacted to Julia's demand. The actress herself was unapologetic. 'It had nothing to with acting and everything to do with just getting everybody as naked and cold as I was. And I think everybody was silently very thrilled by it. It was the bonding thing, you know.'

Thrilled or not, the crew members who did participate apparently weren't angry because they came up with a practical joke that suggests they found the incident amusing rather than degrading. On some pretext, they lured Julia into a room where the whole crew had assembled and then mooned her. 'She screamed with laughter,' a crew member said.

For all her bravado, Ruben still detected the vulnerable actress who had to be held in Garry Marshall's arms between takes on the set of *Pretty Woman*. Even in rehearsals, Julia would recall scenes from her own life to help get her in the mood and then suddenly burst into tears. The director said, 'It's as if she has the thinnest skin imaginable. There's a vulnerability there that knocks you out. She's got two things going on. There's something that happens photographically with her, that star quality you hear about. And she's got this emotional vulnerability that lets you see and feel everything that's going on with her. And the two of them together – bam!'

Julia resented being called fragile or temperamental during an interview with *Playboy*, although 'temperamental' might be the kindest term to describe her strip-and-shoot orders to the crew. The most annoying cliché about actresses, she told the magazine, is 'that they are temperamental and have to be coddled and have to have their egos stroked. I guess you have to treat some people as if they were fragile. But speaking for myself, I don't need to be treated that way. I don't need to be treated badly; I don't need to be abused for the sake of a performance, because I'll find my performance. But I don't have to have people tip-toeing around me, either, trying not hurt my feelings. If my performance is bad, the best thing you can do is tell me, and not in a cruel way, "That's not good."'

Filming *Sleeping with the Enemy* encountered other problems besides a strip search ordered by its star. One ugly incident on the set made national headlines and, again, Julia was the instigator. Although a large part of the story was set in Cape Cod, much of the filming took place in Abbeville and Spartanburg, South Carolina.

A black member of the crew was refused service in a restaurant in Abbeville. Julia, who was with the man at the time, was outraged and let everybody know about it, including the press. She told *Rolling Stone*, 'The people [in Abbeville] were horribly racist, and I had a really hard time. I mean, the town had no restaurants in it [except for the one that had refused to serve the black crew member].' At the end of each day's shooting, Julia found herself with nothing to do but meditate upon her abysmal location. 'I would go home and sit in this small room with my dog and say, "So, there's nothing to eat . . . You wanna go to sleep?" I didn't feel like I was on location any more. I didn't feel like I had a job. I felt like this hell was where I lived . . . In Abbeville, I felt so assaulted and insulted by these people that I just didn't want to be nice any more.'

Julia didn't just vent her anger in the press. She expressed her outrage directly to the perpetrators, according to biographer Aileen Joyce, who claimed the actress stormed into the restaurant and yelled loud enough for everyone in the place to hear, 'You shouldn't call this place Michael's, you should call it Bigot's!'

The citizens of Abbeville were outraged, and a local radio talk-show host circulated a petition denouncing the star and paid for a quarter-page ad in *Daily Variety*, which asked the rhetorical question in a banner headline, 'Pretty Woman? Pretty Low!'

Julia's outrage seemed more than justified when the mayor of Abbeville, Joe Savitz, blamed her and not the restaurant. Savitz called her naïve for expecting anything else from 'a real redneck type place in Abbeville that does not allow black customers. No self-respecting person would want to go there,' Savitz said.

Even so, she backtracked a bit after it seemed she had accused the entire South of racism, rather than one little greasy-spoon in a South Carolina backwater. She had her publicist release this statement to the press: 'I was born in the South so in no way am I trying to create a stereotype. I was shocked that this type of treatment still exists in America in the '90s – in the South or anywhere else.'

Despite the mayor's obtuse comment that Julia should have known better than to expect a redneck hangout to serve blacks, Julia also felt obliged to phone the mayor and clarify her comments in *Rolling Stone*. 'She said she was "a little misquoted" in the *Rolling Stone* article,' Savitz said. 'She said she was talking about one person she met, but the magazine made it sound like she was talking about the whole town. I think the residents were a little upset – I think anybody would be upset if somebody said something like that about their town – but it was really a big flap over nothing. I think everybody has kind of forgotten about what she said.'

Julia's mother defended her daughter. 'Julie grew up in the South and is not naïve about the fact that there's prejudice. But she was very shocked [by the restaurant incident]. I'm proud that she spoke up,' Betty told *People* magazine. 'Julia has never picked friends by colour. She always had a lot of black friends in school. What happened is she became friends with a crew member; they went to a place of business; her friend was black; and they were refused service. Julie was shocked. She'd never had that happen around Smyrna or Atlanta. I think she saw enough [racism in Abbeville] that she thought it was condoned.'

Betty was wrong when she claimed Julia had no first-hand experience with racism – the vandalising of her locker in the sixth grade after she entered a dance contest with a black partner was something she had not forgotten.

Julia had another reason to have bad memories of her stay below the Mason-Dixon Line. On location in Spartanburg, she recalled, 'I was at home and really tired when the doorbell rang. So I went to the door, and there's this guy there. I say, "Can I help you?" He says, "Hi, Julia. I'm so-and-so, how are you doing?" Like he was just going to chat with me. I tried to be really nice and said, "That's really nice, see you later." An hour goes by, I hear a knock on the door, and it's the same guy again. He said, "I don't mean to bother you . . ." He came back four times that day. So now there's a cop outside my door [on the set]. There's a part of me that wants to say, "Do you know how badly you're annoying me?" but I can't. When people [flatter you] the only person who would say "fuck off" is the kind of person that would kick their dog.'

While shooting *Sleeping with the Enemy*, Julia underwent a transformation which, among other things, may explain why she felt powerful enough to condemn an entire region of the country – not to mention imposing an 'undress' code on the crew.

Halfway through the shoot, *Pretty Woman* hit cinema screens and its immense opening weekend take suggested that it would end up being the year's number-one hit. Julia went from successful actress to major motion-picture star that weekend.

'When they called me the first weekend that *Pretty Woman* opened, I didn't believe what they were telling me until I read it in the paper. It was *that* out of my realm of imagination. So I was grateful, I was suspended, I kind of believed it and I kind of didn't. So I just tried to get along.'

Joseph Ruben couldn't believe his good fortune to find himself suddenly working with the hottest actress in the country. He had gone from working with B-list actors in low-budget films like *The Stepfather* to directing the star of the number-one movie in America.

'We were ecstatic about *Pretty Woman*'s success,' Ruben said, 'because we started with a very hot, up-and-coming actress, and we ended up with a major film star. So we were just congratulating ourselves on how "smart" we were. But it was all kind of taking place far away in big cities, and we were in little towns. We still had the same problems every day – putting film in the can – and that's what we concentrated on.'

Making *Sleeping with the Enemy* had been a mixed bag of happy and obnoxious elements. The incident in the Abbeville restaurant had caused emotional pain; getting beaten up by Patrick Bergin caused physical pain. But at least one pleasant thing occurred to Julia during the shoot – the realisation that she was on her way to major stardom in the wake of *Pretty Woman*'s box-office bonanza.

When Julia returned to Los Angeles from North Carolina, things would only get better.

Chapter Twelve

NEAR-CAREER-DEATH EXPERIENCE

Julia had purchased her Nichols Canyon home in the Hollywood Hills just before leaving for South Carolina and she hadn't had time to do anything with the place, which was a mess. She hated the furnishings, which included tacky mirrored tiles and the previous owner's even tackier furniture.

When she returned to Los Angeles, she found a practical demonstration of Kiefer's affection and consideration. During her absence, he had made the place habitable, a monumental task. He had transported all her stuff from the Venice apartment to the hillside home and even managed to organise the clothes in her wardrobe.

'There were books and papers scattered all over my apartment, the house needed a paint job, and it was just too much. I had so much in storage that my girlfriends and I joked about a whole town called Storage, California. You know, "Where's your stuff?" "In Storage." But while I was gone, Kiefer took care of the whole thing. I came home to find the house all ready. Even my clothes were hanging in the closet. Astonishing!' Julia said.

The three months she had spent away from Sutherland made her realise how much she missed him. She was also aware that long separations could kill a romance. Commuter relationships rarely work. Absence, it seems, doesn't make the heart grow fonder; all it does is turn lovers into strangers. Julia vowed that from now on they would take turns working. If Sutherland had a film assignment, she'd play *Hausfrau* on location. He agreed to do the same. But Julia was simply too hot at this time, and the excellent scripts that came in the wake of *Pretty Woman* eventually made her break her promise, with disastrous results for the relationship.

For a while, though, she kept her workaholism at bay and kept her promise. Both of them had a few months off after *Sleeping with the Enemy*, and they partied hearty. Kiefer indulged his love of pool-playing at local dives, and the two were hounded by paparazzi at the clubs where they seemed to go dancing almost nightly.

In October 1990 Sutherland accepted a role in the drama, *Article 99*, which was being shot on location in Kansas City. Julia, the hottest actress in Hollywood, accompanied him to the movie set. Her resolve to remain unemployed while Kiefer worked didn't last longer than a few weeks. She was lured out of a 'retirement' – and a boring sojourn in Kansas – by a script that was so good it made her forget domestic bliss in favour of artistic satisfaction.

'Acting is a true love of mine, but it's not *the* true love. There are times when I get so bogged down by the politics of this business that I just have these great domestic fantasies. Being at home, and being quiet, and reading, and having a garden, and doing all that stuff. Taking care of a family. Those are the most important things. Movies will come and go, but family is a real kind of rich consistency,' she insisted.

Ironically, 'family', however transitory, was exactly what a welcoming movie crew offered her. Julia flew to Mendocino, California, in early November 1990 to begin a project she loved. Unfortunately, the critics and public would not share her enthusiasm, and the film that disrupted her relationship with Kiefer would also almost kill her career.

Even the title of the film, *Dying Young*, might have seemed to the superstitious a bad omen. After popcorn movies like *Pretty Woman* and *Flatliners*, and a commercial thriller like *Sleeping with the Enemy*, Julia may have been attracted to a character drama that would allow her to show she was a serious actress, not just a movie star whose grace and beauty compensated for low-brow scripts.

Dying Young cast Julia as Hilary O'Neil, a nurse hired to take care of a rich, handsome young man named Victor Geddes, who is in the terminal stages of leukaemia. Geddes was played by Campbell Scott, a Dylan McDermott lookalike who also happened to be the son of the actor George C. Scott. *Dying Young* was a three-hanky movie, and Julia looked forward to playing something other than a pretty abused woman.

Sally Field was the 'angel' on this production. In 1988 she bought the rights to the novel on which the film was based and intended to turn it into a vehicle for her protégée. Field's timing was off, however. *Steel Magnolias* hadn't been released when she tried to sell Twentieth Century Fox on the project, and Julia was hardly a big enough star to open a picture, especially one with such a tragic subject. Field buttonholed executives with her pitch, but no one was interested in her product. 'I told them I had this girl, Julia Roberts, who would be wonderful, but they wanted someone better known,' Field said.

It's amazing what a difference a little thing like a $450 million box-office hit can do to indifferent studio chiefs. Two years after Field had unsuccessfully flogged the project around town, *Pretty Woman* came out and Field renewed her assault on the Fox beachhead, which was now happy to surrender.

'By then we had a script. I went to Fox and said, "I repeat. There's this girl I know who would be wonderful in this part." The good thing was I didn't have to say, "You don't know her yet,"' Field recalled archly.

Field was further helped by the fact that Fox's chairman, Joe Roth, had already fallen in love with Julia when he cast her in *Sleeping with the Enemy*. He had taken a chance on her when she was just a promising newcomer, before *Pretty Woman* turned her into pretty bankable. Roth practically grabbed the script out of Field's hands when she pitched the project to the studio the second time.

'When you have Julia's name on the marquee, you have the biggest female star in the world, one of fewer than ten people in the world who can open a picture simply because she's in it,' Roth said. He put his money where his mouth was by offering Julia $3 million, a million-dollar pay rise from *Sleeping with the Enemy*.

Julia made it a point to thank Field publicly for all her professional mothering. When a reporter repeated the cliché that there are few good roles for women in Hollywood, Julia begged to differ. 'I haven't been affected by it as a lot of people have, but I know it exists,' she said of the dearth of multi-dimensional female characters in the movies. 'I also think that women are starting to develop projects and characters and scripts for themselves that give them a part that they want to play. *Dying Young* is from a book Sally Field developed for me – a great gift because it's an incredible part to play.' For her efforts, Field only received a co-producer credit on the film, despite the fact that she had been the moving force behind the project and its star.

Besides the great role and the big payday, *Dying Young* had something else that Julia found irresistible. The film would reunite her with another big fan, Joel Schumacher, the director of *Flatliners*. Timing again played a role in finessing the project – not to mention Julia's taking personal control of her future.

Schumacher said, 'I was going to do *Phantom of the Opera* with Andrew Lloyd Webber, then he postponed the production because of his divorce. A dream had ended and I needed to move on. Emotionally, I couldn't afford to be attached to it any longer. I didn't want to get disappointed again.'

While Schumacher was looking for a script to console himself for losing one of the most sought-after prizes in the industry, the phone rang, and it was his fairy goddaughter on the line. Julia begged him to direct *Dying Young*. Schumacher was already familiar with the project, and his affection for Julia outweighed his business and artistic instincts, which told him *Dying Young* had terminal flaws.

'This was the first time a star had ever asked me to direct, and I don't think I would have made that particular movie if Julia hadn't asked me. I'm in love with Julia,' Schumacher said. 'She's a combination of many things, which is why she's so fascinating on-screen: sexy but ladylike, guileless yet sophisticated, fragile but strong. She's street smart rather than educated, but extremely well-read.'

Artistically, though, theirs would prove to be a disastrous love affair. Years later, Schumacher was still so traumatised by the failure of the project that he found it hard to talk about it. All he could plead was blind faith and love of Julia. 'I was blinded by my passion to be around her, and

I wasn't thinking clearly,' he said. 'This is still a disturbing subject for me,' he added, two years after the release of the film.

At the time, all Schumacher could think of was how much fun he'd have collaborating with his surrogate daughter, a young woman he felt so connected to they communicated in shorthand and sometimes, it seemed, almost telepathically. 'Julia and I early on worked out a symbiotic emotional dance. We don't talk a lot. We discuss maybe in one sentence what the scene is. She has some preparation she does emotionally, then I have some preparation to help, some things we do that are private. There are ways we talk, not about the scene but something from our past or current lives that is relevant to the emotional fibre of what is going on. Sometimes we don't talk at all, we just look at each other,' Schumacher said.

Dying Young's story was set in New England, but it was cheaper to film closer to the home of the movie business. Mendocino County in northern California, with its gingerbread Victorian houses and picket fences, looks more like Cape Cod than a distant suburb of San Francisco. (A hit TV series of the time, *Murder, She Wrote*, also set in New England, took advantage of Mendocino's East Coast look and shot there as well.) Interiors, which included the wealthy young man's palatial townhouse, were filmed in nearby San Francisco. In addition to Victor's sumptuous place in the city, he has a seaside retreat. Instead of renting a house on the beach, Fox built from scratch a 7,000-square-foot retreat on a bluff overlooking the Pacific Ocean.

During a break in filming, Julia confided to a reporter from the *New York Times* that *Dying Young*'s depressing plot was getting her down. 'Yesterday I shot a scene with Campbell that was very sad, and I didn't anticipate it being that sad. That's the hardest part of doing things like this; you don't anticipate how much will really happen.'

The director was having problems of his own with the film. His previous efforts tended to employ large ensemble casts, like those of *St Elmo's Fire* and *The Lost Boys*, which didn't count on only two actors to carry the film. 'I had always done ensemble movies, using six or seven points of view to tell a story,' Schumacher told Julie Lew of the *New York Times* when the reporter visited the Mendocino location. 'Making a movie is like building a 747 while you're flying it. You invent as you go along, and it never is what you think it is. I didn't realise the relationship between Julia and Campbell would lessen the need for other elements. We didn't realise on paper how strong the two of them were going to be.'

Schumacher became so intrigued with his two leads that he found himself pruning the other roles. Colleen Dewhurst, Scott's one-time stepmother in real life, played a winery owner, and her beefy part was made leaner. The young construction worker played by Vincent D'Onofrio was virtually castrated. In the novel on which the film was based, the blue-collar worker forms a love triangle with the characters played by Scott and Julia. By the time Schumacher had finished cutting, D'Onofrio's assignment had been reduced to that of a bit player.

Perhaps the most interesting thing about the making of *Dying Young* was what *didn't* happen on the set. Julia's co-star, Campbell Scott, had the looks of a matinee idol. He bore no physical resemblance to his father, a character actor whose talent turned him into a leading man despite his looks. Scott's and Julia's characters fall in love in the movie. Schumacher attested to the bountiful on-screen chemistry between the two stars. And, with Julia's track record of turning the crew into surrogate family and her co-star into a real-life boyfriend, a Scott–Roberts match seemed a real possibility. But it just didn't happen. All the chemistry remained on the screen. Maybe Julia's love for Kiefer blinded her to the much more handsome Campbell. As for Scott, he had nothing but praise for his leading lady and her ability to cope with the burden of instant fame. 'I think she's handling this whole thing unbelievably well,' he said. 'As an actress she has beautiful presence. People find her identifiable and accessible.'

*

In late 1990, while Julia was filming *Dying Young*, her agents Elaine Goldsmith and Risa Shapiro left the William Morris Agency. For decades, William Morris had been *the* talent agency in Hollywood, with more stars 'than in the heavens' as MGM used to say in its long-gone heyday. But in the 1970s, after the defections of several powerful agents, including Mike Ovitz and Ron Meyer, who founded the Creative Artists Agency, William Morris was beginning to look like an old war-horse that should have been put out to pasture – or, considering the cut-throat nature of the business, a more appropriate metaphor might be 'sent to the glue factory'. CAA reigned supreme as Morris's clients defected to the new agency. Its only rival – and a distant one at that – was International Creative Management (ICM).

Goldsmith, however, didn't leave William Morris because of its declining power in the industry. She was miffed at the agency for firing her mentor, Sue Mengers, one of Hollywood's legendary movers and shakers. Through intermediaries, Goldsmith first tried to move over to CAA, which would have been a natural fit for her client, since CAA represented Julia's surrogate mother, Sally Field, her boyfriend, Kiefer Sutherland, and her favourite director, Joel Schumacher. CAA desperately wanted Julia but, for some inexplicable reason, it refused to take her agent as part of the package. Julia wasn't going anywhere without Goldsmith, the architect of her stunning rise in the movie industry. She felt her loyalties lay with her agents rather than her agency, so when Goldsmith and Shapiro moved around the corner to ICM's Wilshire Boulevard headquarters in Beverly Hills, Julia made the trip with them.

She explained her loyalty with typically colourful language: 'I heard "Your agent is never your friend", but it's a complete and total fucking piece-of-shit lie. I also heard that "All producers are scumbags", which is also untrue of the producers I've worked with. So everybody was wrong. But my brother told me something that was true: "You have to remember that this is show business, not show friendship."'

Keeping her brother's dictum in mind, Julia didn't express even a twinge of guilt for dumping the agency that had overseen her birth as a movie star. 'William Morris is a fine company, but I wasn't so much a company man as a client of Risa and Elaine. They're smart. They care about me. If they told me they were forming Elaine and Risa Inc., I would have said okay.'

Julia's arrival at ICM reportedly wreaked havoc with the agency's clients of a similar age. Their clients – among whom were Holly Hunter, Daryl Hannah, Meg Ryan and Kim Basinger – feared Julia would get first crack at the best scripts offered to ICM, and they would get sloppy seconds. Goldsmith denied the potential for a catfight and felt Julia's presence would have a synergistic effect, attracting even more scripts which would benefit all of ICM's clients. 'Julia's arrival is great for the actresses here. I read all the scripts and she can't do everything. We expand rather than contract their possibilities,' Goldsmith claimed.

A year later, Julia dumped Risa Shapiro and kept Elaine Goldsmith. No explanation was given to the press, but Goldsmith may have won sole possession of this box-office prize because she was much more than an agent to her needy client. Her non-business-related services for Julia, which included babysitting her basset-hound and delivering clothing the actress had bought, make Goldsmith sound more like a personal assistant than a top agent at a top talent agency. Stories, true or not, abound in Hollywood lore that some agents are so desperate to hold on to their big money-makers that they pick up their clients' dry-cleaning and run other personal errands.

While we don't know if Goldsmith ever did grocery shopping for Julia, it's easy to understand the star's desire to continue their business relationship. Goldsmith was a rainmaker, and the colour of the rain was green. She had got her client, then a virtual unknown, $90,000 for *Steel Magnolias*, with the added sweetener that Julia would be rubbing shoulders with big names like Shirley MacLaine and Sally Field. One picture later, Goldsmith had more than tripled the star's salary, to $300,000 for *Pretty Woman*. And before the release of that hit, she managed to pump up Julia's take for her next film, *Flatliners*, to a cool half a million dollars. *Pretty Woman* still hadn't hit cinemas when Goldsmith doubled Julia's fee to $1 million for *Sleeping with the Enemy*, then tripled it for *Dying Young*. Even if Goldsmith didn't pick up Julia's dry-cleaning or babysit her dog, she truly earned her 10 per cent commission.

*

When Julia finished principal photography on *Dying Young* in early 1991, she was dying to take a break. She had made seven films in just four years. She promised herself a year off, a promise she would break almost immediately. 'I think it's time for me to go away for a little while. I just want to slow down,' Julia told friends who worried that she looked close to collapsing from fatigue after returning from northern California.

She postponed her next film, *Renegades*, even though it would pair her with Kiefer and allow them to spend more time together. Julia had arrived at a point in her career where she called the shots, and she was calling a time out. 'I don't have to do anything I don't want to. Your life is as pressure-filled as you allow it to be. Sometimes I feel people try to make it more difficult, to see how absolutely taxing they can make your life,' she said.

Soon enough, without anyone's help, except possibly Kiefer's, Julia would make her life very pressure-filled and tax herself to the point of hospitalisation.

Chapter Thirteen

RUNAWAY BRIDE

When Julia returned to Los Angeles in February 1991, she moved back to the hillside home Kiefer had so thoughtfully refurbished for her.

Although she would later become notoriously tight-lipped about her romantic liaisons, at this time in her life Julia was happy to tell journalists the state of her mind and her relationship with Kiefer. 'We're just real happy. I've been lucky to find someone whom I not only like and is my best friend, but whom I so admire and respect and have fallen madly in love with. I've been immensely blessed in the discovery of this person,' she said.

It was probably a mixture of love and respect for her boyfriend's talent that prompted her to sign on for *Renegades*, a Western originally conceived as a vehicle for Mel Gibson, who left the project due to scheduling conflicts. Kiefer stepped into Gibson's role of a nineteenth-century bounty hunter who falls in love with a Native American bank robber, to be played by Julia. The project was perfect high-concept, a 'sagebrush *Bonnie and Clyde*', as one reporter dubbed it. For her participation, Julia would receive yet another raise, this time to $7 million, making her the highest-paid actress in the business. Kiefer got the less princely but still royal fee of $2.5 million.

A month after her return to Los Angeles, Julia was back in the spotlight again – twice, actually, as a presenter at the Academy Awards and as a guest on a special hosted by America's most respected celebrity interviewer, Barbara Walters, which followed the broadcast on 25 March 1991. Just in case anyone had missed her declarations of love in print, Julia repeated them on the air during her chat with Walters.

In retrospect, her words would reek of irony, but at the time they were heart-felt. 'Kiefer and I will be together forever,' Julia said. When Walters expressed scepticism, since Hollywood romances seem to have the shelf life of dairy products, Julia persisted. 'Yeah. Forever love. I believe in that and I believe this is it. We live together and we are happy and we are in love with each other – and isn't that what being married is?'

This was the first time Julia had uttered the 'm' word in regard to Kiefer, and she chose to say it in front of the huge audience that Walters' post-Oscar specials always attract.

'He is the love of my life. He is the person I love and admire and respect the most in the world. Kiefer is probably the most wonderful, understanding person I have ever met,' she told perhaps half a billion viewers.

The interview with Walters had been pre-recorded, and by the time it was aired in March, rumours were already circulating among her friends and in the press that there was trouble in the paradise Julia claimed she and Kiefer inhabited. The tabloids reported that Julia's career and bigger paycheques were making Kiefer jealous and poisoning the relationship. Three weeks before Julia declared her love for Kiefer on international television, *People* magazine ran an article that must have really rankled with the actor. And if indeed he was jealous of his girlfriend's success, the piece would only have exacerbated his jealousy. People claimed Kiefer couldn't find a job and snidely noted that of his last four movies, the only one to turn a profit – *Flatliners* – just happened to star his eminently more successful girlfriend.

By now, Julia was commanding more than three times Kiefer's fee per film. 'There is definitely a problem and the problem is work-related,' an unnamed friend told the *Los Angeles Times*, which usually avoids tabloid-style coverage of the private lives of celebrities. 'Kiefer is not getting offers for roles, and Julia's phone is ringing every two minutes. But she is madly in love with him and wants the relationship to work.'

With hindsight, the intensity with which Julia described her love for

Kiefer on the Walters special made some suspect she was actually address-ing Kiefer, not the TV audience. The interview seemed like an attempt to salvage a relationship through the sheer power of her desire to make it work – when apparently it wasn't, as the reports in the reliable main-stream press suggested. Less reputable media outlets alleged that Kiefer was furious that Julia demanded he sign a prenuptial agreement. A more worrying rumour claimed Kiefer had been stepping out with a Hollywood stripper while Julia was on location in Mendocino. Just as everyone was predicting an imminent split, the couple trumped the press and other scandal-mongers by announcing their wedding, which would take place on 14 June 1991.

The announcement didn't stop the rumours about their troubled relationship for long, though. Two weeks later, the *National Enquirer* published an alleged interview with Amanda Rice, a stripper at a La Brea Avenue club in Hollywood. Rice, whose stage name was Raven, claimed she and Kiefer had been dating since January, a month before Julia returned to Los Angeles from location on *Dying Young*. According to the *Enquirer*, Rice described her pillow talk with Kiefer, which seemed to focus on Julia – in particular, Julia's flaws. Kiefer told Rice that the actress hated her body, and Kiefer seemed to agree, complaining that she was too pale and thin. He also allegedly said Julia was a 'cold fish' in bed and had become an 'ice princess' after *Pretty Woman* turned her into a super hot star. 'Making love to her was like making love to a corpse,' Rice quoted him as saying.

By itself, the *Enquirer* story wouldn't have caused much trouble. The tabloids are better known for their creative fiction than for their accurate reporting, and outrageous stories like Rice's are rarely picked up by the mainstream press.

Kiefer's publicist insisted her client had not been cheating on Julia. 'He has never denied that he met [Amanda], because he likes to play pool,' his publicist, Annett Wolf, said. 'He's denying that he had a relationship with her.' A friend of Kiefer's backed up Wolf's statement, saying, 'He is extremely upset about this thing with Rice. There was nothing sexual.'

But Kiefer's behaviour during this time lent some credence to the *Enquirer* story. In January 1991, while Julia was on the set of *Dying Young*, he moved out of their elegant home and checked into a fleabag hotel, the St Francis, on Western Avenue in a blighted area of Hollywood. There was a legitimate reason to explain why he went slumming. Kiefer was researching a role for *In from the Cold*, a movie that was never made. He wasn't leaving Julia or their home. In fact, two weeks later, he left the hotel and returned to their Nichols Canyon residence.

But those two weeks were fateful for his future with Julia. While he was staying at the St Francis, he visited Hollywood Billiards across the street. It was there that he met Amanda/Raven, who was just as gorgeous as Kiefer's pretty woman but who, as pictures of her curvaceous figure show, probably didn't have any problems with body image.

Rice invited him to check out her act at the Crazy Girls Club on La Brea, and Kiefer soon became a regular there. 'He always came in just before closing, and I saw them leave together,' Marwan Khalaf, the assistant manager of the strip club, said. The new couple were seen about town. Another stripper at the club claimed she double-dated with Amanda and Kiefer. Kiefer even took Amanda, her son and his daughter to Disneyland.

Although it wasn't discreet, the relationship was brief, lasting only the two weeks Kiefer spent at the St Francis. Shortly after Julia returned to Los Angeles in February, the couple flew to Kiefer's three-hundred-acre ranch in Whitefish. The rumours about Kiefer and the stripper had apparently never reached Julia or it's unlikely she would have gone with him to Montana.

It may have been a coincidence, but two days after the *Enquirer* interview with Amanda ran, Julia checked into Cedars-Sinai Hospital in West Hollywood under an assumed name. Her anonymity didn't last long, and a hospital spokesman released a statement saying that the actress had a 'severe viral infection, headaches and a high fever'.

Some people speculated that distress over Kiefer's infidelity had caused her illness. But an even nastier rumour gained widespread credence at the time and claimed Julia had checked into Cedars to detox from heroin. When these stories made their way into the mainstream press, Julia finally felt compelled to address them: 'I was exhausted. I had a fever, a bad fever. That was the worst symptom. It was like 104 [degrees

Fahrenheit]. That's why I was in the hospital so long. People should be allowed to be sick without enduring tales that they've got a needle stuck in their arm. I had the flu. I was sick. Fuck off!'

The drug rumours started, Julia presumed, because of her emaciated appearance, caused by the flu rather than by opiates. 'I don't nor have I ever done drugs. I'm just naturally thin. I guess it's boring to be a young actor in Hollywood and not have a drug problem. Well, then, I'm boring, but that's okay because I've got clear skin and clean arms.'

Despite the *Enquirer* story, Julia didn't banish Kiefer from her hospital room, where he camped out during the entire five days she stayed there.

She recovered quickly from both the virus and the Rice scandal. Soon, there were sightings of the couple at the Moonlight Tango Café and the Great Greek Café, both in the San Fernando Valley.

Nights out on the town were rare for Julia, however, because she was busy filming *Hook* on a soundstage in Burbank. Directed by Steven Spielberg, the film starred Dustin Hoffman in the title role, Robin Williams as a grown-up Peter Pan, and Julia as Tinkerbell.

She did take time off to attend a bridal shower on 2 June thrown by her agent, Elaine Goldsmith, at Goldsmith's home in Marina del Rey. Her mother Betty and a high-school friend flew in from Smyrna for the party of twenty-five. A guest described Julia as 'extraordinarily happy and glowing', a far cry from the pale and emaciated flu sufferer of only a month before.

The wedding was only two weeks away, and everything was coming together. The four-tiered wedding cake was a major production designed by the bride herself. Ominously, however, instead of the traditional bride and groom figurines, the top of the cake was decorated with violet flowers made of icing.

Julia's favourite designer, Richard Tyler of trendy Melrose Avenue, created her wedding dress for the bargain price of $2,500. As she had with the cake, Julia collaborated with Tyler on her bridesmaids' gowns, which were made of seafoam green silk. Elaine Goldsmith personally picked up the bridesmaids' shoes from Fred Hayman's on Rodeo Drive in Beverly Hills.

Julia and Kiefer wanted a quiet ceremony. They had both had a lifetime's worth of press attention and hoped to avoid turning the happy day into an orgy of helicopter-borne paparazzi reinforced with ground troops. For some reason, though, Joe Roth, who was Julia's favourite studio chief, changed their minds and got them to agree to a lavish wedding on the backlot at Twentieth Century Fox. Maybe it was because he agreed to pay for the big blowout; or maybe it was because the enclosed soundstage set aside for the ceremony would preclude flying paparazzi; or maybe it was Roth's promise to spend $100,000 on security to keep the ground-level press away as well – the extra protection would be necessary, since the cream of Hollywood royalty received invitations and included her much-loved directors Joel Schumacher and Garry Marshall, along with Richard Gere, Michael J. Fox, Charlie Sheen and his brother Emilio Estevez, Bruce Willis and Demi Moore, and Lou Diamond Phillips. Also on the invitation list were her friends from *Steel Magnolias*, Dolly Parton, Daryl Hannah, Shirley MacLaine and, of course, Sally Field.

The wedding turned into a full-blown Hollywood production. Stage 14 was decorated to resemble the antebellum home in *Steel Magnolias*, the studio's first collaboration with Julia. Everything was ready for the most talked-about event of that summer. The invitations had gone out, the food, tables, chairs, linen, dishes and silverware had been ordered. Florists' shops throughout Los Angeles were being emptied of their roses, which would fill the cavernous soundstage.

Overwhelmed by the preparations and expectations, Julia and Kiefer decided to flee Los Angeles before the big day on 14 June. Strangely, they fled to separate locations. Kiefer sought solace on his Montana ranch. Julia and her bridesmaids created the female equivalent of an extended stag party at the ritzy Canyon Ranch Spa in Tucson, Arizona, for three days.

When Julia returned to Los Angeles four days before the wedding, she didn't move back to her home in the Hollywood Hills but stayed with her mother at Elaine Goldsmith's place in Marina del Rey. That was an omen of the next day's headline-making shocker.

On 11 June Goldsmith once again more than earned her 10 per cent commission. According to one account, Julia had her agent phone Kiefer and tell him the wedding was off. According to a friend of Kiefer, Julia didn't even have the courtesy to notify her fiancé that he was now her ex-fiancé. The friend called Kiefer after hearing about the cancellation on the news!

Kiefer phoned and asked to speak to Julia, but she refused to take the call, which may explain why she had decamped at Goldsmith's instead of returning to the home she shared with Kiefer. Betty knew that all hell would break loose when the wedding of the summer turned into the scandal of the year, and it was she who had suggested Julia would be safe from enquiring minds and eyes by staying at Goldsmith's. It turned out to be wishful thinking. Helicopters swooped in and around the Marina del Rey residence, while ground troops of photographers and reporters turned the quiet beach-front suburb into a Cecil B. DeMille spectacle.

A helpful but naïve Betty explained: 'I took Julia to her agent's house, where we thought we'd be safe. But we looked out the window in the morning and we could not believe it. There must have been 150 photographers ringing the house. They were flying over in helicopters.' Julia's fearless mother ran outside and scolded the mob, shouting, 'C'mon, you guys! All she did was break off an engagement! People are starving in the world, you know? Go home!' The photographers didn't budge and treated Betty's exhortations like a photo opportunity.

The assault continued over the telephone. Somehow one of the tabloids got hold of Goldsmith's unlisted phone number and tried to get the inside scoop from the agent's home. Betty said, 'These people from the *National Enquirer* would call [Goldsmith] and lie about where they were from. Once they even said it was *The Times* of London calling. But we checked and there was no such person there. Once they said the US News Agency, and there is no such thing. Anytime you get a British accent from a Florida area code, it's a tabloid.' Someone also called claiming to be her husband, even though Betty had been divorced from Michael Motes for years.

The tabloids love a good morality tale where evil and good are clearly defined with a hissable villain and a pitiable heroine. That's how they had originally portrayed Kiefer and Julia when his dalliance with Amanda Rice had surfaced a month earlier. Now, Julia was the fall girl, condemned for leaving Kiefer if not at the altar, at least near Soundstage 14. Even the *New York Times* took sides, predicting that Julia might turn out to be the 'Liz Taylor of her day, going through men like diamond necklaces . . .'

The morality tale gained extra drama and condemnation when it was discovered that Julia had not merely dumped Kiefer, she had run off with his best friend, the handsome actor Jason Patric.

For a change, it was Julia's mother, not her agent, who had to do the dirty work, namely, justify her daughter's behaviour to the press. 'Julia's been working very hard. She has been under an incredible amount of pressure and stress. So many things have happened to her so quickly. She's talked this over with us and I think she feels she should allow a little more time before making such an important decision as marriage,' Betty told the press.

This time Julia, who had once called her mother a dozen times while preparing Thanksgiving dinner for cooking tips, didn't seek Betty's counsel. 'Julia did not ask my advice about Sutherland, and I wouldn't have had the vaguest idea of what to tell her if she had. Julia knows that I respect her decisions – that's why we're so close. She's handled this whole thing with maturity. She's ignored the press,' Betty said.

It turned out that Julia's 'stag party' with her girlfriends at the Canyon Ranch in Tucson had been a cover. She actually spent three days there with Patric. Jason was described as 'comforting' Julia in the Ranch's restaurant. Friends said the new twosome had become inseparable. Indeed, on 14 July, the day of the aborted wedding, the couple had dinner at the Nowhere Café on Melrose Avenue in West Hollywood. On the same day, Kiefer moved out of their Hollywood Hills home.

A day later, Julia and Jason flew to Ireland. In a feckless attempt at propriety they checked into separate rooms at Dublin's swank Sherborne Hotel. A passenger on the plane to Europe reported that the two were 'practically making love' on the flight. Their apparent happiness wasn't reflected in Julia's appearance, however. An employee at the Sherborne Hotel said, 'The engagement ring was off her finger. She was wearing jeans and looked very drawn. She had lost a lot of weight and her hair was a pale orange, like a dye job gone wrong.'

The next day, the couple checked out of the hotel and moved to a secluded cottage in Galway owned by U2's bassist, Adam Clayton. It was also Father's Day, and Kiefer sought refuge with his ex-wife Camelia and their three-year-old daughter Sarah.

What had caused the split? There seemed to be as many theories as there were writers covering the story. Kiefer's drinking, his alleged affair with Amanda Rice, the disparity in his career and income compared to Julia's, a prenuptial agreement he reportedly refused to sign – maybe all of the above and many more reasons only the two of them will ever know. The reputable *Newsweek* magazine suggested that Julia had a lesbian lover. Perhaps the most unlikely scenario claimed that the wedding wasn't off. To avoid a media orgy, Julia and Kiefer planned to hold the ceremony at an undisclosed location.

Amanda Rice helped spike one rumour at least. She denied having given an interview to the *National Enquirer* in which Kiefer allegedly dissed his fiancée. Rice went even further and insisted that she and Kiefer had never had a sexual relationship. 'I have never given any interviews about having an affair or a relationship with Kiefer Sutherland. Kiefer is a friend. We have not had an affair. Everything that has appeared about us in print has been manufactured and blown out of proportion,' she said in a statement released to the press after the wedding fiasco.

Months later, in an interview with *Entertainment Weekly*, Julia made it clear that she didn't believe Amanda's denials. The information in the *Enquirer* about Julia's negative body image was too perceptive for the tabloid to have made it up. Kiefer, it seemed, must have been Amanda's source.

After the *Enquirer* story broke, Julia claimed she had 'swallowed her pride' for a while. But she soon found herself gagging on it. 'I mean, this [the Rice affair] had been going on for a really long time. So then I had to say, "Well, I have made an enormous mistake in agreeing to get married. Then I made an even greater mistake by letting it all get so big. I'm not going to make the final mistake of actually getting married." At that point I just realised that this had all turned into an enormous joke, and that it wasn't going to be respectable, it wasn't going to be honest, it wasn't going to be simple. And it could have been all those things.'

It's understandable that Julia would want to call off the wedding if she believed that her fiancé was not only having an affair, but was also criticising his future wife's physical shortcomings to his mistress. What's not understandable is why Julia waited until two days before the wedding to make her decision.

In her 1993 biography, *Julia: The Untold Story of America's Pretty Woman*, Aileen Joyce offered this delectable theory: the actress wanted revenge for being publicly humiliated in the pages of the *Enquirer*. 'Hell hath no fury like a woman scorned,' Joyce explained. What better way to exact the maximum amount of revenge by waiting until the last minute to cancel the wedding, then trump Kiefer's humiliation by running off with another man – and his best friend to boot! Kiefer had had his Amanda. Now Julia had her Jason.

People magazine played armchair psychologist and attributed the split to Julia's fear of intimacy. Quoting a 'Hollywood insider', the magazine said, 'Julia is very much Miss Tinkerbell romantic. One minute she's in love with this guy, the next in love with another . . . Every time she gets close, she just shies away.'

There's just one problem with this theory, according to Julia at least. In one interview, she claimed Kiefer beat her to the punch, cancelling the wedding before she could. 'I had returned from a trip to Arizona intending to tell Kiefer that I thought it would be best for both of us not to get married. But, before I could call him, he called me. He told me he did not want to marry me. I said nothing. He was far more nasty about it than I was going to be.'

In fact, 'nasty' was probably too negative a term for a decision that was not only mutual but arrived at with equanimity, at least on her part. 'It was all very civil. I was being very civil. I mean, I wasn't pissed off that we weren't going to get married. I wasn't angry that I had come to these decisions. This is something that I think should be celebrated, that you've realised that, oops! It's not the end of the world that I don't want to marry you. It's not like I said, "Kiefer, you're dirt, I don't want to marry you!" I just said that marriage wasn't right for either one of us.'

As for the public condemnation she endured after running off with another man, Julia did a more profane Rhett Butler: 'Frankly, my dear,' she said, slipping back into her Georgia drawl, 'I don't give a shit what the lady down on the farm thinks about me.' Indeed, she claimed that most of the mail she received after the split came from well-wishers, not bad-mouthers. 'It was sort of an outpouring of kindness, people saying, "Hang in there."'

Kiefer himself absolved Julia of dumping him in revenge, telling *Details* magazine that the split was mutually decided on, if not exactly simultaneously. 'If it wasn't on the specific day the wedding was cancelled, it was mutual shortly thereafter. There was a mutual appreciation for the fact that it didn't happen. Julia and I had what I felt was a great two years. It was very unfortunate that the press took it on such a level as they did, and did it in an uninformed way. All that does is take away from whatever great times we had, and that's not right.'

Chapter Fourteen

TINKERBELL IN HELL

Like the Queen's a year later, 1991 was an *annus horribilis* for Julia Roberts. Windsor Castle was ravaged by fire in the summer of 1992; Julia saw her career go up in smoke the summer before.

The messy break with Kiefer Sutherland was just the beginning of a miserable summer for the actress. She spent much of it strapped in a painful harness, which she described as 'industrial bicycle shorts', attached to wires that allowed Tinkerbell to fly on the set of *Hook*. She also complained that flying in the harness made her dizzy. She would earn every penny of the $7 million she was paid to play the tiny sprite. Out of the harness, she found herself fighting rumours that Steven Spielberg planned to fire her.

Once again, the mainstream press reported the rumours. *USA Today* said, 'Don't be surprised if Julia Roberts is dropped from Steven Spielberg's in-the-works movie *Hook*.' The newspaper even named her possible replacements, among them Michelle Pfeiffer, Meg Ryan and Annette Bening. As soon as one of these actresses signed on the dotted line, it seemed, Julia would be officially fired.

Denials by the film's publicist ('categorically untrue') and Julia's personal press agent, Pat Kingsley ('It seems too silly. I keep hearing about Meg and Michelle – and Julia keeps going to work'), still didn't spike the rumours. It took the full weight and credibility of the director to convince the public and the press that *Hook* would fly with Julia.

First, Spielberg called gossip columnist Liz Smith and said, 'Julia is not acting up and is performing well. Julia was my first and only choice for this role from the moment the movie began production – eleven months ago. She has remained my only choice. No other actress has ever been in the running, and no other actress will replace her. Julia is doing a great job. She's been hard at work, very professional – no problems whatsoever.' He added that he had ignored the tabloid reports, but 'when stories about Julia's so-called misbehaviour or her replacement in my film begin to appear in what I consider legitimate print and TV news venues, I think it's time to speak up.'

And yet the press continued to report Julia's imminent dismissal from the project. Finally, in exasperation, Spielberg marched Julia outside the gates of the studio and held an impromptu press conference.

Referring to her cancelled wedding and the drug-abuse rumours, Spielberg said, 'Julia was going through hell at the time for reasons I won't go into. The last thing she needed was to read in the newspaper that I was going to fire her. I called a couple of reporters and told them the truth, but the stories kept appearing in print.' Knowing a photo opportunity when he saw one, Spielberg continued, 'Finally I dragged Julia to the studio gates, and said, in effect, "See. We love each other."'

Spielberg, it turned out, was only telling half the truth. True, Julia was not going to be fired, but the director and the star felt something less than love for each other. It was their troubled working relationship that had fuelled the inaccurate stories about her getting axed.

After *Hook* was released, Spielberg gave an interview to the top-rated news programme, *60 Minutes*. The show's Ed Bradley asked him if he would ever work with Roberts again. After a painfully long pause, Spielberg said tersely, 'No.' It was a rejection heard around the world.

Roberts was among the millions who heard it. She happened to be channel surfing when she caught Spielberg implying that she was a pain to work with.

In an interview in *Premiere* magazine, Roberts was described as being 'on the verge of tears' when she recounted Spielberg's public rejection of her. 'People disappoint me,' she said. 'It's too bad. Steven and I had an enjoyable time. The last day on the set, a friend shot a video of me and

Steven saying, "You are just the greatest Tinkerbell . . . I love you. And you were fabulous. You dealt with all the crazy technical blue-screen isolation, blah, blah, blah." I didn't leave *Hook* on bad terms with Steven. We hugged and kissed and did the whole goodbye thing in what I felt was a genuine way. It was so nice.

'Then to turn on my television unknowingly and watch him on *60 Minutes* . . . that's surprising. He obviously missed some aspect of me as a person. You can only find disappointment in an expectant mind, and I don't really expect anything from Steven.'

One widely reported incident suggested just how prickly the atmosphere on the set had become. Standing in front of the cameras, Roberts grew tired of waiting for filming to begin. Finally she said, 'I'm ready now.' Spielberg had replied, 'We're ready when I say we're ready, Julia.'

Julia had fonder memories of working with Spielberg and found it hard to reconcile her experience on the set with the director's. While she watched Spielberg on *60 Minutes*, she thought to herself, 'Is this the same man I had whipped-cream fights with on the set? Is this the same man who said that he couldn't wait every day to get to our stage because it was more fun than the big stage and more relaxed and easier, and even though it took nine hours to set up the shot, that I got it done so fast and I kept everything moving and was always good-humoured and didn't complain?'

It seemed the director wasn't the only member of the creative team who was less than charmed by Julia. The actress who had made a fetish of virtually adopting her movie crews in the past did not win any popularity contests on the set of *Hook*, where she reportedly earned the nickname 'Tinkerhell'. Crew members described her as 'hell to work with' and claimed she often burst into tears and 'tongue-lashed' her co-workers.

A spokesman for the studio insisted Julia got along with her colleagues. 'She's young. She's incredibly shy and not confident meeting strangers. She doesn't have the wit or the confidence to parry with a Dustin Hoffman or a Robin Williams, so, instead of even trying to get involved with the cast and crew, Julia retreated to her trailer, staying pretty much on her own set, Stage 10, where she got along fine with the special-effects people.'

*

The summer of 1991 only got worse for Julia. The *Los Angeles Times* predicted that a serious film like *Dying Young* coming out that summer would be a test of Julia's drawing power. It was a test she failed.

Dying Young opened nationwide in July and promptly died at the box office, earning reviews that made criticism of her private life seem mild by comparison. *People* magazine called it 'the big summer movie that wasn't'. *Time* labelled it the 'season's major flop with a pitiful $32 million' at the box office.

Prior to the release of the film Julia was the only actress who could 'open' a film, that is, guarantee a huge opening weekend box office, on the strength of her name alone. She was 'bankable', a title shared by a handful of actors like Tom Cruise and Harrison Ford. Julia chose to define her bankability in a feminist context: 'They say I can open movies, and that's nice in that it puts it into people's minds that women can do it. It's not just Kevin Costner, not just Arnold Schwarzenegger. Not just the guys.'

With the death of *Dying Young*, Julia found her bankable title revoked. 'They said Julia Roberts could open any film,' Martin Grove, an industry analyst for *The Hollywood Reporter*, wrote. 'They said she could open a phone book. *Dying Young* proved they were wrong.'

Time magazine also took Fox to task for releasing a film with 'dying' in the title during the summer, when action films and teen-oriented comedies ruled. Indeed, Fox had considered opening the film later that year and changing the title (in one draft, a desperate Fox had even considered having the hero survive leukaemia, which would really have caused problems with the title), but Joel Schumacher, the director, said no one could come up with a satisfactory alternative title. Fox also wanted a huge summer blockbuster on its balance sheet to trumpet at its next stockholders' meeting. The studio blindly hoped *Dying Young* would be that blockbuster. Fox's Joe Roth refused to use the 'd' word when referring to the film and called it a 'love story'. He justified the summer release as 'counterprogramming'.

'All the movies that were released prior to 4 July – *City Slickers*, *Robin Hood*, *Rocketeer*, *Naked Gun 2½*, *Terminator 2* – are male movies drawn by big stars or big concepts. Julia Roberts in a love story is perfect counterprogramming. Why cut out 50 per cent of the audience . . . or make them wait until autumn?' Roth asked rhetorically, although he was being wildly optimistic when he presumed *Dying Young* would attract 50 per cent of cinemagoers.

Time magazine called Julia down for the count. The failure of the film ruined her long run of hits. While *Hook* may have cost her the title of Miss Congeniality, *Dying Young* lost her the more important title of Miss Bankability. 'What *Dying Young* really proved is that you don't call a picture *Dying Young*. Roberts' rapid ascendancy taught Hollywood that she could sell innocence, glamour, pluck. But not even the movies' most reliable female star since Doris Day could peddle leukaemia – particularly not to a summertime audience that wants only the bad guys to die. So *Dying Young* did just that, and Roberts' pristine rep got terminated too.'

Julia offered her own post-mortem on *Dying Young*. 'We weren't trying to make a hit; we were trying to make a good movie, tell a good story. It was also just released at the wrong time – everyone connected to the movie will attest to that. Certainly I don't regret making that movie. I really enjoyed making it. I was very proud of it.'

*

With the assaults on her reputation and career, Julia spent the summer of 1991 in a state of near emotional collapse. A close friend said at the time, 'Julia is all fucked up. She doesn't know what's what. She's still not normal. Every time she thinks she's finally okay, someone will ask her for an autograph and she can feel herself ready to burst into tears. It's a good thing she got $7 million for *Hook* because, with the way she's feeling, it may have been her last film.'

Julia's emotional state wasn't improved by her surroundings off the set either. Although she still maintained her extravagant Hollywood Hills home, she spent little time there. Instead, she virtually moved into Jason Patric's place, which was anything but extravagant. According to some accounts, his apartment was barely habitable.

Patric's duplex on Stanley Street in Hollywood had only one bedroom. To call its furnishings Salvation Army quality would be to exaggerate their value. Bedsheets instead of curtains covered the windows. A friend said with understatement, 'He's into not seeming materialistic, studiously into not seeming that way. It's like he's a rich kid but doesn't want to appear like one, you know? So he goes out of his way to look and live like he's poverty-stricken.' Patric is the son of Pulitzer Prize-winning playwright Jason Miller (*That Championship Season*) and the grandson of the grand old man of '50s TV, Jackie Gleason.

Another friend and colleague, actress Jami Gertz, was even more blunt about the environment Julia now inhabited. 'He doesn't live in a palatial place. There's an old, second-hand couch. I go in there and I'm disgusted.'

Other friends insisted Julia was happy with her downscale lifestyle, cooking and cleaning for her new boyfriend, spending unglamorous evenings in front of the TV instead of carousing, as she had with Kiefer at fashionable nightclubs and restaurants.

Photos of the couple captured by paparazzi who would jump out of the bushes and freak out the solitary Patric show how chameleon-like Julia had become, taking on the coloration of her boyfriend. Julia wore baggy granny dresses or torn jeans. Jason was always unshaven and the holes in his clothes went beyond the raggedy style then fashionable. The couple could easily have been mistaken for the homeless who camped out in Patric's blighted neighbourhood.

After *Hook* finished filming in August 1991, Julia disappeared from public view until the release of the film in December of that year required her to meet with the press to promote the film.

I was a syndicated columnist for United Media at the time, and I interviewed Julia at the Century Plaza Hotel in Los Angeles. She wore her trademark granny dress to the interview and looked oddly out of place at the posh hotel. She also seemed angry and on the defensive, which was understandable considering the drubbing she had taken from my colleagues in the press over her personal and professional life at the time. I was one of several journalists seated at a table, interviewing Julia. Before she entered the room, a studio publicist warned us not to ask her about Jason Patric, whose film *Rush* had come out earlier that month and had promptly bombed at the box office. The critics were also unkind. I timidly obeyed the studio's order, but one of my colleagues, Rod Lurie, had the temerity to ask her what she thought of Jason's film. Puffing on a cigarette, Julia glared at him and refused to answer the question.

She was more voluble when the subject of the press came up. How did she cope with negative publicity, a reporter at the press gathering asked her. 'I don't concern myself with it. I don't follow it. When it follows me around, that's when I sort of react to it. I just wish the public at large would concern themselves with their own lives, with their own personal business and affairs. And then probably divorce rates would be lower, there wouldn't be so many fractured families and troubled people, and things would be a lot easier for everybody.'

Julia's pique was evident, and one reporter asked her, 'You're not happy being here, are you?'

She said, 'I've learned the hard way to be more frugal with words around people like you, which is not necessarily a bad thing to learn. You just sort of figure things out as you go along, I guess. I've made plenty of mistakes and everyone's made sure that I've known about them.'

When *Hook* premièred a few weeks later, it was widely panned by the critics, Julia among them. The *New York Times* said she spent much of the film looking like a 'confused horsefly', referring to the special effects which shrunk her to fairy size. Her mother said, 'Julia saw it and wasn't very pleased with it.'

Her promotional duties for *Hook* over, Julia again disappeared. This time she would spend almost two years out of sight and, surprisingly for the once workaholic actress, out of work.

In 1992 she did come out of 'retirement' briefly to do a cameo at the end of Robert Altman's *The Player*, which satirised her bankability, that is, her presence in a film automatically guaranteeing financing.

Actually, the in-joke about her bankability in *The Player* was more reality than satire. Despite suffering two back-to-back flops, Hollywood still wanted Julia. But Julia didn't want Hollywood. Her agent, Elaine Goldsmith, seemed to be out of touch with her client, since she continued to solicit work for Julia, even though Julia did not want to work.

A producer described an agent and client who seemed to be at cross-purposes with one another: 'In Hollywood, it's not unusual for a star or director to say, "I'm not working for the next year, or until the spring." No one thinks that's strange. But with Julia Roberts, it was odd because about every three months I'd get a call from Elaine, asking if I had any projects for Julia. She'd tell me, "She wants to work. Have you got a comedy, a drama?" I'd send out the scripts and Julia would reject them all. Then, like clockwork, Elaine would call and the cycle would start again. This was strange, even by Hollywood standards.'

During these 'wilderness years', Julia turned down projects that would become huge hits for other actresses. Demi Moore stepped into *Indecent Proposal* with Robert Redford after Julia refused to play a woman who slept with a billionaire for a million bucks, and Meg Ryan became a huge star after *Sleepless in Seattle*, another Julia reject.

Julia's sabbatical also saw the end of her fourteenth-month relationship with Jason Patric, which was attributed to a new man in her life. As usual, her new inamorata was another co-star, Daniel Day-Lewis, who was set to appear with Julia in a low-budget comedy to be filmed in England called *Shakespeare in Love*. Her short-lived affair with Day-Lewis ended when he dropped out of the picture and out of her life. But not before Day-Lewis's former lover, French actress Isabelle Adjani, had a chance to complain that the actor was with Julia and not her when she gave birth to his child. 'I felt incredible sadness and disappointment,' Adjani said.

Julia's departure from *Shakespeare in Love* tarnished her reputation in an industry where being considered 'difficult' can kill a career. When Julia dropped out of the film, expensive sets had already been built and costumes designed. That kind of waste catches the attention of Hollywood's bean-counters. Or as one unnamed studio chief said, her departure 'has definitely gone beyond the range of normal movie-star behaviour. We've reached the point where a lot of people are wondering just what in the world is going on with her.'

*

While Day-Lewis wasn't much more than a blip on the radar screen of Julia's romantic life, her split from Jason Patric was as noisy and public as her break-up with Kiefer Sutherland had been. On the night of 18 January 1993 Jason's neighbours heard loud voices coming from inside his tiny duplex in Hollywood. Soon, the argument spilled into the streets, and the people arguing were Jason and Julia. Standing in the middle of the street, the combatants hurled obscenities at each other. Witnesses said the subject of the argument was Daniel Day-Lewis, whose name kept coming up in between the profanities. An eye-witness was quoted in Aileen Joyce's biography of Julia as saying, 'Jason was almost falling-down drunk, and although Julia wasn't drunk, it was obvious she'd also been drinking. Anyway, Jason kept accusing her of having slept with Daniel Day-Lewis, yelling, "You fucked him. I know you fucked him." Then Julia yelled back at him, "I can fuck anyone I want to!"' At that, Julia slipped into her Porsche and drove off. She never returned to the duplex.

While Julia was apparently relieved to end their tortured relationship, Jason was devastated by the split. He was unable to sleep in the bed they had once shared and ended up on the living-room couch. 'Jason was terribly despondent and obsessed with Julia after they broke up,' according to a source quoted in *US* magazine. Jason even became something of a stalker, going to her house in the Hollywood Hills several times, allegedly in search of love letters written by Day-Lewis to Julia.

The laconic Patric made only one public statement about *l'affaire* Julia, and he chose an outlet far away from Hollywood, a London magazine. 'It was for me the ultimate nightmare. Relationships have their own problems, and the attention didn't help matters,' he said in an interview in *Time Out*.

In an ironic replay of her dismissal of Kiefer, Julia once again called on the services of the helpful Elaine Goldsmith to do the dirty work and tell her distraught boyfriend they were through.

Even more ironically, Patric's jealousy may have been unfounded. Although some reputable publications like *People* magazine claimed that Julia and Day-Lewis did indeed have a brief fling, others insisted their 'relationship' consisted of only one business meeting to discuss their participation in *Shakespeare in Love*.

Although the romantic comedy would go on to sweep the Oscars in 1999 with a different cast, the project fell apart in the autumn of 1992 when Roberts and Day-Lewis decided not to appear in the film. What or who killed *Shakespeare in Love*?

According to one report, Day-Lewis was happy to have an affair with Julia, but he didn't want to make a film with her, or at least not the one she offered him. When Day-Lewis dropped out, Julia suddenly lost interest in the project, since her real interest all along had been her co-star, not the film, according to this theory.

Another account attributed the collapse of the project to nothing more dramatic than scheduling conflicts. Day-Lewis had already agreed to star in a drama about the IRA, *In the Name of the Father*, and the two films' shooting schedules overlapped.

The official explanation for Julia's departure came from Elaine Goldsmith, who said Julia was unhappy with the actors who were suggested as possible replacements for Day-Lewis. 'I think the frustration comes with everyone wanting to go forward with this project and not being able to find the right person once Daniel Day-Lewis passed,' Goldsmith said. She attributed his departure to 'dates not working out' and 'neither the producer nor Julia has found the right actor' to replace Day-Lewis.

Julia's loss would seven years later be Gwyneth Paltrow's gain and the Oscar for Best Actress.

Chapter Fifteen

IN LOVETT WITH LYLE

By the end of 1992 Julia needed help. Her personal and professional life were a mess. The fourteen-month affair with Jason Patric was nearing its end. Her long absence from the screen had industry insiders talking about permanent retirement. Julia needed a white knight to come to the rescue, and she found one in Joe Roth, the former chairman of Twentieth Century Fox, who had turbocharged her career with the box-office hit *Sleeping with the Enemy*, which took $100 million in the US alone.

By late 1992, Roth had left Fox and set up an independent production company called Caravan Pictures. Caravan's toughest assignment was to find projects for Julia Roberts, who had finally decided to come out of retirement and signed on with the company. When their alliance was announced on 3 December 1992, however, Roth had yet to find anything for his skittish new partner. 'There's nothing that we're thinking about specifically,' he said. 'I hope to find something for her by the first half of next year . . . a romantic comedy, a thriller or high romance.'

Julia felt at home with Roth not only because of their past collaboration on *Sleeping with the Enemy*, but also because Roth's Caravan Pictures was headquartered at Disney, which had produced her first really big hit, *Pretty Woman*. 'I have the utmost respect for Joe Roth and I trust his creative instincts,' Roberts said. 'I am delighted to be working with him again, and to be affiliated with his new company. I am equally pleased to be returning to the Disney Studios.'

Unlike Julia, who had been dithering for almost two years, Roth didn't waste any time finding work for the jewel in his crown. Two weeks after the announcement of their pact, Roth found a script Julia loved, a romantic comedy called *I Love Trouble*. The title would prove to be ironically accurate.

Julia's deal with Roth was non-exclusive, which meant she could work elsewhere if a project tickled her fickle fancy. Within weeks of signing on for *I Love Trouble*, Julia agreed to star in a surefire hit, *The Pelican Brief*, based on the best-selling novel by John Grisham. As usual, she got another pay rise, this time $8 million, which in 1992 was the going rate for top actors like Kevin Costner and Mel Gibson.

Julia's two-year vacation ended in May 1993, when she showed up on the New York set of *The Pelican Brief*. She played Darby Shaw, a brilliant law student whose life is threatened after she finds evidence that two Supreme Court Justices have been the victim of foul play.

After playing an abused wife, a fairy and a fairytale hooker, Julia relished the role of a brainy woman in charge of her life, someone who could take care of herself even in the most daunting situations. Describing Darby Shaw, Julia said, 'She's clever and complex and I find her very admirable in her ways and choices. It's nice to see a woman of strength and, regardless of the paralysing situation she finds herself in, she is never without strength. Regardless of how doomed she feels, she always hangs on. I find that very noble.'

Denzel Washington played the investigative reporter who helps her foil the bad guys. Washington was not Warner Bros' choice for the male lead, but Julia insisted on casting him. Indeed, in the Grisham novel, Washington's character was white. During an interview on the set, Julia insisted she wasn't striking a blow for equal rights or affirmative action. She was adamant that Washington's skin colour was not the determining factor in his casting. 'Who cares? White or black – who cares? I just wanted the best man for the part. Who gives a shit?' she said.

If the movie's plot had revolved around an interracial romance, Julia conceded, 'Then I would give a shit. But this movie is not about who's black and who's white, who's the girl and who's the boy. This movie is about intrigue. It's beside the point who's doing what, who's wearing what colour of skin while they're doing it. Who cares? It's about time we stopped casting roles by colour.' Interestingly, though, there would be no love scene between the two stars, although the characters in the novel do fall in love.

A month after filming began, the production moved to Washington, DC, where Julia, Denzel and director Alan J. Pakula held a press conference. Reporters were shocked at the change in Julia's appearance and demeanour. The former bag lady with an angry distrust of the press had been replaced by an elegantly coiffed and coutured beauty who fielded questions from the press with finesse and even graciousness. The same woman who a few years earlier had told the press to 'fuck off' was as gushy and forthcoming as a Barbara Walters interviewee.

When a reporter asked if she had any problems returning to work after a two-year absence, Julia laughed and said, 'I don't feel rusty. Do I look rusty? I think I came back with some renewed vigour . . . I've been giddy.'

Julia's giddiness, it turned out, had less to do with her return to acting and more to do with her return to romance. Six days after the DC press conference, Julia had a much more newsworthy item to announce. She was going to marry country-and-western crooner Lyle Lovett.

Julia and Lyle had met in June 1992 in New Orleans, where she was filming *The Pelican Brief* and Lyle was performing on stage. Contrary to many published stories, they did not meet on the set of *The Player*, in which they had cameo roles, since their scenes were shot on separate days. Shortly after they met, the couple were spotted at nightspots in New Orleans, including Café Brasil, where they were serenaded by the Klezmer All-Stars, an acoustic band that performs Jewish folk music. At one point in the evening, Lyle and Julia got up and danced the hora. Another patron described a couple who were obviously in love. 'They were nuzzling and dancing together. Everyone could see something was happening between them.'

Despite their busy schedules, which kept Lyle on the road with his band much of the year, they managed to make time for each other, with Julia often flying in to cities where Lyle happened to be performing. Fans caught her backstage at his concerts in Memphis; Vienna, West Virginia; and New York City. Lyle made quick trips to Julia's movie locations. She first met Lyle's mother on the phone.

The Lovett clan was apprehensive about Lyle's new object of affection and feared, based on Julia's history with Kiefer Sutherland, that the relationship might provide tragic fodder for one of his melancholic compositions. His cousin, Wanda Hill, said, 'Our whole side of the family was saying, "O Lord, please don't let her back out, because that'd break his heart."' But Hill didn't share the rest of the clan's pessimism, adding, 'They are just so in love. Every time you turned around they were kissing and hugging.'

Lyle was clearly infatuated with his new girlfriend. 'When I'm not singing, I'm talking to Julia,' he confided to a relative. Band members noticed that he seemed to be putting more emotion into his act after he met Julia. 'His songs suddenly took on a different meaning,' a band member said.

To keep their relationship secret as long as possible, Lyle would dedicate songs to 'Fiona', Julia's middle name, during his stage appearances. 'Fiona likes to think I wrote this song for her,' he told an audience at New York's Paramount Theater. The song was aptly titled, 'She Makes Me Feel Good'. But it seemed that the couple just couldn't keep their happiness to themselves and blew their cover during a performance in New York City, when Julia came on stage and introduced him to the audience before he sang 'Stand By Your Man'.

Observers remarked that Lyle's infatuation with Julia seemed to be mutual. A concert organiser in West Virginia, Trish Shuman, said, 'What I really liked about her is how animated she became during Lyle's set. At the end she threw her arms around a crew member, saying how much she had enjoyed the show.'

Julia's friends were surprised that she had fallen in love with Lovett, who was ten years her senior. Previous loves had all been her handsome leading men. Lovett, whose top-heavy hairstyle has been described as a 'thatch of nuclear-radiated alfalfa sprouts', was not 'conventionally studly', as one magazine kindly referred to Lyle's off-kilter looks.

Still, many women, not just Julia, found something ineffably sexy about the lean six-footer. A female friend who had known him for years said, 'What women look for in a man, he's got in spades. He's sweet, kind and gentle and really a catch. And I bet you he'd do anything to make a woman happy. Anything.'

Lyle's friend and fellow country singer Tanya Tucker felt he must have represented a refreshing change from the people in Julia's usual orbit around Planet Hollywood. 'I think Julia's tired of the Hollywood pretence. Maybe she's ready to be treated like a goddess, which Lyle will do.'

A friend of the bride, Terry Tomalin, predicted that their similar roots would make the union thrive. Lyle and Julia, he said, 'were a consummate Southern gentleman and consummate Southern belle'. Tongue in cheek, Lyle's friend, Memphis concert promoter Bob Kelley, noted that both newlyweds were string-beans. 'Tall people like tall people, I guess,' Kelley said.

Julia's sister-in-law, Eliza Roberts, had high hopes for the union: 'Julia wouldn't be getting married unless she planned on staying with Lyle for the rest of her life.' Bridesmaid Deborah Porter described the bride as 'ecstatic, giddy and excited'.

Unlike her previous fiancé, Kiefer Sutherland, whose parents like Julia's had split when he was four, Lyle had a family background that couldn't have been more different. His parents have been married for more than forty years. During her childhood, Julia moved from house to house as her parents' fortunes rose and fell. Lyle still lives in the same clapboard house in Klein, Texas, built by his grandfather. Both, however, come from small Southern towns and, although Lyle hadn't attained Julia's international status, he was a major figure in the country-and-western music world, having won a 1989 Grammy Award as Best Country Male Vocalist. Prospects for the relationship were improved by the fact that they weren't competing in the same arena, the movie business, which may have contributed to the Kiefer débâcle and perhaps the failure of her relationships with other actors. For his part, although he did have a small cameo in *The Player*, Lyle insisted he had no acting aspirations. Despite his lack of screen ambition, Lovett accepted a meaty role in the surprise hit *The Opposite of Sex* (1998).

Seven days after the DC news conference at which reporters noticed a newly radiant Julia, the couple married on 27 June at the St James Lutheran Church in the sleepy hamlet of Marion, Indiana, a suburb of Indianapolis. Julia managed to squeeze the event in during a weekend break from filming *The Pelican Brief*. The unlikely location of Marion was chosen because it happened to be near a stop on Lyle's concert tour.

It was their good fortune that Indiana does not require a waiting period. Fearing another press circus like the Kiefer Sutherland mess, Julia and Lyle wanted to tie the knot before airborne paparazzi could locate ground zero.

'It's funny,' Julia said about the impromptu nature of the wedding. 'We were both just giddy and wanted to get together and get married. Certainly, as an afterthought, you go, "Let's do it now! We love each other. We want to spend our lives together." This way things are calm and quiet and we can do it the way we want to do it without any influences from anybody else. The only downside to it was that I have a handful of really good friends and I didn't have time to arrange for them to come.'

Julia did, however, have time to round up some friends and family and fly them into Marion. Five tour buses and a stretch limo arrived outside the Grant County court house in Marion and disgorged the wedding guests. One of them, Susan Sarandon, said, 'We were all coming in from everywhere, like Noah's Ark.'

Karen Weaver, the court house clerk, climbed into the lead bus to get the couple's signature on the marriage license. The starstruck clerk asked the bride, 'Are you the real Julia Roberts?' Julia politely confirmed her identity then produced a document showing that she had been immunised against German measles, one of the few requirements for getting married in Indiana. Returning to the court house with the signed marriage licence, Weaver told co-workers that the twosome seemed like 'nice people. I was very impressed but not awestruck. I was awestruck when I met Dan Quayle.'

Friends of Lyle were shocked that the couple had known each other less than a month when they decided to tie the knot. Lyle was notorious for being a meticulous, deliberative man who didn't rush into things. His ex-girlfriend, Allison Inman, whose split with Lyle had been amicable, marvelled, 'I'm proud of the old guy, because I've never seen him do anything spontaneous. I have to applaud a woman who can get him to do something like that.'

Unlike their whirlwind courtship, the wedding itself was more conventional. Lyle chartered private jets and flew in his parents, William and Bernell, retired Exxon employees, along with sixteen other relatives. Julia's mother and half-sister Nancy had booked a commercial flight from Smyrna and sat in the second row of St James, while her sister Lisa served as maid of honour. The bridesmaids were Elaine Goldsmith, actresses Deborah Goodrich Porter and Susan Sarandon, and Julia's best friend at Campbell High, Paige Sampson. Unlike the elaborate designer gowns for the Sutherland wedding, the bridesmaids didn't wear matching outfits, just whatever they chose from their closet.

Glaringly absent was Julia's brother Eric, who had been estranged from his sister since his break-up with his girlfriend, Kelly Cunningham, in 1993. Julia had sided with Kelly in the custody battle over the couple's daughter, Emily. Eric later told the press he had been purposely left off the invitation list because his sister feared he might cause trouble at the event, although he failed to say what exactly it was that Julia thought he might do. Eric also mentioned that he never did get a chance to meet his brother-in-law.

Actor Barry Tubb, a friend from her starving actor days, stood in for her late father and gave the bride away. Tubb walked Julia down the aisle as an organist pounded out Bach's 'Jesu, Joy of Man's Desiring', followed by a cellist's rendition of Mendelssohn's 'Wedding March'. Two flower girls, Susan Sarandon's eight-year-old daughter Eva, and Alexandra Porter, aged five, preceded Julia, who carried a bouquet of white roses.

Unlike her haute-couture gown designed by trendy Richard Tyler for the Sutherland wedding, Julia wore a plain white dress – an off-the-rack number from Commes des Garçons which Lovett himself had bought for $2,000. Her only accessory, besides the roses, was a floor-length tulle scarf. Julia really got into the down-home mood and made her way to the altar barefoot.

Despite the informality, bridesmaid Deborah Porter said of the bride, 'She looked gorgeous.' One of Lyle's relatives, however, thought Julia was underdressed for the occasion. 'It looked more like a slip that should go under a wedding dress. You could see her belly button!' Lyle's cousin complained. Lyle wore a plain dark business suit instead of a tuxedo.

The brief twenty-minute ceremony had two ministers officiating. Lyle's childhood pastor, the Revd De Wyth Belz from Lyle's Trinity Lutheran

Church, and St James's pastor, the Revd Mark Carlsen.

At the end of the ceremony, as Julia and Lyle kissed, Francine Reed, a back-up singer in his band, belted out a twangy version of the Lord's Prayer a cappella from the choir loft.

The wedding party didn't wait around in Marion once the church service ended. Lyle had to perform that evening in Nobelsville, Indiana, sixty miles away, and everyone piled back into the tour bus *en route* to the concert.

The reception was held in a white tent near the Deer Park Music Center. Julia gave a little speech, saying, 'He makes me so happy. He's so good to me,' before tossing her wedding bouquet, which Elaine Gold-smith caught. Lyle made a big show of removing Julia's garter belt, then threw it to the male guests.

At his concert that evening, Julia joined her new husband on stage and danced while he sang, 'Stand By Your Man'. The audience, ten thousand-strong, cheered the couple. After he finished the set, Lovett, not known for wearing his emotions on his sleeve, gave Julia a long, passionate kiss that brought the audience to its feet. 'Thank you very much,' he told his screaming fans. 'And welcome to the happiest day of my life.'

Perhaps based on past experiences, Julia sounded a more cautious note. 'It's like a dream. I'm scared it's going to be over, and I don't want to wake up.'

The couple didn't have time for a honeymoon. The next day the bride was back on the set of *The Pelican Brief* in Washington. A crew member dressed as Cupid and armed with a bow and arrow greeted her. Later, the director had an even nicer surprise in store for his star. Julia's first scene that day had her talking on the phone to co-star John Heard. But Alan Pakula arranged for Lyle to be on the other end of the line, reading Heard's lines.

After the director yelled, 'Cut,' Julia shouted at the crew, 'That's my husband!'

The production team threw a reception for Julia that evening. They all wore T-shirts that said 'Welcome Back, Mrs Lovett' on the front. But on the back it said, 'He's A Lovely Boy . . . But You Really Must Do Something About His Hair.'

Julia defended her new husband's curly mop, which she insisted wasn't scraping the ceiling. 'If you spend any time with him, his hair isn't as big as everybody makes it out to be. I've seen some pictures from a few years ago, and that picture is high. But now, it's pretty normal. He's really good-looking.'

Much to the disappointment of the local and national press, no doubt, the filming of *The Pelican Brief* was uneventful. Despite the hellish humidity of the nation's capital in June, the two stars' tempers never flared, and there were no reports of trouble on the set. Denzel Washington, an actor known to speak up when his needs, artistic or personal, are not being met, didn't let out a peep of complaint during the shoot. Julia, in the full flush of her new marriage, was too happy to complain even if she had had something to complain about. And the director, Alan J. Pakula, who is known as a 'woman's director' and had helped Meryl Streep win a Best Actress Oscar for *Sophie's Choice*, continued Julia's run of good luck with nurturers like Garry Marshall and Joel Schumacher.

Pakula, who had worked with such temperamental stars as Warren Beatty and Dustin Hoffman, was no Spielberg when it came to Julia. The former Tinkerhell reverted to the girl who turned crew and cast into temporary family members. 'She gave everything,' Pakula said. 'By the end, she had earned the respect of the entire crew. Julia responds to the other actors, which is what the best people do.'

Interestingly, Pakula decided not to use one of Julia's biggest assets, her stunning beauty, even though her character in the book is not only gorgeous but even shares Julia's long limbs and tendency to hide them in bag-lady clothes. In the novel, John Grisham described Darby Shaw as seen through the eyes of her lover and law school professor, played by Sam Shepard: 'For two brutal years now, one of the few pleasures of law school had been to watch as she graced the halls and rooms with her long legs and baggy sweaters. There was a fabulous body in there somewhere, they could tell. But she was not one to flaunt it.'

Pakula relied on the intricate plot, typical of John Grisham's works, not the natural wonders of Julia Roberts, to hold the audience's attention, and it worked. *The Pelican Brief* opened on 17 December 1993 and was hailed as Julia's comeback picture by the press. *Variety* declared her 'sensational as a law student on the run', called the film a 'crackling thriller', and predicted it would have a 'long, prosperous box-office flight'. Moviegoers here and abroad did indeed flock to see the thriller, which grossed nearly $200 million worldwide.

The Pelican Brief turned out to be a professional triumph for Julia and a personal pleasure to make for two reasons. She had a director who admired her and a co-star whose chemistry with her was palpable on screen. Or, as the *Los Angeles Times* in its otherwise unfavourable review conceded, 'Roberts and Washington do what is expected of them quite nicely and manage a pleasant on-screen rapport . . .'

Unfortunately, the same *bonhomie* did not suffuse the set of her next film, whose title would prove aptly prophetic.

Chapter Sixteen

LOVES TROUBLE, HATES CO-STAR

———⟨⟩———

I Love Trouble was Julia's first film project for Joe Roth's Caravan Pictures. On paper, the production had a lot going for it. A 1940s-style romantic comedy *à la* Spencer Tracy and Katherine Hepburn, the movie focused on the love–hate relationship between two competitive newspaper reporters in Chicago both in pursuit of the same scoop. The people behind the camera were just as promising. The husband and wife team of Nancy Meyers and Charles Shyer (*Father of the Bride*) were the hottest romantic comedy *auteurs* of the moment. Meyers and Shyer, who collaborated on the cult classic *Irreconcilable Differences*, co-wrote the script, with Shyer directing and Meyers producing.

But there was trouble in this artistic paradise almost from the beginning. By now Julia was so bankable, she always got to pick her leading man. Whatever Julia wanted, it seemed, Julia got. Not this time. The problem was that Julia's 'man' didn't want her – or at least didn't want to work with her. The young actress had set her sights on a more mature leading man this time, Harrison Ford, an actor with an enviable ability to make successful action films (*The Fugitive*) as well as frothy romances (*Working Girl*). Julia's choice of Ford showed she was a savvy casting director. Romantic comedies that pair older men with nubile girls represent one of the most enduring genres in the business, ever since an avuncular Gregory Peck showed a pubescent Audrey Hepburn around town in *Roman Holiday*. We'll never know why Ford, one of the most tight-lipped actors on and off screen, passed up the project. Maybe he had read the stories about Tinkerhell and *Hook*, or perhaps the screenplay didn't pass muster with a major star who was also a great script-reader with a knack for sniffing out a hit.

Ford's replacement turned out to be a disaster. Instead of the mature, courtly gentleman whose resumé stretched all the way back to *Star Wars*, Julia found herself paired with Nick Nolte, a much respected actor whose personal demons have been documented in the press for more than two decades.

Julia played cub reporter Sabrina Peterson. Her first name was no doubt the writers' homage to another classic about a May–September romance, 1954's *Sabrina*. Nolte played a burnt-out city columnist for a rival newspaper. Resting on his laurels, Nolte's newsman seemed more interested in chasing women than tracking down stories. The ambitious young reporter and the jaded journalist ended up covering a train wreck story that leads to murder and mayhem.

Unfortunately, the two stars let the mayhem continue after the cameras stopped rolling. The *Los Angeles Times*, a starchy newspaper which rarely reports celebrity feuds, ran a major piece in conjunction with the film's release in June 1994. It quoted members of the crew who claimed Julia threw a few temper tantrums. She allegedly objected to Nolte's machismo and 'would deride and insult her co-star', according to sources on the set. Although no stranger to swearing herself, Julia found Nolte's crude language and behaviour off-putting. Julia's actions also irritated Nolte, and he went out of his way to return the favour. Their antagonism grew so poisonous that eventually the stars found themselves delivering lines to stand-ins more often than to each other.

Other sources claimed the two got along fine. These eyewitnesses said it was the writer-director team of Shyer and Meyers who created tension on the set by ordering Julia and Nolte to improvise their lines while the cameras recorded their painful attempts at ad-libbing. 'It drove them nuts,' a production source said of Julia and Nolte.

Director Shyer apparently didn't notice Julia's irritation and fell in love with her image on his movieola during the editing process. 'We were looking at the film the other day and our editor said, "She's got it!" I think

Julia would have been a movie star in the '30s or '40s, in any era. There is a magic there with her. You just go, "Wow – this is what it's all about!" And she looks unbelievably great. We wanted her to be very stylish, like Julia hasn't looked in any other movie,' Shyer said.

The director, of course, wore rose-tinted glasses while he looked at the screen. The marketing people charged with selling the film to the public had 20-20 vision, and they saw disaster. Whether it was bickering stars or mad *auteurs* improvising, there was no chemistry between Julia and Nolte on screen. Disney, which had a distribution deal with Roth's Caravan Pictures, took a look at the rough cut and drastically revamped its marketing campaign. The studio had originally planned to tout the summer release as a feel-good romance with tart dialogue in the tradition of Tracy and Hepburn. Instead, trailers and TV commercials for the film emphasised the murder-mystery elements. An industry pundit sardonically described the switch: 'It's gone from a Hepburn–Tracy *Woman of the Year* to *Pelican Brief* in a very short time span.'

Julia refused to comment for the *Los Angeles Times* article. Her publicist, Nancy Seltzer, however, came out swinging against the mudslinging by the newspaper. Seltzer flat out denied any trouble on the set of *I Love Trouble*, adding, 'Serious publications only exacerbate the problem by repeating these rumours. By virtue of this kind of reporting they give permission to the less serious publications to do the same without conscience. I'm greatly saddened by the current trend that journalism seems to be taking . . . that of the business of selling copy instead of the search for the truth.'

Maybe Seltzer didn't subscribe to the *New York Times*. Although Julia had refused to talk to the *Los Angeles Times*, she had said in an earlier interview with its East Coast rival, 'From the moment I met him, we sort of gave each other a hard time and naturally we got on each other's nerves. While he can be completely charming and very nice, he's also completely disgusting. He's going to hate me for saying this, but he seems to go out of his way to repel people. He's a kick [comedian].'

In an interview with *Entertainment Weekly*, Roberts later back-tracked a bit and downgraded the 'hard time' to 'needling'. 'We had great, um, high-spirited needling of each other, trying to get a rise out of each other.'

Jim Wiatt, Nolte's agent, took the unusual step of admitting that the lack of on-screen chemistry reflected off-screen resentments, but insisted the alleged feud was nothing more than the 'typical spats' stars often engage in – more of a pie fight than a fistfight.

As unusual as it was for a star to badmouth a co-star in public, during interviews to promote the release of *I Love Trouble*, Julia did something she rarely does – discuss intimate details of her life, especially painful ones. Maybe her openness about the Nolte mess made her feel like opening up about the feud with her brother, Eric. Eric had made a point of letting the press know he had not been invited to Julia's wedding, and his sister confirmed the estrangement when she bluntly told *Rolling Stone* in 1994, 'We don't speak. Actually, in all fairness, we spoke about a week ago, me making an attempt to explain how I felt based on what he and his wife seemed to be up to and that it concerned me.'

Press reports claimed that Julia had sided with her brother's ex-girlfriend in their child custody battle and that Julia had even gone so far as to help pay her legal bills. This tangled family drama got even more convoluted when Eric's wife seemed to blame her husband, not Julia, for the rift. Eliza Rayfiel Roberts told *Redbook* magazine, 'Eric takes responsibility for the separation [from his sister]. He's a wonderful guy who, when depressed, can be short-tempered and impatient. When that happens, feelings get hurt. Julia was not going to be hurt again and again by somebody she cared about.'

Julia hated airing her family's dirty laundry and wished her brother and sister-in-law would stop doing so. 'It's a private matter that for some reason he and his wife have decided to make more public than I think they should,' she said. But Julia was up and running and couldn't resist addressing the split herself. She also took the opportunity to question her sister-in-law's credentials as family spokesperson. 'Eric tells his stories, and his wife tells her stories. What I find most fascinating about Eric's wife and what she says about me and how I feel about things and what I do about things is that I've never even met her.'

Eliza had appeared on the tabloid TV show, *Hard Copy*, and Julia wondered out loud why Eliza represented herself as an authority on the subject. Julia said in response to the *Hard Copy* appearance, 'It's fascinating to listen to someone speak with such authority about me when I wouldn't even have known what she looked like except I saw her on TV talking about me. There's your exclusive authority interview, do you know what I mean?

'It's too bad. My brother knows specifically what our problems are. He's very clear. He can choose to relay them however he sees fit. I've decided just to take the Nancy Kerrigan approach.' (Kerrigan was the Olympic ice skater who declined to discuss publicly the physical assault on her by the boyfriend of rival Tonya Harding.) 'There's always a lot more respectability in being quiet, as opposed to Tonya Harding's "Look at me, I'm here, I'm here, I'll tell you anything".'

Later, Julia apparently changed her mind that less is more when discussing family squabbles. In an interview with *US* magazine in which she exhorted the reporter to 'ask me anything', the emboldened journalist did. Specifically, he asked about Eric's public admission of problems with drugs. Julia said that both she and her sister had tried to help Eric, but their efforts ultimately failed. 'Many moments of our youth were spent in trying to save Eric from the wreckage of his abuse. I am absolutely a person who can sit here and be absent of any kind of remorse or guilt on my behalf or my sister's because of the effort that we put in trying to do things that we were ill-equipped for . . . It can be incredibly taxing and frustrating.'

Her attempts to end their estrangement were also fruitless and weren't helped by her brother's bizarre explanation for the cause of the rift. Julia said, 'I feel like I've put a lot of effort into fixing [the relationship] . . . but my efforts have come to naught over time, and you get to a place where you're at peace with the fact that you're not smart enough to fix something that you don't really understand. I mean, I read somewhere that Eric said the lack of our relationship is a direct result of my being pissed off because he insulted my hair.'

Despite his criticism, Julia sincerely hoped her brother would put his life back in order. 'I wish Eric great success with his recovery. I do, because it's been a long time in coming.'

Much of Julia's public revelations about a deeply painful and private matter came out during interviews to drum up publicity for *I Love Trouble*.

But no amount of sensationalistic publicity could save the troubled project. The critics barbecued the film. Kenneth Turan of the *Los Angeles Times* wrote that 'the repartee is mostly lacklustre [and] the comedy aspects . . . are not especially entrancing despite the star power'. *US* magazine claimed 'even a microscope couldn't detect a chemical reaction between Roberts and co-star Nick Nolte'.

The public agreed with the critical consensus. *I Love Trouble* turned out to be a rarity on Julia's resumé: a complete box-office flop, grossing little over $30 million in the US, approximately what it cost to make. The *Sunday Times* called it her 'one unqualified flop'.

A few years later, Julia found herself agreeing with the critics and the public and offered this post-mortem on the failure of *I Love Trouble*: 'If you read the script, you'd know why I did that film. It was clever banter – sort of '40s-style, hard-driving, a little wacky, a little screwball, a little adventure. But throughout the making of the film those things weren't supported enough by our leaders. It became a '90s movie that didn't really know what it was. I know better questions to ask now,' she said in 1995.

Time didn't heal the wounds inflicted by the failure of *I Love Trouble*. In fact, it seemed to have inflamed her memories of the film. Four years after its release, Julia was dismissing it with a single profanity. 'I don't know what I've already said about *I Love Trouble*, other than that it was a piece of shit.'

One flop doesn't kill a career, of course, and a major talent agent accurately predicted Julia's prospects perfectly in the wake of *I Love Trouble*'s troubles. 'She has weakened her franchise, but I would still take her in a New York minute. If she gets back and has another hit, she'll have the acceptability in this town of a 2,000-pound gorilla – a bankable superstar.'

A Hollywood producer shared the industry consensus about Julia, Inc. 'It's not that the bloom is off Julia Roberts. It's just that she's going to have to gain momentum again. This really is a town of who's the flavour of the month.'

Despite a few misses and because of a string of hits, Julia would ultimately become the flavour of the decade.

Chapter Seventeen

MY BEST FRIEND'S DIVORCE

The trade paper *Variety* overstated the case when it claimed, 'In 1994 and 1995, Roberts probably hit the nadir of her young career.' While 1994 was indeed a low point with the bad press that followed her feud with Nick Nolte and the commercial failure of their collaboration *I Love Trouble,* 1995 saw the revival of her career with the modest hit, *Something to Talk About.*

Her personal life was something everyone wanted to talk about because her twenty-one-month marriage to Lyle Lovett ended in 1995. On 28 March the couple were still tight enough to issue a joint press release announcing the break-up with a single sentence: 'We remain close and in great support of one another.' As they had been during much of their marriage, they were apart when the split was announced. Julia was in London finishing up her Gothic thriller *Mary Reilly.* Lovett, in addition to a broken heart, also had a broken collarbone from a motorcycle accident and was recovering in a Houston hospital.

The timing of the press release was a clever although ultimately fruitless effort to minimise publicity, since it was issued on the same day as the Academy Awards were announced. Their hopes of being buried under an avalanche of Oscar news were dashed when *People* magazine, along with many other publications, splashed the story on the cover of its next issue, bumping Oscar.

Julia and Lyle had made so many public professions of their love that the break-up caught even close friends by surprise. Photographer Peter Nash, a friend of Lovett, said, 'I was shocked when I heard the news. I'm not one of those people who said, "This won't work." I thought they were wonderful together, really in love.'

Julia's words at the time of their wedding almost two years before must have come back to haunt her. In 1993 she described a perfect match. 'I feel liberated in a way. I feel like this really pleasant calm has descended upon my life. It has to do with your own ability to make a perfectly correct decision. I think that's quite a feat, to look at something you've done and say, "This is completely right." Every time I talk to him . . . or look at his picture . . . or think about him, I think, "Wow, I'm so . . . I'm so smart. I'm so lucky."'

Julia wasn't smart enough to realise, however, that absence doesn't make the heart grow fonder – frequent absences make it almost impossible to keep a relationship going. Because of the competing demands of their careers, the couple spent little time together. The marriage started with a bad omen. The day after their wedding, instead of a honeymoon, Julia returned to work on *The Pelican Brief* in Washington, while the groom continued his cross-country tour.

Simply put, Julia had overbooked her professional life at the expense of her private one. She was away on location and away from Lyle making four films in less than two years during their marriage. They had separate homes: her Grammercy Park co-op in New York; his cabin in Klein, Texas. *Hard Copy* reported that during the first eight months of their marriage, Julia and Lyle spent only ten nights under the same roof. *People* magazine offered another grim statistic: during their entire marriage, they rarely spent more than a week together.

Statistically, 'commuter marriages', where spouses live in different cities and travel to see each other, have a high failure rate. This marriage was no exception. Julia tried to fool herself that their relationship on the run could somehow beat the odds. Before the split, she said, 'We are pretending to be a normal couple. We get up in the morning, we have breakfast, he goes off to work, I go off to work, we come home at night. "How was your day, dear?" That whole gig.'

As for Lyle, he resigned himself to making the most of their limited time together. 'We're just so happy to be together when we can be,' he said.

Their public behaviour right up to the announcement of their separation didn't provide a clue that something was wrong with the relationship. Up to the end, they still acted like honeymooners – maybe because they had never gone on that honeymoon.

Less than a month before the announcement, the couple were seen strolling hand in hand on the Champs-Elysées in Paris, where they were filming Robert Altman's *Prêt-à-Porter* (released as *Ready to Wear* in the States). Lyle tried to visit Julia's movie sets as often as his concert schedule allowed. In December 1994, he showed up on the set of her romantic comedy, *Something to Talk About*, in Savannah, Georgia, and one crew member described a picture of a couple still infatuated with each other after almost a year of marriage. 'They would kiss each other hello and goodbye, morning and night,' her co-worker reported. 'Julia always spoke so highly of him. They seemed very much in love.'

Julia didn't make her husband do all the travelling for their rendezvous. If not filming, she was more than likely hopping on a plane to his next concert stop. During a break in the shooting of *I Love Trouble* in February 1994, she showed up at rehearsal with his band at the Wheeler Opera House in Aspen, Colorado. Lovett immediately interrupted the practice session and kicked the band members off the stage so he could be alone with Julia.

Despite all these happy tableaux of a couple in love, some creepy scenes of wedded blisslessness began to appear. In April 1994, a year before their split, husband and wife both happened to be in New York, but they stayed at separate hotels and didn't hang out together. Julia dined out with her social circle, and Lyle kept to his.

At about this time, Julia was spotted at a fashion show without her wedding ring on. Even more ominously, when Lyle left Julia in New York to return to Paris for additional scenes in *Prêt-à-Porter*, Julia had dinner at a restaurant with handsome actor Ethan Hawke on 27 April. According to her handlers, it was purely a business meeting to discuss *Pagan Babies*, a film Julia and Hawke planned to make but never did. Photos that appeared in the *New York Post* the next day, however, suggested that the two actors were mixing business with pleasure. *Time* magazine said Julia was seen looking 'dreamily into the eyes' of Hawke and 'dancing, hugging and amorously holding hands' with him. Julia's publicist, Nancy Seltzer, tried to defuse the inflammatory incident, saying, 'I'm so glad Julia and Ethan went out dancing because, prior to this, I had no idea dancing was a crime,' adding that the two were 'friends, just friends'. *Time* archly noted that the press agent had said the same thing about Julia and Lyle a few days before they got married.

Meanwhile, Lyle was no monk while his wife went out on the town with another man. In October 1993, he was photographed leaving a hotel room in Austin, Texas, with another pretty woman, country singer Kelly Willis.

Conflicting schedules stopped them from celebrating their first anniversary on 27 June 1994 together, since Julia was in New York promoting *I Love Trouble*, while Lyle was in Los Angeles shooting a video for his *I Love Everybody* album.

Documentary proof of the troubled marriage began to pile up. Later in June, *Hard Copy* aired footage of Julia sobbing on the shoulder of Jason Patric. Despite their noisy break-up in the street outside his duplex a few years earlier, the two had turned into best (platonic) friends and confidants. It was the same kind of relationship Julia would maintain with Lyle after their relationship ended.

Even innocent get-togethers were turned into Scenes from a Failing Marriage. The less reputable media reported on a romance between Julia and Richard Gere after the two were spotted on the beach in Malibu. For a change, Julia's publicist wasn't spreading disinformation when she insisted that this ocean stroll, like the Hawke dinner, was purely business. 'They were just talking about a *Pretty Woman* sequel,' an overworked Nancy Seltzer insisted.

Robert Altman, who directed the couple in both *The Player* and *Prêt-à-Porter*, felt the press was creating the illusion of a marriage on the rocks when the reality was that the relationship was solid. 'It's a true romance,' Altman declared at about the time Julia was dining and dancing with Ethan Hawke. 'It'll survive long after the trashy media wagon has moved on.'

Julia didn't leave the denials of trouble in paradise to her publicist. The day after the *New York Post* ran photos of her and Hawke together, she personally phoned a reporter at *Vogue* and said, 'I have a deep, tremendous love for Lyle. I think he is one of the poetic geniuses of our time.' When the reporter asked if she believed in monogamy, she answered his question, then asked that her reply be kept off the record.

Lyle was also making equivocal comments about the state of their marriage. In December 1993 at a concert in Buffalo, New York, a fan shouted, 'Where's Julia?' He responded, 'She's . . . she's everywhere.' Later, during a break in his set, he told the audience, 'No matter how well you may have planned, things don't always come out as you intended.'

Ironically, only three months earlier, he revealed plans for a visit from the stork. 'We have been discussing having a child after Julia finishes *Mary Reilly*,' he said, referring to a Victorian melodrama she was filming in London and Ireland.

Lyle kept the news of their break-up from his close-knit family until a public announcement let everyone know. His aunt Bernice said, 'I am shocked. I had no hint this was coming.' Lyle didn't even confide in his favorite uncle, Calvin, whose wife, Sheila, said, 'We heard nothing about it.' Lyle's camp placed the odds on a reconciliation at zero. 'Lyle sees no solution but divorce,' a source said.

Meanwhile Julia avoided the press onslaught by hiding behind the secured gates of Pinewood Studios outside London, where she was finishing *Mary Reilly*.

Heartless fans of the singer may have taken some comfort in the separation since a broken heart is a staple of country-and-western songs. Lovett seemed to agree. A year before they broke up, he said, 'It's harder to write songs when you're happy than it is when you're miserable. Who wants to hear how happy you are?'

*

Julia couldn't hide out from the press for long. In May 1995 she found herself in the middle of a press conference from hell in a country that has often been compared to that place. Following in the friendlier footsteps of Audrey Hepburn, Peter Ustinov and Princess Diana, Julia agreed to be a goodwill ambassador for UNICEF. Her trip to Haiti in that role, however, had pundits calling her an 'ill-will ambassador'.

In mid-May, Julia visited Haiti as a representative of the UN Children's Fund. *The Times* seemed to be puzzled by her presence there, saying, 'What the trip achieves for Haiti's desperate children remains to be seen.' Even her generous offer to spend two weeks as UNICEF's roving ambassador was criticised. UNICEF only wanted her services for two days, since celebrity tours tie up UN personnel whose time could be better spent on other tasks. A compromise was reached, and Julia agreed to a six-day trip to the troubled island.

If her tour was meant to drum up publicity, it certainly did, but not the kind UNICEF wanted. During a visit to a United Nations-funded schoolhouse in a Haitian slum, she felt the accompanying press corps was turning the event into a photo opportunity, which was in part what it was designed to be – publicity for the UN's humanitarian efforts. The swarming paparazzi became too much for Julia in the crowded, sweltering classroom, and one particularly pesky photographer irritated her enough that she snapped at him, 'You – in the orange shirt! Out!'

On another leg of her tour, the UN invited photographers from the Associated Press, who include award-winning photojournalists and definitely not paparazzi, to cover a cocktail party in Julia's honour. The shocked photographers were confronted by security men who placed their hands over the lenses and pushed the cameras away. The next day, after having been invited to cover a barbecue with US military personnel, the press corps suddenly found themselves disinvited and denied access to the event.

While this kind of treatment is *de rigueur* for the much maligned and rightfully despised Hollywood press vulture who jumps out of bushes to capture celebrities on film, the journalists accredited to the United Nations are a classier crew unaccustomed to rudeness which tabloid photographers accept as part of doing business. The security guards who had stiff-armed the photographers were not acting under orders from the UN PR staff. By the end of her trip, a spokesman for the UN Children's Fund apologised to the press accompanying Julia and attributed her behaviour to 'shyness' and 'inexperience in her new role' as a goodwill ambassador. The apology led some to wonder if the order to turn the photo opportunities into photo nightmares had come from Julia's camp of pitbull publicists.

Unlike the UN spokesperson, Julia didn't feel the need to apologise and considered her outburst in the schoolhouse something of a successful publicity stunt that benefited UNICEF's littlest charges. She said of the negative press reports about the incident, 'If that's the worst thing they write about my career, it's not so bad. At least it brings attention to the plight of the poor children of Haiti.'

The mainstream press refused to accept the UN spokesman's explanation of her behaviour at face value. *The Times* attributed her trip to less-than-selfless motives. 'Casting about for something useful and unshowbizzy to do with her time, she alighted on Haitian children,' the newspaper said. Her irritability was attributed to two recent failures, her film, *I Love Trouble*, and her marriage.

For whatever reasons, career or personal, Julia appears to have been a deeply unhappy person at this period in her life. The press were not the only ones to feel her wrath and disdain – fans also got the brush-off.

When Julia returned from Haiti, an admirer sent a bouquet of flowers to her apartment in New York's Grammercy Park. A resident of the building said Julia returned the flowers with a note that said, 'I don't take gifts from strangers.' Her rejection was dutifully reported in the press. By now, she probably wished she never had to talk to another reporter again, but her busy career made that wish virtually impossible.

*

Three months after her tangle with the media in Haiti, she found herself being grilled yet again by the press about her failed marriage and faltering film career when all she wanted to do was do her job – hyping her latest movie, *Something to Talk About*, which opened in the US in August 1995.

In the dramatic comedy, Julia plays Grace Bichon, a top equestrienne who gives up her job to become a full-time housewife. After sacrificing her career for the sake of her husband (Dennis Quaid) and daughter, she discovers that her husband has been wildly unfaithful to her for years. The ensuing squabbles provide the engine for the storyline.

Coincidentally, as her marriage was falling apart on screen, her relationship with Lyle Lovett was also coming to a close. This led interviewers to suggest that her role was autobiographical, providing themselves with a cheap excuse to pry into Julia's private life, especially the dissolution of her marriage.

The actress resisted the notion that she was doing autobiography and would only speak about her failed marriage in general, abstract terms. 'The timing [of the break-up] and the filming of the movie aren't parallel as everyone seems to think because it makes for a little juicier lunch conversation. It wasn't this symbiotic everybody-breaking-up-at-the-same-time sort of thing,' she said.

The most important difference between reel life and her real life was the nature of the two break-ups. On screen, Julia's and Quaid's characters go at it hammer and tongs in their marital squabbles. Based on her description, the split from Lyle sounded as though it involved a lot of friendly hand-holding rather than the fisticuffs of *Something to Talk About*.

Elliptically referring to the end of their marriage, Julia said, 'I feel like I was sincerely lucky with the situation I found myself in, the joy I felt within that situation. And the ultimate demise of the marital structure – the outcome of it. It's actually ridiculously amicable. You'd think people who could be that nice to each other would probably be a couple, but it just sort of wasn't the way it was intended to be. We found our little niche and then overstepped it a little bit. In fact, I think it can just as often be the weaker choice to stay.'

The most telling thing about her discussion of the break-up is her ability to speak about it at length without revealing very much at all. After almost a decade of dealing with an often hostile press, Julia had finally learned how to appear to open up while remaining as tight-lipped as a press secretary for a North Korean head of state.

During interviews for the film, Julia seemed happiest and most voluble when discussing marriage and its problems in the abstract. She could be philosophical and forthcoming without any real self-revelation. 'It's a symptom of childhood, this Cinderella theme that marriage is the beginning of the "Happy". People think when you get married you'll be happy, but it's not a *fait accompli*. When you're a little girl, Barbie and Ken are happy, so are Mickey and Minnie – they've been together forever. Of course, they don't have those important parts,' she said with a laugh.

Making *Something to Talk About* allowed her to revert to the old Julia, the Surrogate Earth Mother of the Soundstage. After the poisonous atmosphere on the sets of *Hook* and *I Love Trouble*, she could recreate a *faux* family complete with the child she didn't have in real life. Co-star Kyra Sedgwick, who played her sister in the film, described how Julia charmed the crew and continued to mother Haley Aull, her daughter in the film, even after the cameras stopped rolling.

'After the second day on the set, she knew everyone's name. She'd come in every single morning, smile and say, "Hello, So-and-So," to every member of the crew. She's constantly cracking jokes, even in the midst of a huge crying scene. She feels she needs to let everyone off the hook for a minute. It's a responsibility she doesn't need to take on, but it makes her feel comfortable knowing everyone else is okay,' Sedgwick recalled.

'Julia is physical – she touches you a lot in a really nice way. From the moment Julia saw the little girl [Aull] on the set she went straight to her, kneeled down to her level and started talking to her,' Sedgwick added.

Something to Talk About received mixed reviews, but Julia's personal notices were largely positive. The *Hollywood Reporter* praised her 'solid, fan-pleasing performance', which the *New York Times* found 'charmingly light'. Perhaps referring to *I Love Trouble*, *Newsweek* said, 'It's nice to see Roberts working with good material again.' And, unlike the commercial and critical failure of *I Love Trouble* the summer before, *Something to Talk About* was a modest box-office hit, grossing more than $50 million in the US alone.

Something to Talk About was described as a departure for Roberts. In so many of her previous films she had used an ear-spanning smile to charm audiences into theatres. Because of *Something to Talk About*'s themes of betrayal and infidelity, critics noted that Julia spent most of the film frowning instead of smiling.

If *Something to Talk About* was a small step away from her patented screen persona, her next film would be a giant leap away from it. She may have been stretched a bit artistically in *Something to Talk About*, but the following project would put her on the rack.

Chapter Eighteen

NOTHING TO SMILE ABOUT

Mary Reilly must have looked good on paper, even if Julia's title role called for her to look anything but good on screen. The project reeked of class in front of and behind the camera. The screenplay told the story of Dr Jekyll and Mr Hyde from the point of view of the film's eponymous maid, Mary Reilly. It was written by the respected playwright Christopher Hampton, who proved himself a master at period pieces with his multi-Oscar-winning *Dangerous Liaisons*, which he adapted for the screen from his own stage play. On *Mary Reilly*, Hampton would be joined by his *Dangerous Liaisons'* producer, Norma Heyman, its director, Stephen Frears, and its stars, John Malkovich as the Victorian physician who suffered multiple personality disorder with disastrous results, and Glenn Close as the proprietor of his favourite brothel.

While the combination of class-act filmmakers and America's number-one female box-office draw must have made *Mary Reilly* seem like a happy marriage, the studio executives at TriStar, which gave the film the go-ahead, apparently neglected to read the script, and in particular the description of its title character.

America's Prettiest Woman was being paid a reported $10 million to look plain. Or, as one critic described this nightmarish bit of miscasting, 'Roberts plays Dr Jekyll's homely maid, swathed in long-sleeved, high-necked servant gear with a bonnet atop a scraggly wig. Without makeup or even eyebrows (she bleached them). Her celebrity presence vanishes and she becomes a humble, rather unremarkable-looking waif.'

Julia was happy to look her worst because it allowed her to get rid of the grin and glitz that had typecast her for most of the decade. 'This role does not call for any ounce of glamour I could ever possess. I was thrilled to pieces to get to do something where no one was at any point going to say, "Could you just give us a smile?"'

Despite her box-office clout, the British team behind *Mary Reilly* initially balked at casting Julia, and it wasn't because of her $10 million fee. Producer Norma Heyman said, 'She was a movie star, so undoubtedly people were concerned. But she just bewitched Stephen [Frears]. She's an extraordinary creature. I remember her walking past me on the way to the set. You just wanted to put your arms around her and say, "It's going to be all right." She just exudes vulnerability and a need for affection in this role.'

Julia suffered a 'bad hair day' for the five months it took to make the film, with a chopped, bleached-blonde wig hiding the prettiest auburn curls in the movie business. Inexplicably, Julia decided to cut and bleach her own hair in the same style after the film finished shooting in Ireland and she returned to New York. For a while, she even continued to bleach her eyebrows.

'I looked like some kind of bizarre, mad alien. My friends were like, "What the hell has happened to you?" Then, when I went and got myself all pasted together, my eyebrows coloured in, I felt like Groucho Marx.'

Even before *Mary Reilly* wrapped, news was leaking out that the film was a major disaster – and an expensive one at that, with a reported budget of $50 million. The rumours gained credibility when the studio kept the film on the shelf for more than a year before its release in February 1996, the time of the year post-Christmas, pre-spring break when the kids are back in school and turkeys are traditionally dumped.

It's hard to say which the critics hated more, *Mary Reilly* or the actress who played her. *Newsweek* suggested she posed no threat to the Queen of Accents, Meryl Streep, when it noted that Julia's Irish brogue seemed to come and go. While the magazine praised her for 'gamely de-glamorising herself', it complained that she lacked the 'technique to plumb this character's psychosexual depths'. The *New York Times* found her performance 'solemnly repetitive without much spark'. *Variety* declared *Mary Reilly* 'DOA, a muddled mix of melodrama and horror'. The film's $5.7 million US gross was grimmer than its storyline and didn't even cover its star's salary.

A year later, Julia herself would be one of the project's harshest critics, saying, '*Mary Reilly* is a hard movie to watch.' The *Sunday Times* speculated that the public embarrassment of *Mary Reilly* made her terrified of 'being in the limelight', and that's why she chose a small, supporting role in her next project, which wouldn't require her to carry the film. If it failed, her ex-boyfriend and its star, Liam Neeson, would take the fall.

Chapter Nineteen

JULIA, WE HARDLY SEE YE

In 1996, Julia seemed to be turning into the incredible shrinking woman, appearing in two films where her roles could be described as large cameos at most.

Written and directed by Neil Jordan, who specialised in offbeat little movies like *The Crying Game* or baroque extravaganzas like *Interview with the Vampire*, *Michael Collins*, was, in contrast, a vast historical epic about the Irish freedom fighter who helped win independence for his country from Great Britain in the early part of the twentieth century.

Tacked on almost as an afterthought amid the important historical events depicted in the big-budget film was a love triangle between Collins (Liam Neeson), his best friend (Aidan Quinn) and the woman they both loved, Kitty Kiernan, played by Julia Roberts. The unimportance of the romance *vis-à-vis* the main story meant that Julia's role was little more than a bit part.

Despite *Mary Reilly*'s failure at the box office, Julia was still a big star, and it was surprising that she actively sought the minor role in *Michael Collins*. Maybe it was the writer-director's track record of getting terrific performances out of his actors, like Bob Hoskins in *Mona Lisa* or Stephen Rea in *The Crying Game*.

Perhaps disingenuously, director Neil Jordan claimed that no one in his native land was quite right for the role of Kitty, and he ended up throwing his casting net across the ocean. 'I couldn't find somebody in

Ireland who was luminous enough to play the part of Kitty Kiernan. There were some wonderful women actors there, but they were all in their thirties. I couldn't find somebody in their twenties, so I started to look abroad. Julia [Roberts] called me and we met. She was unique among all the American actresses because she knew the period and knew the song ['She Moves Through the Fair', which she sings in the movie], so there and then I said, "If you want to do it, you've got the part." '

But as much as Jordan wanted Julia, he had some misgivings about the actress's past history with Liam Neeson and her habit of falling in love with her co-stars, especially since Neeson was by now happily married to actress Natasha Richardson with whom he had a one-year-old son. *Michael Collins*, he felt, had enough melodrama on screen, and Jordan didn't want an off-camera soap opera distracting the cast and attracting irrelevant press. The director conceded, 'I think it was very natural for me to be worried at the start, with these two having been in a relationship. But I spoke to them about it, and we all quickly realised that Liam was terribly wrapped up in that baby of his and that Julia had a very mature attitude. Since I'd never met her, I didn't know quite what to expect. I was delighted to discover that she is straightforward and direct.' And kept her hands off his leading man.

Julia made it clear that she didn't count the number of her lines when she considered a script. It was the quality of the role, not the quantity of screen time that attracted her to this epic about the birth of the Irish republic.

Kitty, she said, was 'a perfect balance of complexity and simplicity. She came from an interesting family, and when she became involved in the lives of Michael Collins and Harry Boland [Quinn], it brought out an untapped source of strength and compassion. And certainly she was no fool. She had both of these men in love with her and I think she enjoyed that. But I think that ultimately she was truly and deeply in love and devoted to Michael Collins. It's almost unbelievable how much she loved him. I don't think you see that very much in films – a love based on something so pure and simple. She loved him for her whole life.'

Julia must have read a lot into the script, because her analysis of Kitty's character and relationship with Collins is less than evident on screen.

Maybe much of her part ended up on the cutting-room floor – an expensive excision of a major box-office attraction's participation, if that was indeed the case.

The lavish production opened on 11 October 1996 and earned mixed and negative reviews. The $50 million epic took in a mere $10 million during its US run. The role of Kitty was so small, it probably would have gone unremarked in the reviews if it hadn't been for the fact that a major actress had chosen to play her. *Newsweek* hated the romantic subplot and partially blamed Julia for the fact that it didn't work. 'The love triangle is historical fact; that it fizzles on screen is also a fact. The fault lies both with the rather wan Roberts and with Jordan's failure to write her a part: all we know about Kitty is that she always shows up wearing a new, and improbably smashing, outfit.' *Rolling Stone* described her as 'rather lost' as Kitty. While acknowledging the unimportance of her presence, the *New York Times* was kinder and even praised her singing talent, which in this film and her next would elicit some catty remarks. The paper's Janet Maslin, however, wrote, 'Julia Roberts . . . in her first scene here sweetly sings an Irish standard. ("She's a voice like an angel!" Collins exclaims.) Ms Roberts beams charmingly through this role without adding anything substantial to the film's vision of its hero.'

Newsweek best summed up Julia's problem with period pieces and offered career advice which her handlers should have given before she signed on to the projects: '*Mary Reilly* and *Michael Collins* proved Roberts was not meant to time travel.'

Many critics felt *Michael Collins* and her next film proved Julia Roberts was not meant to sing either. Again, she chose a minor supporting role in Woody Allen's ensemble musical, *Everyone Says I Love You*. Two small roles in a row had one interviewer wondering if Julia was hiding out, cinematically speaking, after the critical drubbing she had taken in recent films. 'It's just a coincidence that two things I was asked to do that I liked and wanted to participate in were smaller parts in these two films,' she explained, referring to *Michael Collins* and the Allen film. 'You can do a big part that's crappy, and then it's just a big crappy part. It always comes down to the quality of what you're doing.'

Although she has only a few scenes in the film, her character Von involved an ingenious plot device. Woody Allen plays Joe, a neurotic writer who, during a visit to Venice, spots a lovely young woman and falls in love at first sight. It turns out that his daughter has been eavesdropping on Von's sessions with her psychotherapist, during which Von describes her ideal mate. Joe's daughter passes the information on to her father, who woos Von by pretending to have all the attributes she seeks in a lover. It's a clever conceit that keeps the audience amused as Joe 'coincidentally' loves everything Von does, from Mahler's Fifth to Tintoretto to even her favourite vacation spot, Bora Bora.

Julia found herself singing in two films back to back, which led some to ask if she was planning a second career in the recording industry. 'Don't count on it,' she said. 'I could not have been more terrified, getting up and singing in front of groups of people. I wanted to do these songs justice, which is just an impossibility. I'm not a singer! It was just my summer of singing and I think that's passed,' she added, laughing.

Woody Allen sidestepped a question about her musical talent, but gushed about their collaboration. 'She has a very broad spectrum,' he said, referring to her vocal range, and added, 'She's bright, beautiful and a pleasure to work with.'

The critics were split on Julia's acting and singing. The *Sunday Times* felt she was miscast in the role and as a singer. 'What is Julia Roberts, cinema's sunniest comedienne, doing with a shrink? It's not just her singing that's flat: so is the part.'

Newsweek both agreed and disagreed with the *Sunday Times*: 'Julia Roberts is charming as an unhappily married woman, but no one is going to be casting her in *Tosca* any time soon.'

America's most influential film critic, Roger Ebert of the *Chicago Sun-Times*, however, claimed she could 'hold her own in a piano bar'. And unlike the *Sunday Times*, *New Times* magazine thought Julia was perfectly cast as a neurotic couch potato. 'Roberts is lovely in the part. Delusion becomes her.'

Like most of Woody Allen's recent films, *Everyone Says I Love You* received mostly favourable reviews when it débuted on 6 December 1996, but performed poorly at the box office with a $9.7 million gross in the US and Canada.

Julia had now starred in three back-to-back commercial failures, and industry commentators were predicting the imminent demise of her career. One pundit called her the 'Farrah Fawcett for the new millennium', referring to the sex symbol whose time had come and gone after a series of professional and personal embarrassments.

A major film director couldn't decide if the fault lay with her handlers or whether Julia herself was her own worst enemy. 'This is a case of a totally mismanaged career. She's surrounded herself with the wrong people, she's made bad script choices, and she's let her private life totally colour her persona – all of which has taken its toll on the public. I don't think people are in love with Julia the way they once were,' the director, who requested anonymity, told *US* magazine.

That epitaph was pronounced in late 1996, when both *Michael Collins* and *Everyone Says I Love You* disappeared from cinemas soon after their release. Would Julia also do another disappearing act as she had for two years during a similar downturn in the early part of the decade?

As it turned out, reports of her career death were greatly exaggerated. Only six months after being declared the cinematic equivalent of a Charlie's Angel, Julia would reappear and rule the summer of 1997 in not one but two blockbusters.

Chapter Twenty

BEST FRIENDS AGAIN WITH MOVIEGOERS

⟫⟫⟪⟪

While one major director hid behind anonymity when he badmouthed Julia and her career prospects in 1996, that same year another top film-maker went on the record to defend one of his favourite actresses and collaborators.

Joel Schumacher, who had guided her through hits (*Flatliners*) and misses (*Dying Young*), felt the critics were missing the point and the bigger picture when it came to charting the ups and downs of a major star's career.

The director had just finished filming *A Time to Kill* with another protégée, Sandra Bullock, an embryonic megastar whom the press were calling the 'new Julia Roberts'. Bullock's media title irked Schumacher, who asked a reporter, 'What's wrong with the old Julia Roberts? She's all of twenty-eight. And what do people mean when they talk about Julia trying to make a comeback? A comeback from what – puberty?' Female stars, Schumacher complained, are 'given so little time to remain successful. Men can be huge draws for many years, but with women it's different.'

Maybe there was so much talk of a 'Julia Roberts comeback' because that's exactly what she pulled off in the summer of 1997.

My Best Friend's Wedding allowed Julia to do what she did best – romantic comedy. Fans had made it clear they didn't want her scrubbing floors in the nineteenth century or warbling along a Venetian lagoon in the twentieth. The film's plot involved a restaurant critic (Julia) and a sports writer (Dermot Mulroney) as ex-lovers who have remained best friends. They make a pact that if neither of them has found a mate by age twenty-eight, they will marry each other. But just before the sports reporter's pivotal birthday, he finds a dream girl (Cameron Diaz) to marry. Julia's food critic isn't happy for her best friend. In fact, she does everything in her power to destroy the relationship so she can rekindle her own romance. The inherent meanness of this concept sounds like Pretty Ugly Woman, but it is testament to the power of Julia's on-screen grace, especially that amazing grin, that she manages to make her devious character likeable. It also helps that, by film's end, she has had a change of character and heart. Co-star Mulroney described how she pulled it off: 'Julia's smile is like a thousand-watt bulb. Everybody falls for it, but there's nothing like it when she smiles and laughs. You can't help but be drawn into it.'

Other felt the 'eyes' had it, in particular Chris Lee, the president of TriStar Pictures, which produced the film and paid Julia $12 million. 'If you look at her performance closely, you realise it's not just the smile, it's all in her eyes. That was a very tough role. The big question-mark with the script was, who do we get to play this part? Because, easily, the audience could have hated that character. It's a testament to Julia and how the audience feels about her. They just went with it completely.'

The film reunited her with screenwriter Ron Bass, who had written another, wildly different, hit for her, *Sleeping with the Enemy*. The director, P.J. Hogan, had made the sleeper Australian hit, *Muriel's Wedding*, and was clearly a man who knew how to film marital unions to full comedic effect.

After years of bad press for her on- and off-screen performances, the old nurturing Julia was back. Despite filming in the humid hell of Chicago during the summer, she once again turned the crew into family. She performed the impressive feat of memorising the names of all one hundred crew members and addressing each by name. She also found out their birthdays and presented each one with a cake – fourteen in all during the shoot. For one celebration, she stopped shooting by picking up a bullhorn and bellowing 'happy birthday to you'. Then she turned the bullhorn on the gawking spectators and thanked them for keeping quiet during filming and allowing the production to tie up traffic in the middle of the city. 'We just want to thank you,' she shouted at the sweating Chicagoans. 'We know this is a hassle for you, but we're thrilled to be here.'

The same bitter woman who once returned unsolicited flowers from a fan had turned into the People's Princess on location. During the Chicago shoot, she was walking Diego, her three-year-old German shepherd-husky mix, when she passed police officer Jim Meir, who was selling T-shirts to raise funds for the Special Olympics. Julia apologised for not having any cash, but promised to return. 'Yeah, right,' Meir thought to himself. 'But lo and behold, at about eleven the next day, here she comes, walking across the street . . . She said, "I promised I would come back, and here I am."' Julia bought $100 worth of T-shirts from the cop.

Her extrovert's accessibility may have been overcompensation for a bad reputation, which she insisted was undeserved and propagated by ill-willed strangers. 'I can't tell you how many times on a set, whether it be two weeks into it or the day we wrap, I have people come up and say, "I thought you were the biggest bitch and, wow, you're really nice," and I say, "Thanks." I don't overcompensate, because I'm not going to beg someone to like me. Take it or leave it, it's all up to you. But anybody who has had anything particularly nasty to say about me, I'd lay odds they've never met me.'

Julia was such a good sport, she even kept her cool when co-star Rupert Everett copped a feel during filming. Everett plays her gay boss, who is reluctantly commandeered into pretending to be her fiancé to make Mulroney's character jealous. Everett improvised a scene in which he is supposed to make the sports writer jealous by adding an unscripted lunge at Julia's breasts in a taxicab. Julia loved the improvisation, but put her foot – and Everett's hands – down when he groped her off camera. 'Julia does not like people touching her tits,' Everett said. 'She did get pissed off at me once – I did it again when we were playing around.'

Julia's attitude at this time may have in part been due to the strong ties she maintained with her ex, Lyle Lovett. In real life, an associate joked, the two seemed to be starring in 'My Best Friend's Divorce'.

Long after they split up, Lyle and Julia were often spotted about town, and he visited her in Taos, New Mexico, at her fifty-acre spread, which she purchased for $2 million in 1995. Lyle reportedly still calls Betty 'Mom'. Lovett, even more reticent than his ex, denied a rekindled romance but conceded, 'Julia and I are very close, and we do see each other socially.' She seconded the sentiment, saying, 'I can't imagine Lyle not being in my life. I can't imagine us not being friends.'

A mutual friend said, 'Their relationship was based on something true and real, and that will always be there.'

*

Not all Julia's relationships were platonic during this time. Typically, she fell for one of her co-stars, Matthew Perry, when she did a guest slot on his TV sitcom *Friends* in January 1996. (She once sent him a note, dripping with *double entendre*, that said, 'I love a man who can fax me five times a day!' Less generously, Perry implied that Julia was unlikely to win any good housekeeping awards: 'She leaves her panties on the bathroom floor and toothpaste all over the sink.') Maybe because of cracks like that, their liaison lasted only a few months, although Julia later claimed there had been no romance period. 'I wouldn't classify [it] as a relationship. We were friends. We *are* friends. Went out on a bunch of dates, had fun, but the "love affair" never existed. For that to happen, I think people being in love with each other probably helps.'

While Julia dated Pat Manocchia, a personal trainer with a celebrity clientèle, her publicist was forced to address rumours that her ferociously heterosexual client was gay. On the night of 8 September 1996, Julia was with her date, Manocchia, at a New York after-hours bar called Hogs & Heifers, when she jumped up on the bar, ripped off her bra (dutifully reported by *Vanity Fair* as a Maidenform 34B) and danced with one Margaret Emery. Then, according to a photographer for the *New York Post*, Gary Miller, 'There was one big, long, tongue-to-tongue kiss that lasted between thirty and fifty seconds.' An eyewitness and the owner of the bar, Allan Dell, insisted that the smooch never happened. So did the alleged object of Julia's impulsiveness. 'Julia Roberts did not kiss me. That's a long time for a first kiss. I don't know whether I could even do that with a guy,' Margaret Emery told the *New York Daily News*. Indeed, a photo showed

Julia and the tube-topped Emery simply dancing shoulder to shoulder but not kissing. Her publicist, Nancy Seltzer, spent the rest of the next day telling the press, 'No, Julia isn't gay, she was just having fun, out dancing with friends. The only person who got a serious kiss that night was Pat Manocchia.'

Manocchia and Lovett both accompanied Julia to the première of *My Best Friend's Wedding* in New York, but her official escort was Rupert Everett. This time, however, there wasn't the slightest chance that history had repeated itself and Julia had fallen in love with yet another co-star, since Everett has been openly gay for years. Like her other escorts that evening, Manocchia and Lovett, Julia and Rupert were just friends.

My Best Friend's Wedding had originally been set to open nationwide in the US on 27 June to avoid the summer's box-office monster, *Batman & Robin*, which would début the weekend before. But TriStar, which had lost millions on its previous Roberts project, *Mary Reilly*, was so bullish on the film, it moved the date up to 20 June to open on the same day as the *Batman* sequel (which, ironically, was directed by one of her best friends, Joel Schumacher).

Some industry analysts called TriStar's move madness; the correct term turned out to be counterprogramming. The thinking behind the company's decision was that people who didn't want to see a loud action film would flock to a gentle romantic comedy. The studio was right. Although the Caped Crusader trounced *My Best Friend's Wedding* $42 million v. $21 million during its first three days of release, Julia's film broke the all-time record set by *Sleepless in Seattle* for a romantic comedy's opening weekend. (Breaking that record must have given Julia delicious comfort since she had passed on that film. Two years later, she would break her own record with *Notting Hill*.)

For once, the critics agreed with the public. 'Julia Roberts glitters like gold dust,' *Rolling Stone* raved. *Newsweek* proclaimed, 'Julia Roberts is back in glorious comic form!' Even the usually curmudgeonly critic for the *Los Angeles Times*, Kenneth Turan, anointed her the comeback kid: 'After a run of roles dour enough to do credit to Calvin Coolidge, Julia Roberts returns to the kind of smart romantic comedy she's especially good at.' And while *Time* magazine panned the film as a 'romantic comedy that doesn't quite know where its heart belongs', it paid tribute to the new, viewer-friendly Julia by calling her 'the realest of nice girls'.

The harshest criticism came from a source not usually known for disseminating movie reviews. First Lady Hillary Rodham Clinton took the film to task for its nicotine addiction. Julia, Mrs Clinton complained in her nationally syndicated newspaper column, 'smokes when she's upset. She smokes when she's tired. She smokes when she's happy. In fact, she seems to smoke throughout the movie.' On the plus side, Julia's character didn't smoke a cigar.

Except for one cranky inhabitant of the White House, the whole world, it seemed, loved Julia. *My Best Friend's Wedding* grossed $126 million in the US, but did even better overseas, earning another $165 million, despite the fact that chatty comedies often do not travel well because of the language barrier. Julia's smile, however, seemed to be a *lingua franca* with audiences around the globe.

June 1997 was just the beginning of the Julia juggernaut, which ended the summer with another hit that showed romantic comedy wasn't the only genre she flourished in.

Conspiracy Theory reunited the team behind the ultra-successful *Lethal Weapon* series, director Richard Donner, producer Joel Silver, and of course, the star, Mel Gibson. Warner Bros was so happy to get this gang together again on another possible film franchise (*Conspiracy Theories I to III*, perhaps) that studio heads Terry Semel and Bob Daly signed off the $80 million budget without even seeing a script. One of the reasons the film cost so much, besides the car chases that shut down traffic in mid-town Manhattan and Los Angeles, was Gibson's $20 million salary.

Although Warner Bros was happy to write the team of Donner, Gibson and Silver what amounted to more or less a blank cheque, it baulked at hiring Julia Roberts for several reasons. As Donner diplomatically described her reputation from films like *I Love Trouble* and *Hook*, 'She comes with baggage . . .' But what really made the studio choke on its chequebook was Julia's price tag – $12 million, the highest fee paid to an actress up to that time. Plus, with a huge star like Gibson already on board, any number of less famous actresses (say, Rene Russo in two *Lethal Weapons*) would have been satisfactory in the female lead.

But Mel wanted Julia, and whatever Mel wanted, the star of the billion-dollar *Lethal Weapon* franchise got. Although the actor agreed she was an 'expensive luxury on a movie that already boasts such a pricey marquee . . . it seemed like a jolly good idea. She is the queen of subtext. She's very expressive, very smart about the way she acts. Just watch her.'

In the script by Brian Helgeland, who would go on to win an Oscar for co-writing the classier *LA Confidential*, Gibson plays a crazy cabdriver who sees conspiracies everywhere. But proving the old adage that even paranoid people have enemies, Gibson's Jerry Fletcher stumbles upon a real government conspiracy and convinces a Justice Department attorney, Alice Sutton (Julia), to help him bring the bad guys down.

Gibson is notorious for playing practical jokes, and as much as he wanted to work with Julia, he didn't treat 'the queen of subtext' like royalty. On the first day of filming in New York, he set the tone for the rest of the shoot by sending Julia a lavishly wrapped gift, which contained a freeze-dried rat. 'It's basically just a horrible object. I think it affected her on a deep, primeval level,' Gibson said.

Julia didn't get mad; she got even. She was not only a good sport about such low-brow, fratboy humour, she showed she could give as good as she got, and got even with her co-star in an even more ingenious way – and possibly an even cruder one. Julia covered the toilet seat in Gibson's dressing room with clingfilm, which, according to more than one magazine account, caused him to urinate on a pair of expensive boots. Gibson was delighted at being one-upped. 'She's rather more relaxed and a lot more fun than one would expect,' he said.

Not that artistic differences didn't flare up between Julia and what she called the 'boys' club', which consisted of the star, director and producer. Julia wanted some lovin' from her handsome leading man. The director felt that their relationship should be more maternal, since her no-nonsense character takes Gibson's wacko cabbie under her wing.

Whenever the script put them in a romantic situation, Julia lobbied for a lip-lock, but all she ever got was a peck on the cheek. 'I always want more,' she said, and complained that similar requests for her romantic scenes with Denzel Washington in *The Pelican Brief* also ended up U-rated. 'Put me and Mel in a movie, and people are going to be waiting for a little smoochie. I hope people realised the value of the reality we give them rather than waiting to see us smooch,' she said with resignation.

One interviewer noted that in 1996 Julia kissed two very different leading men on screen, Woody Allen and Mel Gibson. This enquiring mind wanted to know who was the better kisser. 'Umm, I kissed Woody more. I only did a little smoochie on Mel. Just a little smooch, the way, you know, I kiss my mama or something. Just a little smooch. My kiss with Woody was a bit longer. I was able to assess more. And it was very nice. But the Mel smooch was good, you know. They're just different. It's like an apple and an orange. One's a smooch and one was more a kiss.'

Warner Bros paid Julia $12 million for, in Gibson's term, 'subtext', and the director felt she earned every penny when he described just how good she was at delivering more than what appeared on the written page. Donner said: 'There was one little scene where Alice [Julia] comes into the hospital and, knowing Jerry's fears about being killed in his sick-bed, spots a body on a gurney in the corridor. For a moment, she thinks it's Jerry, and as she pulls back the sheet, someone says the FBI wants to see her. As usual, I had written a series of notes – guilt; my career down the tubes; why does the FBI want to see me? – so if she was floundering, I'd have something to throw at her. But she came in on the first take, did the whole thing, and as she leaned back against the wall I saw every one of my ideas roll across her eyes. She's a great little actress.'

Producer Joel Silver agreed that 'the eyes had it' when it came to Julia speaking volumes without opening her mouth. 'There's always so much going on behind her eyes. She's the eyes and the voice of the audience as she watches this crackpot suffer and discover the truth about himself and, like them, she slowly falls in love with Jerry,' Silver said.

*

My Best Friend's Wedding had already grossed $100 million in the US when *Conspiracy Theory* opened on 8 August 1997. Its weekend tally of $19 million was enough to knock another action star vehicle, *Air Force One*, out of the top spot, which the Harrison Ford film had held for the previous three weeks. Despite the drawing power of two major stars, *Conspiracy Theory*, although a *bona fide* hit, didn't come close to matching the performance of *My Best Friend's Wedding*, even though the latter had only one bankable star above the title. *Conspiracy Theory* garnered a hefty worldwide total of $137 million, compared to *My Best Friend's Wedding's* heftier $275 million. Even in foreign markets, where action films with minimal dialogue do better than talky romantic comedies, Julia's solo effort trounced her collaboration with Mel, $148 million to $60 million. Plus, with a budget of $40 million, *My Best Friend's Wedding* cost only half what it took to make *Conspiracy Theory*.

Like the public, the critics also liked Julia's romantic comedy better than her foray into high-octane adventure. Roger Ebert of the *Chicago Sun Times* seemed to agree with Julia that the two stars needed more face-to-face, lip-to-lip contact on screen. He called *Conspiracy Theory's* 'love story unconvincing' and felt the film got 'buried beneath the deadening layers of thriller clichés'.

Because so much of their advertising revenue comes from movie studios, the Hollywood trade papers tend to deliver their pans with kid gloves, but *Daily Variety* took off its mitts and slammed the film as 'a below-par star vehicle for Mel Gibson and Julia Roberts'. Even worse, the trade paper inaccurately predicted that the expensive film would not live up to the studio's great expectations. 'Appeal of the lead thesps will carry this mild suspenser a certain distance in the marketplace, but the dream-teaming of two of Hollywood's most attractive actors won't be the cash-cow it could have been . . .'

At the end of the summer of 1997, with two huge hits in cinemas simultaneously, a cheeky reporter had the nerve to ask Julia the same question which had so irked her mentor, Joel Schumacher: Who would be the next Julia Roberts?

The old press-paranoid Julia might have lashed out at such a ludicrous question in the light of her current box-office performance. Instead, the actress flashed the smile that had contributed to her popularity and said, 'You're looking at her, honey. The original, the one and only.'

Chapter Twenty-One

WEEPING ALL THE WAY TO THE BANK

After the testosterone-fuelled buddy picture *Conspiracy Theory*, for her next project Julia chose what in the 1940s was called a 'woman's picture'. Think Joan Crawford in *Mildred Pierce* or Bette Davis in, well, just about any Bette Davis movie, where the male lead plays a distant second banana to the heroine and her emotional life.

Actually, *Stepmom* might be better described as a *women's* picture, since it focused on two heroines, real-life best friends Susan Sarandon and Julia Roberts. Despite an age difference of more than twenty years, the two actresses were close confidantes ever since they met on the set of *The Player*, in which Julia and Sarandon's long-time companion, Tim Robbins, appeared. Sarandon also served as a bridesmaid at the wedding of Julia and Lyle Lovett. 'Susan is the ideal woman to me. I think I'm secretly in love with her,' Julia said, laughing. 'You know, if anything ever happens to Tim [Robbins], I'm more than willing to step in there. She's loving and generous and infinitely clever and smart.'

The original script of *Stepmom* was found by Julia's invaluable agent, Elaine Goldsmith-Thomas. (Goldsmith's 1995 marriage had given her the double-barrelled name.) The film's title was something of a misnomer, however. As the lover of a New York attorney played by Ed Harris, Julia's photographer Isabel actually plays a 'step-girlfriend' to Sarandon's two children. At first, the women are nasty rivals for the kids' affections, with Sarandon's Jackie especially bitter since her husband has dumped her for the younger Isabel. But soon the rivals are forced to become allies when Jackie is diagnosed with the cinema's favourite disease, terminal cancer. They have to work together to ensure a smooth transition of the children's affections to Isabel after Jackie is gone.

The original story and first draft were written by Gigi Levangie, but after two powerhouses like Julia and the Oscar-winning Sarandon signed on, *four* additional writers were drafted in for box-office insurance. The best insurance was no doubt provided by hiring Ron Bass, who had written two of Julia's biggest hits, *Sleeping with the Enemy* and *My Best Friend's Wedding*.

But the script doctoring didn't stop with the credited writers. For the first time in her career, Julia wore another hat on this movie, executive producer. As such, she felt obligated to immerse herself in the rewrites. With Sarandon, who also had a producer credit, and the director, Chris Columbus, the trio had frequent meetings to 'hash and rehash, hire and rehire, structure and restructure' the production, Julia said.

Despite her added clout as a producer, Julia always deferred to the director, who had made the enormously successful *Home Alone* and *Mrs Doubtfire*. She credited him with keeping the story chugging along. 'If it flows smoothly, it's because of Chris. There were times when I said this scene doesn't seem right and he'd say, "Well, what doesn't seem right?" And I'd say, "I just want it to be better. I want it to be more forceful. I think she should be more aggressive here. Or wherever." It's easy to make this wish list, but you don't always get what you want. But the next day, we'd come into rehearsal and he'd pass out little scenes for everybody. Pretty amazing.'

Julia never abused her power as executive producer, and as soon as the cameras started rolling in the autumn of 1997, she doffed her producer's hat altogether and stuck to her day job, acting. 'Once we got on the set, I never considered myself a producer. Once we started shooting, I was an actor. I mean, that's what I do. And that was enough, particularly with this movie. I had enough on my plate.'

An outspoken feminist and left-wing activist, Sarandon took a more hands-on approach than Julia. Sarandon claimed that both she and Julia 'would keep telling Chris that you don't have to telegraph everything out front so much'. More likely, it was the outspoken Sarandon who was giving the director orders. One 'suggestion' Sarandon made was later criticised by the *New York Times*. While she was exercising on her treadmill, the actress heard Marvin Gaye's rendition of the Motown classic, 'Ain't No Mountain High Enough'. She convinced the director to have her and the kids dance to this song after she reveals she's dying of cancer. In her review of the film, Janet Maslin complained, 'Motown music is tacked on as heavily as possible, working overtime to make feeling bad another way of feeling good . . . Ms Sarandon's Jackie is together enough to bop with the children to a Motown song just after they've heard the really bad news.'

To flesh out her role, Sarandon called on her own experiences as the mother of three children, which led interviewers to ask if Julia had found any autobiographical elements in Isabel. Julia's response: 'My trying-to-be-amusing and slightly curt answer is that we're the same height and weight. At the same time, I have a certain understanding for particular aspects of her life. I can relate to the fact that we're both into our careers and not yet ready to raise a family. At the same time, I want to say to reporters, "Do you really want to know where these things interact?" And I include myself as an avid moviegoer when I find myself wondering how much an actor and a character are alike. And I say, "What difference does it make?" You know? Just go and listen to the story and believe in the characters and let that be the joy, instead of approaching it as a puzzle where you try figuring out the components of the actor in the character. That's like seeing the strings. And where's the joy in that?'

Isabel and Julia shared one obvious trait: both are childless. By the time of *Stepmom*'s première in December 1998, Julia was getting a little tired of the emphasis the press was putting on this fact and the inevitable question of when she planned to do something about it. After one reporter too many at the Los Angeles première asked when we might be expecting some little Robertses, Julia was sufficiently annoyed to ask an interviewer from one of the TV entertainment news shows covering the event, 'Why is everybody so obsessed with my uterus?'

Despite its heavy subject matter, *Stepmom* opened on Christmas Day 1998, and collected a whopping $19 million over the holiday. Critics complained it was a manipulative three-hanky movie, more interested in jerking tears than eliciting more sophisticated emotions. The *New York Times*, which actually liked the picture, still called it a 'story with enough suds to take care of all your 1999 laundry needs', but reviewer Janet Maslin held back her venom long enough to praise Julia and Sarandon, whom she called the film's 'secret weapons. These two actresses are so galvanised and team up so well [they] make the film a lot more watchable than it has any right to be.'

The *Village Voice* really hated the movie, but loved Julia: 'Loathsome though *Stepmom* is, the eternally coltish Roberts is always a pleasure to watch.' The *Los Angeles Times* even felt Julia acted the more experienced Sarandon off the screen: 'Roberts does an especially appealing job as the striving stepparent. Though Sarandon is one of those actresses who never gives a bad performance, her work here is not among her best, suffering in subtlety and credibility.'

The public apparently didn't resent being manipulated emotionally and turned *Stepmom* into an international hit with a worldwide box office of $155 million, a huge amount for a non-action movie with squealing kids rather than squealing tyres.

Chapter Twenty-Two

RUNAWAY BOX OFFICE

Julia now had three monster hits back to back, so it was no surprise when ShoWest, the Las Vegas gala put on by the National Association of Theater Owners, named her International Star of the Year in 1998. What was surprising was that she was the first woman in the organisation's twenty-year history to be so honoured. Julia had joined the previously all-boys club whose members included Arnold, Harrison, Sylvester and assorted Toms. But despite this official recognition of her box-office clout, Julia actually took a pay cut to make her next film, *Notting Hill*.

When Julia was told the plot of *Notting Hill* – American superstar falls in love with shy London bookseller – her first reaction was, 'How boring. How tedious – what a stupid thing for me to do.' She only agreed to read the script by Richard Curtis because she loved his previous film, *Four Weddings and a Funeral*, and had once called him a 'genius' on a TV talk show. Although Julia hated the concept, since it sounded as though she'd be playing a thinly veiled version of herself, once she read Curtis's script, it reaffirmed her assessment of him as a genius. Or as she elegantly put it, 'Fuck, I'm gonna do this movie!'

Duncan Kenworthy, the producer of *Four Weddings and a Funeral*, was already attached to the project, and the acclaimed director of Jane Austen's *Persuasion*, Roger Michell, added a high-brow sheen. Despite their success-ful track records, Julia did, in Mel Gibson's words, carry a lot of baggage with her, and when she first met with the trio at the Four Seasons Hotel in New York, the men were so intimidated by her movie queen status that they donned suits for the first time in their lives, or so screenwriter Curtis claimed. Curtis and his collaborators felt like schoolboys called to the headmistress's office when they entered Julia's hotel suite. 'It was an extraordinary experience to see the real Julia Roberts waiting at the dining-room table. She was ten years younger than some of us – twenty years younger than one of us – and yet so obviously in charge that it was alarming.'

Julia did not reveal her enthusiasm for the script immediately. Curtis described her as 'aloof' during the meeting. Finally, she kissed the director and said non-committally, 'Good luck with your film.' A few days later, America's reigning box-office queen agreed to star in the quirky little British comedy for a fraction of her usual fee, which by then had ballooned to near Schwarzenegger pumpitude of $17 million.

Hugh Grant would play the owner of the bookshop in the London neighbourhood which gave the film its name. The actor had met Julia in 1992, when he auditioned for the abortive *Shakespeare in Love*. 'I was a very, very unemployed, pathetic actor at the time,' Grant recalled. 'I remember being so intimidated by the fact that she was in the room that I got myself in a sort of kerfuffle and missed the chair when I sat down. I sat on the arm of the chair, then had that very awkward inner debate about whether to say, "Actually, I've missed the chair," or to pretend that I was really a slightly quirky sort of character who always sits on the arm.'

Six years and several hit films later, Grant was still intimidated by Julia when they met on the set of *Notting Hill* outside London in the spring of 1998. Like the director and the rest of the team who had cringed in her presence at the Four Seasons, Grant described his primary emotion at their second meeting as fear. 'When he's nervous, his voice goes up an octave,' screenwriter Curtis said and, for a while, Grant complained that her voice was much deeper than his!

Ironically, although she hid it better than her collaborators, Julia shared the same fear. Here she was, an actress with no formal training, working with men who had cut their teeth on Jane Austen and Shakespeare. Julia, whose formal education ended at high school, would be working with Grant, who had studied at Oxford. Also, playing a movie star wasn't the walk in the park she had expected since she definitely was not playing herself. 'I was struggling with playing a person who really only shares an occupation and a height and a weight and a status with me. Just because you share an occupation with someone doesn't mean you're the same person.'

Notting Hill's American movie star, Anna Scott, was definitely not the American movie star, Julia Roberts. 'Anna is still unsure of her own worth, whether as an actor or as a person. What is written about her [in the press] concerns her a lot more than it would concern me: she's a lot more fragile.' (After claiming indifference to the press, she promised a reporter from *Vanity Fair*, 'Then again, if a reporter were to jump out of a hedge tonight, I would bust some ass.')

Unlike Julia, Anna is also much less judicious in her career moves. A major plot twist in the movie has Anna suffering mightily after the tabloids publish a nude photo spread she did years earlier during her starving-actress days. That's Madonna's personal history, not Julia's. 'I didn't agree with what [Anna] did. Didn't agree with how she got into this mess – I would never have been in that situation.'

Julia also had problems with the obnoxious way Anna dealt with the scandal she had inadvertently created. To escape the paparazzi, Anna hides out in the modest townhouse of Grant's bookseller, then throws a hissy fit when photographers track her there, accusing him of alerting the tabloids to her whereabouts. When Julia complained that Anna was far too obnoxious, the director reminded her of something she had been insisting on all along: 'Anna Scott – different person.'

Julia also had some quibbles with the screenwriter. Curtis may have been a genius in her opinion, but not when he wrote Anna's speech in which she quotes Rita Hayworth's line about her title role in the 1946 film *Gilda*: 'They go to bed with Gilda; they wake up with me.' Julia really feared audiences would think that the statement, filled with obvious self-loathing, was autobiographical. 'I hate to say anything negative about what Richard wrote, because he's a genius, but I hated saying that line. To me, it was like nails on a chalkboard. I don't really believe any of that.'

To which the screenwriter, if he still hadn't been so scared of her, might have replied, 'That's why they call it "acting", Julia.'

In its review of the film, *Newsweek* agreed with Julia that Anna Scott is a bit too unappealing for a heroine in what is supposed to be a glossy fairytale. Although the magazine called *Notting Hill* 'adorable', it regretted that 'Roberts . . . becomes increasingly less lovable as we get to know her better'. The reviewer, Jeff Giles, praised Julia's talent in the same breath he condemned her character. 'Roberts is so convincingly uppity that you wouldn't wish her on anybody.'

Time magazine, on the other hand, gave the film an unequivocal rave review, calling the film 'utterly charming and very smart', and praising Julia's 'irresistible glow'.

For once, the public and the critics were in synch. *Notting Hill*'s three-day opening beginning on 28 May 1999, took in $22 million, beating the record of any romantic comedy up to that time. In its story about the film's spectacular début, the *Los Angeles Times* predicted that *Notting Hill* would join Julia Roberts' $100 million movie club, which included *My Best Friend's Wedding* and *Pretty Woman*. Less than two weeks after the story ran, *Notting Hill* fulfilled the paper's prediction and passed the magic $100 million mark, which put Julia in the record books as the only actress to have six films gross that figure. By midway through the summer of 1999 *Notting Hill* had so far grossed $155 million worldwide. To date, her twenty-one films have taken $1.2 billion. In a cover story headlined 'Women on Top', *Entertainment Weekly* claimed that Julia has shown the most consistent drawing power of any modern actress. One studio executive felt she was a bigger box-office draw than her male counterparts. 'When she wants to do a picture that appeals to everybody,' when she plays a pretty woman instead of, say, a grotty Victorian scullery maid, 'there's no one – male or female – who can touch her,' said Columbia's president of worldwide distribution, Jeff Blake, whose studio released *Stepmom*.

*

Julia didn't rest on her laurels or ticket sales after the release of *Notting Hill*. The summer of 1999 looked like it might be the summer of 1997 all over again, when Julia had two box-office leviathans in cinemas, *My Best Friend's Wedding* and *Conspiracy Theory*.

The second entrant in the Roberts box-office derby of 1999 was

Runaway Bride, which, after a decade in development, finally reunited Julia with her *Pretty Woman* collaborators, Garry Marshall and Richard Gere.

The official story for the script's exceedingly long gestation period was that both Julia and Gere had spent the better part of the past decade trying to find another project they both liked. Julia said in an interview that every script she liked, he loathed, and vice versa. The more likely scenario is that after a series of film failures, Gere was the one searching for a vehicle that the queen of the box office would deign to appear in with him. Indeed, a few years earlier Gere found the script for *Runaway Bride*, which told a vaguely Roberts-esque story about a woman who jilts her bridegrooms at the altar – although in the script, she does it four times! Gere would play a cynical big-city newspaper columnist who writes a mocking article about her wedding blues. Julia turned down Gere's offering. At various stages of its incarnations, Geena Davis, Harrison Ford, Demi Moore, Ellen DeGeneres and Sandra Bullock flirted with the script, but, like the title character, they all ultimately jilted the project.

With amazing candour, Julia summed up why it took the stars of *Pretty Woman* the better part of the 1990s to reconnect on screen. 'We have incredibly dissimilar tastes, as our careers would attest,' she said, perhaps alluding to her rising and Gere's falling star. 'So it never really seemed like anything would come to pass.' However, after one more rewrite on *Runaway Bride*, Julia found the new script acceptable, but still she hesitated. After the Noel Coward sophistication of *Notting Hill*, she found the broad farcical elements of *Runaway Bride* a little too down-market for her newly refined comedic tastes. So she called on the man she trusted most in the world, her current beau, actor Benjamin Bratt. Over the phone, she told him, 'I think it's really funny, but I can't tell.' Bratt, she said, could hear the frantic tone in her voice, so he raced through the script after she 'sent it to him Johnny-on-the-spot'. His verdict confirmed her instincts. 'This is the no-brainer [obvious choice] of all time,' he said, referring of course to the decision to appear in the film, not the quality of the script.

Runaway Bride went on location in Maryland in October 1998. Garry

Marshall, who had dubbed her the 'schlumpy girl' for her awkwardness and bad posture on the set of *Pretty Woman*, marvelled at how the gangly duckling of eight years before had turned into a sophisticated swan. Her emotional transformation had been almost as dramatic as her improved posture. Marshall said, 'She's got it much more together, as they say, in her craft and in her life. Back then, she was with these various boyfriends, breaking up, starting over, all of that. But now she has a regular fella, you know. I think she likes that boy. I mean, sometimes he came to Baltimore just to say hello. That, to me, says something. Where are you gonna find a guy who does that?' Marshall, whose recent films had mirrored Gere's disappointing box-office performance, may have had another motive for praising Bratt, since it was Bratt's script-reading savvy that compelled Julia to sign on to a project that could well resuscitate Marshall's out-of-breath career.

While Julia's posture had improved with age, Marshall jokingly noted that her co-star's hair also reflected the passage of time. 'Richard looks great,' Marshall cracked, 'but his hair is now so white I told Julia that if she stood close enough to him, I wouldn't have to light her.'

As she had with *Notting Hill*, Julia couldn't avoid suggestions that her role as the fickle bride was autobiographical. 'Look, *Runaway Bride* is a great title, incredibly evocative, but it doesn't attach to my life at all,' she said. It's not surprising that Julia resisted comparisons between her life and *Runaway Bride*'s Maggie Carpenter, since she described the character as 'increasingly unconsciously psychotic in her behaviour' as she keeps leaving 'em at the altar.

Besides the emotional strain of portraying psychosis on screen, Julia's role was physically strenuous as well. One of Maggie's hobbies is kickboxing (perhaps as a defence against all those disgruntled suitors). Marshall said, 'Julia had to be in great shape for this film because we made the character quite an athlete. She kickboxes, she jumps rope, and she runs from her weddings!'

Runaway Bride depicts five wedding ceremonies in all, and two of them sound like dead-ringers for Julia's own flings at the altar. One wonders if she experienced any flashbacks or perhaps a touch of post-traumatic stress when she had to re-enact a formal, overblown ceremony that sounds a lot like the Normandy Invasion-style of her aborted wedding to Kiefer Sutherland. Another wedding in the film echoed her barefoot bride, flower-child union with Lyle Lovett.

Unlike Julia, who simply slipped away to a health spa in Tucson after splitting up with Sutherland, her Maggie Carpenter escapes the altar in a variety of dramatic ways, including via horseback and motorcycle.

For the flower-child, counterculture wedding, Maggie was supposed to jump from a trampoline to the altar. (Don't ask. Or better yet, ask the screenwriters, Josann McGibbon and Sara Parriott.) Instead, the skittish bride leaps from the trampoline on to the back of motorcycle and makes her escape.

It's a safe bet that without Julia's participation, *Runaway Bride* would have remained on the shelf forever. Her co-star and director weren't bankable, and the screenwriters' biggest prior credit was the flop farce *Three Men and a Little Lady*, which was most notable for pounding the final nails in the big-screen careers of TV stars Tom Selleck and Ted Danson.

The critics, who had loved Julia's recent film efforts, treated *Runaway Bride* like a recent Richard Gere movie, in other words they panned it. The *Los Angeles Times*' banner headline said, 'It Looked Good on Paper', then devoted the rest of the review to explaining why it looked so awful on screen, although it spared Julia the brunt of its venom: 'Roberts, as she was in the more successful *Notting Hill*, is in full movie-star mode, lithe, smiling and game for all kinds of physical humour . . .' Even so, the reviewer felt moviegoers would leave the cinema 'with a bad taste in their mouths'.

The *New York Times* complained that the *Pretty Woman* chemistry between Gere and Julia was missing in their long-awaited reunion: 'Gere's and Marshall's reunion with Ms Roberts guarantees a comedy that's easy on the eyes and dependable in the laugh department. But *Runaway Bride* shows signs of strain. Chemistry-wise, it can't bode well for a romantic comedy to feature two stars who apparently posed for the poster art on separate days.'

The *Hollywood Reporter* disagreed and felt the stars still sparkled but that the script was flat: 'Remarkably, the actors have only gotten better-looking with age, and there's no question the chemistry between them still works for a light romantic comedy. But an overcalculated, under-nourished screenplay undermines much of the effort.'

Only *Daily Variety* gave the film an unqualified rave and, more importantly, predicted *Notting Hill*-size box office, praising *Runaway Bride* as 'an ultra-commercial mainstream romantic comedy that delivers all the laughs and smiles it intends to . . . this Paramount release can hardly miss'. The *Variety* reviewer proved that his crystal ball wasn't cloudy, and Julia proved once again that she was bankable. *Runaway Bride* opened on 30 July 1999 at number one, with a whopping $34.5 million in its first three days of release. It was Julia's best début ever and broke the previous record for a romantic comedy opening held by her own *Notting Hill*.

*

Julia probably ignored *Runaway Bride*'s mediocre reviews because she was too busy filming a serious project with a serious director, which would allow her to escape typecasting as America's favourite fairytale protagonist.

Erin Brockovich, which began filming in Ventura County, California, on 25 May 1999, represented a huge departure for a woman who had built her career on big-budget productions. Based on a real-life story, the plot sounded more like an issues-orientated TV movie than something the notoriously risk-averse world of big-budget feature-filmmaking would take on.

Erin Brockovich was a college drop-out who was working as a secretary at a law firm in suburban Los Angeles when she came across legal documents from an obscure case that involved poisoning of the water supply by Pacific Gas & Electric. A divorced mother of three, Julia's character joins her boss, played by Albert Finney, in filing a $400 million class-action lawsuit against the gas company. With the guts and gluttony for punishment of a northern Norma Rae, Brockovich fights the case through endless appeals and ultimately wins.

The *New York Times* predicted that *Brockovich* might be the film that finally won the twice-nominated actress an Oscar. Its prediction was strengthened by the talent behind the camera, director Steven Soderbergh, whose quirky 1989 feature film début, *sex, lies and videotape*, won him an Academy Award nomination for Best Screenplay and the Cannes Film Festival's top prize, the Palme d'Or. In the ensuing decade, Soderbergh specialised in small-budget, character-driven films, something which could not be said of Julia's resumé.

At $55 million, *Erin Brockovich* would also be Soderbergh's most expensive film (his most recent movie, *The Limey*, cost $9 million to make – lunch money in Hollywood), although the cost was inflated by Julia's fee, the record-breaking $20 million that put her in the nose-bleed altitude of male movie-star compensation. Universal and Sony, which are nervously splitting the cost of the somewhat iffy production, may have felt a bit less anxious because of *Erin Brockovich*'s screenwriters, Susannah Grant, who penned Drew Barrymore's sleeper hit, *Ever After*, a reworking of Cinderella, and Richard Lagravenese, who wrote *The Fisher King*, a grim urban fairytale that earned Robin Williams an Oscar nomination. The bean-counters at the Black Tower and the old MGM backlot knew the famous equation: Julia + fairytale = blockbuster.

Julia would earn every penny of her $20 million salary – and not just as insurance for the film's big budget. Soderbergh said, 'I've never made a movie in which a female character had that much time on the screen. She's in virtually every scene in this film.'

With no big-name co-star to help her carry the drama, the success or failure of the film would lie directly on Julia's thirty-one-year-old shoulders. Or, as Soderbergh said, 'I guess what I liked is that this is a high-wire act for her.' If her track record is any indication, Julia will float across the tightrope gracefully, flawlessly, then make a movie about dirty water and dirtier deeds burn up the box office on its opening weekend.

All that will remain is the early-morning announcement the following spring of that year's Academy Award nominees for Best Actress. Will *Erin Brockovich* turn out to be Julia's *Norma Rae* (the film for which Sally Field won her first Oscar), not only for its socially conscious theme but for her personal Oscar glory?

Stay tuned to CNN or Sky TV at three in the morning Pacific Standard Time in California, when bleary-eyed reporters from around the world will gather at the Academy's Beverly Hills headquarters for every actor's penultimate benediction: 'And the nominees are . . .'

Chapter Twenty-Three

THE MAN IN HER LIFE

—⸺∿⸻—

'It would take a brave man to date me' – *Julia Roberts, 1997, before
she met Benjamin Bratt*

As 1999 drew to a close, thirty-two-year-old Julia Fiona Roberts could look
at her life and career and be pleased with what she saw. Like Gloria
Vanderbilt's famous biography, Julia's work in progress might be titled
Little Julia, Happy at Last!

The actress wouldn't disagree with that assessment as she described her
life at this time. 'I work when I want to work, and I work with people that
I want to work with. I travel hither and yon to fabulous places. I'm surrounded by wonderful, interesting people. I live a privileged life – hugely
privileged. It's an excellent life. I'm rich. I'm happy. I have a great job. It
would be absurd to pretend that it's anything different. I'm like a pig in
shit.'

A close friend confirmed – less evocatively – that her claim to happiness was not just made for public consumption and good press: 'Julia is
incredibly happy right now. The relationship is so special that none of us
wants to comment,' the friend said.

The 'special relationship' was with the man who had convinced her to
make *Runaway Bride*, actor Benjamin Bratt. And while friends refused to
comment, Julia practically became a motor-mouth when talking about
the man in her happy life.

After dating just about every other man she ever co-starred with, Julia finally seemed to be settling down with yet another co-star, thirty-five-year-old Benjamin Bratt, in whose television drama *Law and Order* she graciously guest-starred on 5 May 1999. This, though, was not another on-the-set romance, since their relationship began long before she went slumming on episodic TV as a favour to Bratt – and for scale wages ($4,000).

A visitor to Julia's production office in Manhattan at this time noticed that there were no photos of Bratt on the walls or her desk. There was, however, a picture of her ex, Lyle Lovett!

In the past Julia had always been tight-lipped about her lovelife. Journalists at the junket to promote *Hook* were warned that Julia would take a hike if the forbidden subject of Jason Patric were mentioned. In the summer of 1999 by contrast, during a series of interviews to promote her two films, Julia was garrulous on the subject of Benjamin Bratt. Although there were no visual references to him in her office, she was happy to rhapsodise about the man who had been in her life for the past two years. 'He's kind. And good to his bones. I realised immediately that he is someone who will always challenge me in that great way that keeps you moving forward in your life. His presence raises the quality of my life. And dare I say that all my friends echo that sentiment,' she replied when asked if Bratt was a major contributing factor to her current happy state.

Julia had fun with the press and created a mythological meeting between the two, which she repeated in several interviews, only to deny it in another. 'We met in a restaurant. He walked in, and I looked up at him, and it was like something hit me over the head with a bat.' She told that story to *US* magazine as fact, told the same story to *Vanity Fair*, but later in the interview confessed that she didn't feel like sharing the true version of their first encounter. 'The actual story is wildly interesting and calamity-filled and hilarious and wonderful and all these great things that are incredibly personal and private to us.' And she made it clear to the interviewer that the story would remain private. 'So the expedient, for-the-world-publication answer is: "We met in a restaurant." Now by definition, that's not even true. We didn't even speak to each other that night.'

Julia believed that the strength of their relationship derived from the fact that they were both actors and knew what each other was going through on a daily basis. That explanation, of course, failed to explain why her liaisons with so many other men in the same profession, from Neeson through McDermott, Sutherland, Patric, Day-Lewis, Hawke and Perry, had failed.

'My boyfriend is an actor so we understand what goes through the course of each other's day, that in a relationship you have to meet in the middle. It's not coach and player. It's a team. The beauty of the whole tangled wonder is I don't have to give up anything,' Julia said, then hinted at why at least one previous romance didn't work, although she neglected to name names. 'The idea that a woman just serves her man, that you just stand down in the background and be the caretaker, and the man's persona is head of the household? Well, there was something of that within the framework of how I entered into relationships as a young person. But I'm thirty-one now, and I've become an adult in a lot of ways,' she said in 1998.

So who is this man who has managed to keep her attention and affection for two years running?

If Lyle Lovett was just weird-looking, the Peruvian-German-English Benjamin Bratt was an exotic bird of Julia's prey. She made it clear that it wasn't just sharing the same occupation that bonded them. The attraction wasn't purely physical, but it was powerfully so. 'He's very good-looking, and his handsomeness pales in comparison to his kindness. That is all a girl could ask for, really,' she said.

A female reporter felt the same sexual incandescence in his presence and wrote, 'If possible, [Bratt] is prettier than the Pretty Woman, though in a decidedly masculine way.' The writer went on to lose all journalistic objectivity by describing his 'perfect full lips, tiger cheekbones and velvety eyes'.

Indeed, *People* magazine named him one of the fifty Most Beautiful People of 1999, citing his 'mile-high cheekbones, caffè latte complexion and six-foot-two-inch frame'. And women weren't the only ones who felt the tug of Bratt's handsome gravitas. His *Law and Order* co-star, Jerry Orbach, enthused, 'We don't see too many classically handsome people.

Benjamin's a hunk to the women. He gets an immediate reaction.'

Julia and Benjamin shared similar family backgrounds. She lost her father to cancer when she was ten. At four, Benjamin lost his father, a sheet-metal-worker, to divorce; like Julia's penurious early years, money was tight in the single-parent household, which included four siblings. Like Julia's mother, who upgraded from secretary to realtor, Benjamin's mother, a Quechua Indian who emigrated from Peru at the age of fourteen and settled in San Francisco, managed to raise her brood on her own and at the same time put herself through nursing school. Like Roberts' parents, who promoted interracial contact with their integrated theatre productions in Atlanta, Mrs Bratt campaigned for Native American rights. In 1969 she packed up the kids and spent weekends with them on Alcatraz Island during a nineteen-month occupation to protest against the treatment of Native Americans. Their activism provided a family bond that continues to this day. Benjamin remains as close to his mother as Julia does to Betty. 'At five years old,' Bratt says, 'I had little understanding of the reasons behind the occupation [of Alcatraz] and my mother's participation in it. I will say, however, that it felt like a natural place to be – very welcoming, very much like a village. Only in hindsight can I grasp the fortitude it took her to single-handedly raise five young kids and be as politically active as she was. I am in awe of her strength and will.'

During high school, Benjamin went to live with his father in San Francisco. Why did he leave his adored mother? 'I had a need to know who my father was, what my second half was,' he said. His father seemed to know what his son needed to be – an actor. Dad suggested he try out for the senior class play. Benjamin landed the starring role in a musical version of the Western movie classic *Destry Rides Again*. Since then, Bratt has proudly said that he has held no other jobs besides acting.

Unlike Julia, who is an instinctive actress with no formal training, Bratt attended the Harvard of acting schools, the American Conservatory Theater in San Francisco, and earned a bachelor of fine arts degree in theatre from the University of California at Santa Barbara.

Bratt never had to take a day job because he found almost non-stop work on the big and small screens. He starred in the 1987 TV movie

Juarez, about a young Mexican-American detective in El Paso, Texas. He also did guest shots on episodic television and had minor parts in major feature films like *A Clear and Present Danger* and *The River Wild*. A stint on the short-lived TV cop series, *Nasty Boys*, in 1990 led to his career breakthrough five years later when the producer, Dick Wolf, asked him to join the cast of his more prestigious series, *Law and Order*, American TV's longest-running night-time drama. Bratt was cast against type (politically) as a conservative Latino police officer, Detective Reynaldo Curtis.

Following in his mother's footsteps, Bratt has become a champion of more participation by minority actors in prime-time television, which *Time* magazine dubbed 'The Vast Whiteland' after the four major networks' autumn 1999 seasons were unveiled without a single series starring a black person.

'The idea of fair and equal representation for people of colour in this business is a joke,' Bratt said in a rare moment when his trademark courtliness wasn't present. 'How can we as artists remain optimistic about our prospects when the personification of this industry is an overpampered, self-satisfied, middle-aged white male whose only contact with people of colour is the people who clean his house? We can't.' It was Julia's own political activism, however poorly demonstrated in her ill-fated trip to Haiti in 1995, that first made him aware of her identity as something more than just another gorgeous Hollywood movie star.

Sadly, each of them also suffers a bitter family estrangement. Julia's rift with brother Eric is famous. For reasons which Bratt refuses to disclose, his father cut off all contact with the family when his son was twenty-five. Unlike Julia's and Eric's very public airing of their differences, Bratt will only say, 'I've made attempts to get in touch with him, and he won't respond. It's a deep pain for me.'

On a happier note, the couple also love an endorphin rush; both are exercise addicts. Julia runs six miles a day, which may be a better explanation of her whippet-like frame than the old drug-abuse rumours. A surfer junkie who has been known to hop on a plane to California when the surf's dramatically up, Benjamin finds it more convenient to rollerblade through New York's Central Park and cross-train with weights at a Manhattan gym. 'I've found that I can't go more than three days without doing something physically invigorating, because it makes me uptight and tense. When I'm physically fit, it balances my whole well-being,' he said. His addiction to surfing and working out may be an attempt to compensate for being extremely thin as a youth, when he was nicknamed 'Scarecrow' – just the opposite of Julia's slight weight problem in high school.

On Benjamin's thirty-fifth birthday, 16 December 1998, Julia sent a bouquet of thirty-five long-stemmed red roses to his dressing-room on the set of *Law and Order*. And while Julia's office has no visual mementos of the man in her life, Bratt's dressing-room walls are festooned with snapshots of his Pretty Woman.

Less auspiciously for the long-term prospects of their relationship, they maintain, Lovett-like, separate residences. But while Lyle had the excuse of concert tours and a love of the South to justify a home in his native Texas, Julia and Benjamin both live in New York City – although his Chelsea loft is only a four-dollar cab ride away from her Grammercy Park co-op. Even so, different digs more than hint at some vestigial fear of commitment.

Another potential landmine in their life together is his decision at the end of the 1998–99 season to leave the safe haven of his highly rated TV show and enter the more prestigious but riskier arena of feature films. If his movie career flounders while hers flourishes, will their relationship take a Kiefer-like turn of duelling box-office grosses?

Complicating things more – or enriching them, depending whether your crystal ball is half empty or half full – Julia will soon become his boss when, as executive producer, she works on a cable TV movie bio-pic about Pancho Gonzalez, with Bratt playing the tennis star.

But Bratt's first project post-*Law and Order* is a feature film, *The Next Best Thing*, a comedy of bad manners in which he, Madonna and Rupert Everett form a quirky love triangle that fits perfectly with the pre-millennial 'Gay Nineties'. Madonna plays a free spirit who gets drunk with her best friend, a gay man played by Rupert Everett. They end up in bed together and Madonna's character accidentally finds herself pregnant with her gay friend's child. They decide to have the child and form a happy if non-traditional nuclear family until a handsome straight man (Bratt, typecast) enters the picture and bowls the mother off her feet. One wonders if Julia suffered a *soupçon* of jealousy when Benjamin signed on to co-star opposite the Material Omnivore, since Madonna is well known to have a liking for Latin men – in fact, the father of her daughter, Lourdes, is Hispanic. And, like Julia, Madonna has a track record of falling for her leading men (Warren Beatty, Sean Penn).

*

And what is Julia's next best thing after she finishes battling corporate polluters of our drinking water? Nothing is set in stone or even in a deal memo, but one possible project is *Martha and Arthur*, written by Rupert Everett, who would again play gay, this time as a macho James Bond-type movie star, Arthur, who hides his homosexuality in a phony marriage to Julia's Martha.

If Julia agrees to star, Everett's script, currently in some circle of development hell at Disney, will get the go-ahead faster than you can say 'bankable'. Everett's hopes for the project must be encouraged by Julia's rapturous description of her co-star from *My Best Friend's Wedding*: 'Gay or straight doesn't matter any more than long-haired or short-haired. What's so appealing about [Everett] is his intelligence and his humour. He's incredibly smart. He energises a moment. I just love to be around him and experience his "Rupertness". I think the planet is a better place with him on it.'

With that kind of enthusiasm and clout behind it, *Martha and Arthur* could happen any day now. But whither Julia Roberts years from now? His Rupertness himself offers a prediction that suggests, in light of the unfortunate Haitian visitation, he's a much better actor than fortune-teller. 'Just wait and see,' Everett said in the summer of 1999. 'When she's fifty, she'll have her shirtsleeves rolled up, and she'll be scrubbing babies in Calcutta.' Given Julia's desire to stretch in roles that don't typecast her, a much better prediction for the actress at midlife is that she will be playing Mother Teresa in a film, scrubbing babies on a soundstage standing in for impossible Calcutta.

And if their union on and off screen is truly blessed with affection and longevity, Benjamin Bratt will play, perhaps, a greying but still handsome doctor of unspecified Latin descent who gives Mother Teresa a hand with her baby-wrangling.

FILMOGRAPHY

Blood Red

(1986, a Hemdale release)

CREDITS: Executive producers, John Daly, Derek Gibson; producers, Judd Bernard, Patricia Casey; director, Peter Masterson; screenplay, Ron Cutler; camera, Toyomichi Kurita; editor, Randy Thornton; music, Darmine Coppola; sound, Doug Axtell; production design, Bruno Rubeo; costume design, Ruth Myers; assistant director, Stephen McEveety.

Rating, R; running time, 91 minutes; released 11 November 1986.

CAST: Eric Roberts (Marco Collogero), Giancarlo Giannini (Sebastian Collogero), Dennis Hopper (Berrigan), Burt Young (Andrews), Carlin Glynn (Miss Jeffreys), Lara Harris (Angelica), Francesca de Sapio (Rosa Collogero), Julia Roberts (Maria Collogero).

Satisfaction

(1988, a Twentieth Century Fox release)

CREDITS: Executive producers, Rob Aiden, Armyan Bernstein; producers, Aaron Spelling, Alan Greisman; director, Joan Freeman; screenplay, Charles Purpura; camera, Thomas Del Ruth; editor, Joel Goodman; music, Michael Colombier; sound, Willy Burton; production designer, Lynda Paradise; set decorator, Ernie Bishop; costume designer, Eugenie Bafaloukos; associate producer, Ilene Chaiken; assistant director, Jerry Ketcham; casting, Johanna Ray.

Rating, PG-13; running time, 92 minutes; released 13 February 1988.

CAST: Justine Bateman (Jennie Lee), Liam Neeson (Martin Falcon), Trini Alvarado (May [Mooch] Stark), Scott Coffey (Nickie Longo), Britta Phillips (Brilly Swan), Julia Roberts (Daryle Shane), Debbie Harry (Tina).

Mystic Pizza

(1988, a Samuel Goldwyn Co. release)

CREDITS: Executive producer, Samuel Goldwyn, Jr.; producers, Mark Levinson, Scott Rosenfelt; line producer, Susan Vogelfang; director, Donald Petrie; screenplay, Amy Jones, Perry Hoze, Randy Howze, Alfred Uhry; story, Amy Jones; camera, Tim Suhrstedt; editors, Marion Rothman, Don Brochu; music, David McHugh; production design, David Chapman; art director, Mark Haack; set decoration, Mark Haack; costume designer, Jennifer Von Mayrhauser; sound, Russel Fager; assistant director, Mark Radcliffe; unit production manager, Scott Rosenfelt.

Rating, R; running time, 104 minutes; released 21 October 1988.

CAST: Julia Roberts (Daisy Araujo), Annabeth Gish (Kat Araujo), Lili Taylor (Jojo Barboza), Vincent Phillip D'Onofrio (Bill Montijo), William R. Moses (Tim Travers), Adam Storke (Charlie Winsor), Conchata Ferrell (Leona Valsouano), Joanna Merlin (Margaret).

Steel Magnolias

(1989, A TriStar Pictures presentation)

CREDITS: producer, Ray Stark; director, Herbert Ross; screenplay, Robert Harling, based on his play; camera, John A. Alonzo; editor, Paul Hirsch; music, Georges Delarue.

Rating PG; running time, 118 minutes; released 17 November 1989.

CAST: Sally Field (M'Lynn Eatenton), Dolly Parton (Truvy Jones), Shirley MacLaine (Ouiser Boudreaux), Daryl Hannah (Annelle Dupuy Desoto), Olympia Dukakis (Clairee Belcher), Julia Roberts (Shelby Eatenton Latcherie), Tom Skerritt (Drum Eatenton), Sam Shepard (Spud Jones), Dylan McDermott (Jackson Latcherie).

Pretty Woman

(1990, a Buena Vista release of a Touchstone Pictures presentation)
CREDITS: Executive producer, Laura Ziskin; producers, Arnon Milchan, Steven Reuther; director, Garry Marshall; screenplay, J.F. Lawton; camera, Charles Minsky; editor, Priscilla Nedd; music, James Newton Howard; sound, Jim Webb; production design, Albert Brenner; art direction, David Haber; set decoration, Garrett Lewis; costume design, Marilyn Vance-Straker; production manager, Roger Joseph Pugliese; assistant director, Ellen H. Schwartz; second unit director-associate producer, Walter Von Huene; co-producer, Gary W. Goldstein; casting, Dianne Crittenden.
Rating, R; running time, 117 minutes; released 23 March 1990.
CAST: Richard Gere (Edward Lewis), Julia Roberts (Vivian Ward), Ralph Bellamy (James Morse), Jason Alexander (Philip Stuckey), Laura San Giacomo (Kit De Luca), Hector Elizondo (hotel manager), Alex Hyde-White (David Morse); Amy Yasbeck (Elizabeth Stuckey).

Flatliners

(1990, a Columbia Pictures release)
CREDITS: Producers, Michael Douglas, Rick Bieber; director, Joel Schumacher; screenplay, Peter Filardi; director of photography, Jan de Bont; editor, Robert Brown; music, James Newton Howard; production designer, Eugenio Zanetti.
Rating, R; running time, 111 minutes; released 10 August 1990.
CAST: Kiefer Sutherland (Nelson), Julia Roberts (Rachel), Kevin Bacon (Labraccio), William Baldwin (Joe), Oliver Platt (Steckle).

Sleeping with the Enemy

(1991, a Twentieth Century Fox release)
CREDITS: Executive producer, Jeffrey Chernov; producer, Leonard Goldberg; director, Joseph Ruben; screenplay, Ronald Bass; based on the novel by Nancy Price; camera, John W. Lindley; editor, George Bowers; music, Jerry Goldsmith; production design, Doug Kraner; costume design, Richard Hornung; art direction, Joseph P. Lucky; set design, Stan Tropp; sound, Susumu Tokunow; associate producers, C. Tad Devlin, Michael E. Steele; assistant director, Michael E. Steele; casting, Karen Rea.

Rating, R; running time, 98 minutes; released 8 February 1991.

CAST: Julia Roberts (Sara/Laura), Patrick Bergin (Martin), Kevin Anderson (Ben), Elizabeth Lawrence (Chloe).

Dying Young

(1991, a Twentieth Century Fox release)

CREDITS: Producers, Sally Field, Kevin McCormick; director, Joel Schumacher; screenplay, Richard Friedenberg; based on the novel by Marti Leimbach; co-producer, Duncan Henderson; camera, Juan Ruiz Anchia; art director, Guy J. Comtois; editor, Robert Brown; costume designer, Susan Becker; music, James Newton Howard; casting, Mary Goldberg; associate producer, Mauri Gayton.

Rating, R; running time, 105 minutes; released 21 June 1991.

CAST: Julia Roberts (Hilary O'Neil), Campbell Scott (Victor), Vincent D'Onofrio (Gordon), Colleen Dewhurst (Estelle), David Selvy (Richard), Ellen Burstyn (Mrs O'Neil), Dion Anderson (Cappy), George Martin (Malachi).

Hook

(1991, a TriStar Pictures release)

CREDITS: Executive producers, Dodi Fayed, Jim V. Hart; producers, Kathleen Kennedy, Frank Marshall, Gerald R. Molen; director, Steven Spielberg; screenplay, Jim V. Hart, Malia Scotch Marmo; story, Jim V. Hart, Nick Castle; co-producers, Gary Adelson, Craig Baumgarten; camera, Dean Cundey; production designer, Norman Garwood; editor, Michael Kahn; music, John Williams; costume designer, Anthony Powell; casting, Janet Hirshenson, Jane Jenkins, Michael Hirshenson; visual consultant, John Napier; visual effects supervisor, Eric Brevig; sound mixer, Ron Judkins; special visual effects, Industrial Light & Magic; visual effects producer, Kimberly K. Nelson.

Rating, PG; running time, 135 minutes; released 11 December 1991.

CAST: Dustin Hoffman (Captain Hook), Robin Williams (Peter Banning-Peter Pan), Julia Roberts (Tinkerbell), Bob Hoskins (Smee), Maggie Smith (Granny Wendy), Caroline Goodall (Moira), Charlie Korsmo (Jack), Amber Scott (Maggie), Laurel Cronin (Liza), Phil Collins (Inspector Good), Arthur Malet (Tootles).

The Player

(1992, a Fine Line Features release)

CREDITS: Executive producer, Cary Brokaw; producers, David Brown, Michael Tolkin, Nick Wechsler; co-producer, Scott Bushnell; co-executive producer, William S. Gillmore; director, Robert Altman; screenplay, Michael Tolkin, based on his novel; camera, Jean Lepine; editor, Geraldine Peroni; music, Thomas Newman; production design, Stephen Altman; art director, Jerry Fleming; set decorator, Susan Emshwiller; costume design, Alexander Julia; sound, John Pritchett; associate producer, David Levy; assistant director, Allan Nichols.

Rating, R; running time, 123 minutes; released 10 April 1992.

CAST: Tim Robbins (Griffin Mill), Greta Scacchi (June Gudmundsdottir), Fred Ward (Walter Stuckel), Whoopi Goldberg (Detective Avery), Peter Gallagher (Larry Levy), Brion James (Joel Levison), Cynthia Stevenson (Bonnie Sherow), Vincent D'Onofrio (David Kahane), Dean Stockwell (Andy Civella), Richard E. Grant (Tom Oakley), Sydney Pollack (Dick Mellen), Lyle Lovett (Detective DeLongpre), Dina Merrill (Celia), Angela Hall (Jan), Leah Ayres (Sandy), Paul Hewitt (Jimmy Chase), Randal Batinkoff (Reg Goldman), Jeremy Piven (Steve Reeves), Gina Gershon (Whitney Gersh), Frank Baryhydt (Frank Murphy), Mike E. Kaplan (Marty Grossman), Kevin Scannell (Gar Girard); as themselves: Steve Allen, Richard Anderson, Rene Auberjonois, Harry Belafonte, Shari Belafonte, Karen Black, Michael Bowen, Gary Busey, Robert Carradine, Charles Champlin, Cher, James Coburn, Cathy Lee Crosby, John Cusack, Brad Davis, Paul Dooley, Thereza Ellis, Peter Falk, Felicia Farr, Kasia Figura, Louise Fletcher, Dennis Franz, Teri Garr, Leeza Gibbons, Scott Glenn, Jeff Goldblum, Elliott Gould, Joel Grey, David Alan Grier, Buck Henry, Anjelica Huston, Kathy Ireland, Steve James, Maxine John-James, Sally Kellerman, Sally Kirkland, Jack Lemmon, Marlee Matlin, Andie MacDowell, Malcolm McDowell, Jayne Meadows, Martin Mull, Jennifer Nash, Nick Nolte, Alexandra Powers, Bert Remsen, Guy Remsen, Patricia Resnick, Burt Reynolds, Jack Riley, Julia Roberts, Mimi Rogers, Annie Ross, Alan Rudolph, Jill St John, Susan Sarandon, Adam Simon, Rod Steiger, Joan Tewkesbury, Brian Tochi, Lily Tomlin, Robert Wagner, Ray Walston, Bruce Willis, Marvin Young.

The Pelican Brief

(1993, a Warner Bros release)

CREDITS: Producers, Alan J. Pakula, Pieter Jan Brugge; director, Alan J. Pakula; screenplay, Alan J. Pakula; based on the novel by John Grisham; camera, Stephen Goldblatt; editors, Tom Rolf, Trudy Ship; music, James Horner; production design, Philip Rosenberg; art direction, Robert Guerra; set design, Sarah Stollman, Monroe Kelly; set decoration, Lisa Fischer, Rick Simpson; costume design, Albert Wolsky; sound, James J. Sabat; associate producer, Donald Laventhal; assistant director, Peter Kohn; casting, Alixe Gordon.

Rating, PG-13; running time, 141 minutes; released 17 December 1993.

CAST: Julia Roberts (Darby Shaw), Denzel Washington (Gray Grantham), Sam Shepard (Thomas Callahan), John Heard (Gavin Verheek), Tony Goldwyn (Fletcher Coal), James B. Sikking (Denton Voyles), William Atherton (Bob Gminski), Robert Culp (President), Stanley Tucci (Khamel), Hume Cronyn (Justice Rosenberg), John Lithgow (Smith Keen).

I Love Trouble

(1994, a Touchstone Pictures presentation in association with Caravan Pictures)

CREDITS: Producer, Nancy Meyers; director, Charles Shyer; screenplay, Nancy Meyers and Charles Shyer; camera, John Lindley; editors, Paul Hirsch, Walter Murch, Adam Bernardi; costumes, Susan Becker; music, David Newman; production design, Dean Tavoularis; art director, Alex Tavloularis; set decorator, Gary Fetts; set designers, Sean Haworth, James J. Murakami, Nick Novarro, William O'Brien, Nancy Tobias.

Rating, PG; running time, 123 minutes; released 29 June 1994.

CAST: Julia Roberts (Sabrina Peterson), Nick Nolte (Peter Brackett), Saul Rubinek (Sam Smotherman), Robert Loggia (Matt Greenfield), James Rebhorn (The Thin Man).

Prêt-à-Porter (Ready to Wear in USA)

(1994, a Miramax release)

CREDITS: Executive producers, Bob Weinstein, Harvey Weinstein, Ian Jessel; producer, director, Robert Altman; screenplay, Robert Altman,

Barbara Shulgasser; co-producers, Scott Bushnell, Jon Kilik; camera, Pierre Mignot, Jean Lepine; editor, Geraldine Peroni; production designer, Stephen Altman; costume designer, Catherine Leterrier; music, Michel Legrand.

Rating, R; running time, 132 minutes; released 23 December 1994.

CAST: Danny Aiello (Major Hamilton), Anouk Aimee (Simone Lowenthal), Lauren Bacall (Slim Chrysler), Kim Basinger (Kitty Potter), Michel Blanc (Daniel Forget), Rupert Everett (Jack Owenthal), Teri Garr (Louise Hamilton), Richard E. Grant (Cort Romney), Linda Hunt (Regina Krumm), Sally Kellerman (Sissy Wanamaker), Ute Lemper (Albertine), Sophia Loren (Isabella de la Fontaine), Lyle Lovett (Clint Lammereaux), Chiara Mastroianni (Sophie Chiozet), Tim Robbins (Joe Flynn), Julia Roberts (Anne Eisenhower).

Something to Talk About

(1995, a Warner Bros release)

CREDITS: Executive producer, Goldie Hawn; producers, Anthea Sylbert, Paula Weinstein; director, Lasse Hallstrom; camera, Sven Nykvist; production designer, Mel Bourne; editor, Mia Goldman; co-producer, William Beasley; music, Hans Zimmer, Graham Preskett; costume designer, Aggie Guerard Rodgers; casting, Marion Dougherty.

Rating, R; running time, 105 minutes; released 4 August 1995.

CAST: Julia Roberts (Grace), Dennis Quaid (Eddie), Robert Duvall (Wyly King), Gena Rowlands (Georgia King), Kyra Sedgwick (Emma Rae), Brett Cullen (Jamie Johnson), Haley Aull (Caroline), Muse Watson (Hank Corrigan), Anne Shropshire (Aunt Rae).

Mary Reilly

(1996, a Sony Pictures Entertainment release of a TriStar Pictures presentation)

CREDITS: Executive producer, Lynne Pleshette; producers, Ned Tanen, Nancy Graham Tanen, Norma Heyman; director, Stephen Frears; screenplay, Christopher Hampton, based on the novel by Valerie Martin; camera, Philippe Rousselot; editor, Lesley Walker; music, George Fenton; production design, Stuart Craig; art direction, John King; set decoration,

Stephenie McMillan; costume design, Consolata Boyle; sound, Clive Winter; special effects, Richard Conway; assistant director, David Tringham; casting, Leo Davis, Juliet Taylor.

Rating, R; running time, 108 minutes; released 23 February 1996.

CAST: Julia Roberts (Mary Reilly), John Malkovich (Dr Jekyll/Mr Hyde), George Cole (Mr Poole), Michael Gambon (Mary's father), Kathy Staff (Mary's mother), Glenn Close (Mrs Farraday), Michael Sheen (Bradshaw), Bronagh Gallagher (Annie), Linda Bassett (Mary's Mother), Henry Goodman (Haffinger), Ciaran Hinds (Sir Danvers Carew), Sasha Hanav (Young Mary).

Michael Collins

(1996, a Warner Bros release)

CREDITS: Producer, Stephen Woolley; writer-director, Neil Jordan; co-producer, Redmond Morris; camera, Chris Menges; production designer, Anthony Pratt; editors, J. Patrick Duffner, Tony Lawson; music, Elliot Goldenthal; costume designer, Sandy Powell; casting, Susie Figgis.

Rating, R; running time, 133 minutes; released 11 October 1996.

CAST: Liam Neeson (Michael Collins), Aidan Quinn (Harry Boland), Alan Rickman (Eamon De Valera), Stephen Rea (Ned Broy), Julia Roberts (Kitty Kiernan), Charles Dance (Soames).

Everyone Says I Love You

(1996, a Miramax release)

CREDITS: Producer, Robert Greenhut; writer-director, Woody Allen; camera, Carlo DiPalma; editor, Susan E. Morse; music arranged and conducted by Dick Hyman; choreography, Graciela Daniele; production designer, Santo Loquasto; costumes, Jeffrey Kurland.

Rating, R; running time, 97 minutes; released 6 December 1996.

CAST: Edward Norton (Holden), Goldie Hawn (Steffi), Woody Allen (Joe), Alan Alda (Bob), Gaby Hoffman (Lane), Natalie Portman (Laura), Drew Barrymore (Skylar), Natasha Lyonne (DJ), Lukas Haas (Scott), Julia Roberts (Von), Tim Roth (Charles Ferry).

My Best Friend's Wedding

(1997, a Sony Pictures release of a TriStar Pictures presentation)

CREDITS: Executive producers, Gil Netter, Patricia Whitcher; producers, Jerry Zucker, Ronald Bass; director, P.J. Hogan; screenplay, Ron Bass; camera, Laszlo Kovacs; editor, Garth Craven, Lisa Fruchtman; music, James Newton Howard; production design, Richard Sylbert; art direction, Karen Fletcher Trujillo; costume design, Jeffrey Kurland; sound, Ed Novick; associate producers, Patricia Cullen, Bill Johnson; assistant director, Eric Heffron; casting, David Rubin;

Rating, PG-13; running time, 105 minutes; released 20 June 1997.

CAST: Julia Roberts (Julianne Potter), Dermot Mulroney (Michael O'Neal), Cameron Diaz (Kimmy Wallace), Rupert Everett (George Downes), Philip Bosco (Walter Wallace), M. Emmet Walsh (Joe O'Neal), Rachel Griffiths (Samantha Newhouse), Carrie Preston (Amanda Newhouse), Susan Sullivan (Isabelle), Chris Masterson (Scott), Paul Giamatti (Richard).

Conspiracy Theory

(1997, a Warner Bros release)

CREDITS: Executive producer, Jim Van Wyck; producers, Joel Silver, Richard Donner; co-producers, Dan Cracchiolo, J. Mills Goodloe, Rick Solomon; director, Richard Donner; screenplay, Brian Helgeland; camera, John Schwartzman; editors, Frank J. Urioste, Kevin Stitt; music, Carter Burwell; production design, Paul Sylbert; art direction, Gregory Wm. Bolton, Chris Shriver (NY); set design, Lauren Cory, Joseph G. Pacelli, Jr., Thomas Betts; set decoration, Casey Hallenbeck, Leslie Bloom (NY); costume design, Ha Nguyen; sound, Tim Cooney, James Sabat (NY); associate producers, Ilyse Reutlinger, Julie Durk; assistant director, Jim Van Wyck; stunt co-ordinator/second unit director, Conrad Palmisano; second unit camera, John M. Stephens; casting, Marion Dougherty.

Rating, R; running time, 135 minutes; released 8 August 1997.

CAST: Mel Gibson (Jerry Fletcher), Julia Roberts (Alice Sutton), Patrick Stewart (Dr Jonas), Cylk Cozart (Agent Lowry).

Stepmom

(1998, a TriStar Pictures presentation)

CREDITS: Executive producers, Patrick McCormick, Ron Bass, Margaret French Isaac, Julia Roberts, Susan Sarandon, Pliny Porter; producers, Wendy Finerman, Chris Columbus, Mark Radcliffe, Michael Barnathan; director, Chris Columbus; screenplay, Gigi Levangie, Jessie Nelson, Steven Rogers, Karen Leigh Hopkins and Ron Bass; camera, Donald M. McAlpine; editor, Neil Travis; costumes, Joseph G. Aulisi; music, John Williams; production design, Stuart Wurtzel.

Rating, PG-13; running time, 124 minutes; released 25 December 1998.

CAST: Julia Roberts (Isabel), Susan Sarandon (Jackie), Ed Harris (Luke), Jena Malone (Anna), Liam Aiken (Ben).

Notting Hill

(1999, a Polygram Films presentation of a Universal Pictures release)

CREDITS: Executive producers, Tim Bevan, Richard Curtis, Eric Fellner; producer, Duncan Kenworthy; director, Roger Michell; screenplay, Richard Curtis; camera, Michael Coulter; editor, Nick Moore; costume designer, Shuna Harwood; production designer, Stuart Craig; music, Trevor Jones; casting, Mary Selway; sound, David Stephenson; set decorator, Stephenie McMillan.

Rating, PG-13; running time, 125 minutes; released 28 May 1999.

CAST: Julia Roberts (Anna Scott), Hugh Grant (William Thacker), Richard McCabe (Tony), Rhys Ifans (Spike), Emma Chambers (Honey), Gina McKee (Bella), Tim McInnerny (Max), Hugh Bonneville (Bernie).

Runaway Bride

(1999, a Paramount Pictures and Touchstone Pictures presentation)

CREDITS: Executive producers, Ted Tannebaum, David Madden, Gary Lucchesi; producers, Ted Field, Tom Rosenberg, Scott Kroopf, Robert Cort; director, Garry Marshall; writers, Josann McGibbon, Sara Parriott; camera, Stuart Dryburgh; editor, Bruce Green; costumes, Albert Wolsky; music, James Newton Howard; production design, Mark Friedberg; art director, Wray Steven Graham; set decorator, Stephanie Carroll.

Rating, PG; running time, 116 minutes; released 30 July 1999.

CAST: Julia Roberts (Maggie Carpenter), Richard Gere (Ike Graham), Joan Cusack (Peggy Fleming), Hector Elizondo (Fisher), Rita Wilson (Ellie), Paul Dooley (Walter), Christopher Meloni (Coach Bob), Jane Morris (Mrs Pressman), Laurie Metcalf (Mrs Trout).

Erin Brockovich

(2000, a Universal Pictures presentation)

CREDITS: Executive producers, Carla Santos Shamberg, John Hardy; producers, Danny DeVito, Michael Shamberg, Stacey Sher; director, Steven Soderbergh; screenplay, Susannah Grant, Richard Lagravenese; camera, Ed Lachman; editor, Anne V. Coates; production design, Phil Messina; art direction, Christa Munro; set decorator, Kristen Toscano Messina; costumes, Jeffrey Kurland; sound, Thomas Causey; casting, Margery Simkin;

CAST: Julia Roberts, Albert Finney, Aaron Eckhart, Marg Helgenberger.

ACKNOWLEDGEMENTS

Academy of Motion Picture Arts and Sciences (Margaret Herrick Library), Kris Andersson, Dr Dan Berrios, Ellen Bersh, Dr Daniel Bowers, William Campbell, Louis Chunovic, Anita Edson, Marcy Engleman, Sarah Edwards, Cyrus Godfrey, Elaine Goldsmith-Thomas, Mary and Art Goodale, Mitchell (Mike) Hamilburg, David Izenman, Professor Benjamin Sifuentes Jauregui, Richard Johnson, Gary Kirkland, Lin and John Knorr, Dr David Krefetz, Robert Lent, Rod Lurie, Christina Madej, Paul Manchester, Jim Murphy, Donald J. Myers, Sia Prospero, Linda Reinle, Doris Romeo, Marjorie Rothstein, Professor Anthony Sabedra, Catherine Seipp, Guy Shalem, Dorie Simmonds, Stadtlander's and Dr Brent Walta. Special thanks to Ms Aileen Joyce for her immensely helpful *Julia: The Untold Story of America's Pretty Woman*.